## RIT - WALLACE LIBRARY
# CIRCULATING LIBRARY BOOKS

| JUL 2 5 2000 | |
|---|---|
| | |
| | |
| | |
| | |
| | |

OVERDUE FINES AND FEES FOR <u>ALL</u> BORROWERS

*Recalled = $1/ day overdue (no grace period)
*Billed = $10.00/ item when returned 4 or more weeks overdue
*Lost Items = replacement cost+$10 fee
*All materials must be returned or renewed by the duedate.

# FACULTY AND STUDENT CHALLENGES IN FACING CULTURAL AND LINGUISTIC DIVERSITY

# FACULTY AND STUDENT CHALLENGES IN FACING CULTURAL AND LINGUISTIC DIVERSITY

*Editor*

## LYNNE W. CLARK, Ph.D.

*Associate Professor*
*Program Director of Communication Sciences Program*
*School of Health Sciences of Hunter College*
*City University of New York*
*Faculty Member of The Hunter/Mount Sinai Geriatric*
*Education Center*
*Fellow of Brookdale Center on Aging*
*New York, New York*

*Associate Editor*

## Dava E. Waltzman, M.A., M.Phil.

*Lecturer of Communication Sciences Program*
*School of Health Sciences of Hunter College*
*City University of New York*
*Doctoral Candidate of Speech and Hearing Program*
*The Graduate School of City University of New York*
*New York, New York*

CHARLES C THOMAS • PUBLISHER
*Springfield • Illinois • U.S.A.*

*Published and Distributed Throughout the World by*

**CHARLES C THOMAS • PUBLISHER**
2600 South First Street
Springfield, Illinois 62794-9265

© *1993 by* CHARLES C THOMAS • PUBLISHER

ISBN 0-398-05853-9

Library of Congress Catalog Card Number: 93-18205

*With* THOMAS BOOKS *careful attention is given to all details of manufacturing
and design. It is the Publisher's desire to present books that are satisfactory as to
their physical qualities and artistic possibilities and appropriate for their particular
use.* THOMAS BOOKS *will be true to those laws of quality that assure a good
name and good will.*

*Printed in the United States of America*
*SC-R-3*

**Library of Congress Cataloging-in-Publication Data**

Faculty and student challenges in facing cultural and linguistic
    diversity / editor, Lynne W. Clark ; associate editor, Dava E.
    Waltzman.
        p.    cm.
    Includes bibliographical references and index.
    ISBN 0-398-05853-9
    1. Paramedical education.   2. Intercultural education.   I. Clark,
Lynne W.   II. Waltzman, Dava E.
R847.5.F33   1993
610.69′6—dc20                                                        93-18205
                                                                          CIP

# CONTRIBUTORS

**DOLORES E. BATTLE, Ph.D.**
*Associate Professor, Speech and Hearing Department*
*State University of Buffalo*
*Buffalo, New York*

**LI-RONG LILLY CHENG, Ph.D.**
*Professor, Department of Communicative Disorders*
*Assistant Dean of Student Affairs and*
*International Development*
*San Diego State University*
*San Diego, California*

**LYNNE W. CLARK, Ph.D.**
*Associate Professor and Program Director*
*Communication Sciences Program*
*School of Health Sciences of Hunter College*
*City University of New York*
*Faculty Member, Hunter/Mount Sinai*
*Geriatric Education Center*
*New York, New York*

**ELLA INGLEBRET, M.A.**
*Program Coordinator of Native Americans*
*Communication Disorders Training Project*
*Department of Speech and Hearing Sciences*
*Washington State University*
*Pullman, Washington*

**HENRIETTE W. LANGDON, Ed.D.**
*Bilingual Speech and Language Specialist*
*Private Practice*
*Cupertino, California*

v

**MARILYN A. PIPES, M.S.**
*Program Coordinator of American Indian*
*Professional Training Program in Speech-Language*
*Pathology and Audiology*
*University of Arizona*
*Tucson, Arizona*

**ANNETTE RAMIREZ dE ARELLANO, Dr.PH.**
*Educational Consultant*
*Formerly, Associate Dean of the*
*School of Health Sciences*
*Hunter College of City University of New York*
*New York, New York*

**GERALDINE RODRIGUEZ ROUSE, M.S.**
*Formerly Lecture and Clinical Supervisor*
*Multicultural Education Program*
*in Communicative Disorders*
*University of New Mexico*
*Albuquerque, New Mexico*
*Doctoral Candidate of Department of Audiology*
*and Speech Pathology*
*Memphis State University*
*Memphis, Tennessee*

**GLORIAJEAN L. WALLACE, Ph.D.**
*Associate Professor*
*Department of Audiology and Speech Pathology*
*University of Tennessee*
*Knoxville, Tennessee*

**DAVA E. WALTZMAN, M.A., M.Phil.**
*Adjunct Lecturer of Communication Sciences Program*
*School of Health Sciences of Hunter College*
*City University of New York*
*Doctoral Candidate of Speech and Hearing Program*
*The Graduate School of City University of New York*
*New York, New York*

**CAROL E. WESTBY, Ph.D.**
*Research Associate*
*University Affiliated Program*
*University of New Mexico*
*Albuquerque, New Mexico*

*To* M *and* M,
the new generation to appreciate and embrace
cultural and linguistic diversity.

# PREFACE

*The meaning of life is felt through*
  *relationship . . .*
*Relationship with others and with one's own*
  *self.*
*From what it is at birth to whom we become*
  *as a child,*
*Adult, parent grand parent and ultimately,*
  *as ancestor.*
*The meaning of life flowers through*
  *relationship . . .*
*Parenting teaching serving creating.*
*Learning from nature, the sages, our peers,*
*From our emerging selves in a state of*
  *becoming.*[*]
(Jonas Salk and Carol Anne Bundy, 1992)

With the current and projected future demographic changes in the United States population, institutions of higher education are witnessing increasing enrollment of students from diverse cultural, ethnic, and linguistic backgrounds. This shift to a more diverse student population presents a challenge for faculty in effectively teaching all students. With the increasing demand to provide health care and educational services to diverse client populations, faculty in the professional education programs of allied health are also concerned with how they can recruit and retain more bilingual and minority students in their programs. Finally, faculty are concerned with how they can professionally prepare students to competently service culturally diverse client populations by imparting to students relevant cultural and linguistic information.

Ideally, students need to receive an education from faculty who are knowledgeable and competent in their own culture, and who speak the

---

[*]Salk, Jonas & Bundy, C.A.: The meaning of life. In Friend, David (Ed.): *More Reflections on the Meaning of Life.* New York, Time Life, 1992, pp. 50.

ix

same language. However, the current match between faculty and students in higher education is far from perfect. However, this does not mean that students will not receive a quality education. It means that faculty, as well as students, must become cross-cultural and communicatively competent. Additionally, it means that faculty must teach in sensitive, and perhaps different ways than they did in the past. It is hoped that this book will serve as a starting place for such efforts.

In researching and pursuing knowledge for the content of this book, the editor as well as chapter authors encountered a paucity of published information on culturally and linguistically diverse students in higher education. Thus, in some instances information from secondary educational practices has been applied to students in higher education. Much information and insight came directly from our contributing authors, some of whom are bicultural, bilingual and many of whom administrate special, federally funded educational training programs at their own institutional settings. In fact, many of our contributing authors were selected for their dual expertise, first hand knowledge of the culture and their experience in teaching diverse student groups.

The book's content is designed to be useful to administrators, faculty and clinical training supervisors in the professional education programs of allied health (e.g., nursing, social work, nutrition, occupational therapy, physical therapy, medical laboratory sciences, environmental health, speech-language pathology, audiology and public health). Additionally, faculty in medicine, psychology, education, anthropology, linguistics and the other health-related and educational programs will find the information useful. Last, practicing professionals in the health care and educational fields will find the information of value for the persons they service.

The perspectives of the book are based on the following assumptions. First, a prerequisite to effectively teaching all students is based on an understanding of one's own culture, ethnic, language and communicative backgrounds, and the values and beliefs that we hold about individuals who are different from ourselves. Second, each student is a unique individual. Although students may be influenced by their culture and ethnic backgrounds, they are not fully defined by them. While faculty's understanding of students' cultural and ethnic differences should serve to enhance interactions and learning between faculty and students, faculty should be cautious about over generalizing, stereotyping, and using cultural characteristics as the sole determiner in teaching students. Third, faculty have an obligation to develop teaching methods and strategies that are culturally sensitive to all students. Fourth, faculty have a responsibility to students to interpret the educational views and practices of the mainstream higher educational system, as well as to help students find ways to easily negotiate and adapt to the environment of mainstream higher education.

This book is organized in three major sections. The first section provides the reader with an introduction to the many issues and challenges facing faculty in educating students from diverse cultural, ethnic and linguistic groups. Chapter 1 provides demographic data, and discusses what is meant by cultural and communicative competency, and the hidden curriculum. Chapter 2 discusses the pragmatics of addressing race, ethnicity and diversity in the academic setting. Chapter 3 describes how social cultural bias and prejudice develops as a natural developmental process, and provides suggestions on how faculty can overcome bias.

The second part of the book introduces the reader to a number of major American cultural, ethnic student groups. Chapters 4, 5, 6 and 7 separately profile African American, Hispanic/Latino, Asian and Pacific Islander and Native American students, respectively. Each of these student groups is described in terms of how their historical, religious and cultural beliefs are reflected in their communication and learning styles, as well as in their views of education and health. These cultural groups were selected since they represented a large segment of the present and future student populations in higher education. While the information in these four chapters is intended for faculty to better understand the students they teach, much of the basic information can also serve as a beginning source to faculty for infusing cultural information into the content of their academic and clinical lecture courses. We included Chapter 8 for we wanted to address the common educational obstacles that foreign-born, non-American students encounter when they come to the United States to pursue studies in higher education.

The third and final section of this book, provides specific strategies to help minority students academically achieve, as well as provides faculty with specific approaches for the inclusion of multicultural content into the curriculum. Chapter 9 outlines factors impacting on the academic performance of minority students, and provides language-learning and text strategies to facilitate the successful retention of diverse students. Additionally, the information in Chapter 9 can be specifically applied by faculty and clinical supervisors in speech-language pathology to the management of school age children with language-learning impairments. Where Chapter 10 provides various curriculum approaches for the successful inclusion of multicultural content that applies to the professional knowledge base of each specific allied health discipline, Chapter 11 discusses the importance of a cross-cultural curriculum approach for the effective preparation of future health care professionals.

The reader should note that while the specific examples cited in the text deal with the professional programs of speech-language pathology and audiology, the general content of chapters readily applies to all allied health professional programs.

With respect to the terminology used in this text, terms were chosen by chapter authors. Most terms reflect what is nationally accepted. The terms, mainstream U.S. culture or mainstream Americans, were chosen to refer to Anglo-European Americans who currently comprise the dominant culture in the United States. Any inconsistency in use of terms was preserved to represent the different cultural perspectives of chapter authors. As Chapter 2 points out, the reader should be aware that the terms used in the text may change over time. Thus, the reader should use those terms that a person within a particular cultural group prefers.

In closing, we would like to add that while the heart (and soul) of the challenge to competently teach all students should commence at the elementary and secondary educational levels, faculty in higher education cannot wait and assume that this will happen. Therefore, the challenge is now before faculty in higher education to provide all students with a quality education.

# ACKNOWLEDGMENTS

This manuscript was prepared with the generous and continuing efforts of numerous individuals. The text was inspired by a faculty development conference entitled *Teaching Cultural-Linguistic Diversity in the Professional Curriculums of Speech-Language Pathology and Audiology* held at Hunter College in May 1991 for faculty members from university programs within the New York City Metropolitan area. The conference was sponsored by Hunter College's Communication Sciences Program by awards graciously received from The President's Plural and Diversity and Faculty Development Funds. I am grateful to Everlena Holmes, Dean of the School of Health Sciences for her encouragement to write a book for all faculty in the professional education programs of allied health. I would also wish to extend my deepest gratitude to my Associate Editor, Dava Waltzman, for her enthusiasm and support, for assisting with the endless editing of the manuscript, and for her incisive comments and organizational skills. I also want to especially thank Carol Westby for her continuous inspirations and scholarship.

To each of the authors, I offer my sincerest thanks for giving of their knowledge, personal experience, cross-cultural skills, patience and time when preparing their manuscripts. Despite demanding phone calls and schedules, and even personal crises, each author gave her best to the book.

My sincere indebtedness goes to Ann Okon who typed, retyped, alphabetized, numbered, renumbered, inserted, deleted and xeroxed the text for final preparation.

I am also deeply indebted to Helen Sweeney and Kaye Leitzinger, who graciously offered their personal assistance and support while at Hunter College, in the implementation of the conference. Special thanks also to Lynn Waltzman who assisted in typing some of the text, and to Monica Thorne who constantly followed up with phone calls to authors.

Finally, sincerest appreciation to my husband, Art, who continuously encouraged me along the way, to my daughter, Meggan, who screened all phone calls by stating, "She's working and can't be disturbed," and to my son, Matthew, who would ask "Aren't you done, yet?".

A number of authors wish to offer their appreciation to those who helped in the preparation of their chapters. Henriette Langdon wishes to thank and acknowledge the input of several colleagues: Carol Beaumont, Maria Botello, Minnie Galván, Rachel Parada, Charlene Rau and Michele Sánchez-Boyce. Marilyn Pipes, Carol Westby and Ella Inglebret would like to express their gratitude to Ms. Lucinda Wever for assistance in the preparation of this chapter, and to the former and current Native American students in their training programs for their contributions and inspiration. In particular, these latter three authors want to thank their students, John Dodge, Jennifer Enote, and Gari Smith for their insights and editorial comments on the Profile of Native American Students Chapter.

# CONTENTS

## PART ONE
### CHALLENGES BEFORE FACULTY AND STUDENTS

*Chapter*

xv

## PART THREE
### SUCCESSFUL LEARNING STRATEGIES
### AND CURRICULUM APPROACHES

# FACULTY AND STUDENT CHALLENGES IN FACING CULTURAL AND LINGUISTIC DIVERSITY

# PART ONE
# CHALLENGES BEFORE
# FACULTY AND STUDENTS

# Chapter 1

# FACULTY CHALLENGES IN FACING DIVERSITY

LYNNE W. CLARK AND LI-RONG LILLY CHENG

## INTRODUCTION

The increasing ethnic, linguistic and cultural diversity among students in higher education, and more specifically among students in the professional programs of allied health, presents faculty with important educational challenges (Oliver and Johnson, 1988). In order to effectively educate all student groups, faculty will need to achieve cultural literacy and cross-cultural communicative competency. Educational programs will additionally need to broaden their curriculums to reflect multicultural and linguistic information. However, while many educational accrediting and professional certification boards in the allied health professions recommend the inclusion of specific multicultural content into the academic and clinical components of programs, this goal will not be fully realized until faculty achieve cross-cultural and communicative competency with the students they teach. In turn, faculty must encourage students to see the relative importance of their working together with faculty to develop a better understanding of cultural diversity.

Thus, the purpose of this chapter is to describe some of the challenges that faculty may encounter in facing culturally diverse student populations; to address cultural literacy and communicative competency, and to present some strategies for managing diversity within the academic environment.

## EDUCATIONAL CHALLENGES

As we approach a multicultural and multilingual country in the twenty-first century, faculty in the professional programs of allied health are being relied upon to play a vital role in educating and clinically training future professionals to effectively service the diverse client population. With these objectives in mind, faculty are faced with the following challenges:

- To understand and be sensitive to diversity by being aware of the similarities and differences that exist regarding educational views and the learning and communications styles among culturally diverse students;
- To educate and clinically prepare *all* students to effectively service diverse client populations by having students become cross-cultural and communicatively competent;
- To broaden the academic and clinical curriculums to include multi-cultural and linguistic content specific to allied health disciplines;
- To be adaptive and flexible in their own interactions, teaching and communication styles in order to meet the learning needs of all students, including English as a Second Language students;
- To recruit more bilingual, multibilingual and minority American students into their professional programs;
- To recruit more non-American foreign-born students into their professional programs;
- To evaluate whether traditional admission policies are applicable to all student groups.

While cultural and linguistically diverse populations continue to grow at rapid rates, shortages of allied health professionals in both the United States and other countries exist. The most severe shortages have been identified as a shortage of bilingual and minority professionals. For instance, the ASHA's Directory of Bilingual Speech-Language Pathologists and Audiologists (1989) reported that only 0.01 percent of the American Speech, Language and Hearing Association's (ASHA) membership were bilingual. The bilingual ASHA members professed proficiency in Spanish, French, Italian, German, few spoke Chamorro, Chinese, Hindi, Indonesian, Japanese, Korean, Filipino, Thai or Urdu. No members reported speaking Southeast Asian or Pacific Island languages. Further, some of ASHA's bilingual professionals reported servicing only monolingual clients. On the other hand, over one-third of the ASHA monolingual professionals reported servicing clients who were nonnative English speakers (Shewan, 1988). Additionally, of the 67,115 ASHA members in 1992 (Cole, 1992), only 3.7 percent (or 2,461 members) represented ethnic minority groups with 41 percent being African/Black American, 27 percent being Hispanic/Latino American, 26 percent being Asian and Pacific Island American and .06 percent being American Indians including Alaskan Natives.

Given the low incidence of bilingual and minority professionals, monolingual, nonminority professionals must currently meet the needs of minority, culturally diverse clients. However, monolingual, nonminority professionals report a void in their academic preparation and clinical training of the diverse clients groups they service. For instance, A Self Study by ASHA (1982) revealed that 77 percent of those certified speech-language pathologists who were surveyed, felt a need for more multicultural knowledge in order to effectively meet the needs of their minority and multilingual client populations. Also, results of a survey conducted in 1985 by ASHA (1987) of its more than 49,591 members revealed that only 9 percent of its membership had received preservice academic and clinical preparation in multicultural content.

As mentioned, shortages in the allied health professions also exist in other countries around the world. Certain of the allied health disciplines fail to exist in these countries because they do not have professional educational programs in these areas. Thus foreign students come to the United States to pursue allied health degrees so that when they return to their own countries, they can serve as health professionals or faculty members in existing or in developing educational programs in allied health.

Given the reported paucity of academic content (ASHA 1982; 1987), the challenge for faculty is how to effectively educate all students to serve diverse populations. In order to understand the breadth of this educational challenge, faculty will need greater understanding of the culturally and linguistically diverse student populations they teach. The shift in U.S. demographics, detailed in the following section demonstrates that faculty will see increasingly more minority and bilingual students entering higher education.

## CHANGING DEMOGRAPHICS OF THE U.S. POPULATION AND ITS EDUCATIONAL SYSTEM

Demographic data indicate that our nation will continue to become increasingly diverse (U.S. Census Bureau, 1991). Individuals from different linguistic, social, economic, political, religious, and cultural backgrounds bring with them varying sets of values, beliefs, and practices which in turn must be effectively dealt with in the classroom. When faced with such diversity, faculty must be prepared to effectively educate these students.

According to the 1990 Census, between 1980 and 1990 the total U.S. population grew 9.8 percent with minority populations growing much faster than nonminority ones. The Asian/Pacific Island population grew by 107.8 percent; Hispanic/Latino by 53 percent; American Indian by 37.9 percent; Black by 13.2 percent; and the White by 6.0 percent. In exact figures, the 1990 Census Bureau reported that there were 199,686,070 Whites, 29,986,060 Blacks, 22,345,059 Hispanics, 7,273,662 Asian/Pacific Islanders and 1,959,234 American Indians residing in the United States (U.S. Bureau of Census, 1991).

The Hispanic/Latino population constitutes the fastest growing of all ethnic communities in the United States. Currently, there are 23.4 million Hispanic/Latinos residing in the United States (Current Population Report, 1990). By the year 2000 an estimated 30 million, and by the year 2020 an estimated 50 million Hispanic/Latinos will be living in the United States. Asian Americans also represent a growing minority group. The 1990 U.S. Census data reported over 7 million Asians living in the United States, with the largest numbers residing in California and Hawaii. As compared to 1.5 percent or 3 million American Asians in 1980, the current number represents 2.9 percent of the total United States population. Asians are expected to constitute 4 percent of the total United States population by the year 2000; a projected growth of 400 percent in 30 years (Gardner, Robey and Smith, 1985).

While the United States has historically received a large proportion of its immigrants from Europe, the last two decades have witnessed a tremendous influx of immigrants from Pacific Rim countries, including Mexico, Panama, El Salvador, Guatemala, Columbia, Honduras, Taiwan, the People's Republic of China, Hong Kong, Vietnam, Laos and Cambodia (Gordon, 1987). Further, every year more than 80,000 Blacks immigrate to the United States from the Caribbean, Africa and South and Central Americas (Gardner, Robey and Smith, 1985). This shift in immigrants from European to Pacific Rim countries and the Caribbean, Africa and Central and South Americas, has been an important factor in the dramatic change in the overall composition of the United States population. This change in the demographic distribution is illustrated, for example, by the expectation that in the state of California within the next 10 to 20 years, Whites will constitute less than 49 percent of the general population, Hispanic/Latinos will constitute 30 percent, Asians 13 percent, and African American/Blacks 8 percent of the population (*California Faces*, 1989).

As would be expected, these changing demographics are also reflected in the populations of children attending public schools and adults attending institutions of higher education (American Council on Education, 1988). The percentage of U.S. public school children who are minorities rose from 20 percent in 1970 to 29.1 percent in 1986. The U.S. Bureau of Census has further predicted that by the year 2000, 33 percent of all school-age children will be from minority groups and by 2020, 39 percent of our school-age population will be composed of minorities (U.S. Bureau of Census, 1987).

At the present time, approximately half of all U.S. public school minority students are located in 25 of the U.S.'s largest metropolitan areas (Cheng, 1989a). By the year 2000, almost 42 percent of all public school students in the metropolitan areas will be from minority groups. California, which has 1/9th of the nation's public school children, can expect to be particularly affected by these changing demographics (Cheng, 1989a). By the year 2000, the number of limited English proficient (LEP) school-age children will have increased to an estimated 3.4 million with Hispanic/Latino and Asian populations experiencing the most rapid growth (Cheng, 1989a). According to the Status Report on Minorities in Higher Education from the American Council on Education (as cited by McKenna in *On Campus,* 1992), minority college enrollment increased 10 percent between 1988 and 1990. Asian American enrollment climbed 11.7 percent, representing one of the largest increases. Also, the enrollment of African American men which show a decline a few years ago, increased 1 percent between 1988 and 1990. However, since 1985, Hispanic/Latino American enrollment has only increased 1 percent.

This dramatic change in the composition of the United States population will have a significant impact on education within the public school systems. It will additionally have an effect upon American institutions of higher education to produce allied health professionals and educators to meet the health and educational needs of the minority and multilingual client populations. In order for faculty to meet the needs of students from culturally and linguistically diverse populations, faculty must begin first by developing cross-cultural competency.

## CROSS-CULTURAL COMPETENCY

By becoming cross-culturally competent, faculty will better understand, appreciate, support and more effectively teach culturally and linguistically diverse students. In practical terms, Lynch (1991) states:

> Achieving cross-cultural competency requires that we lower our defenses, take risks and practice behaviors that may feel unfamiliar and uncomfortable. It requires a flexible mind, an open heart and a willingness to accept alternative perspectives. It may even mean setting aside some beliefs that are cherished to make room for others whose value is unknown; and it may mean changing what we think, what we say and how we behave (p. 35).

Three aspects involved in becoming cross-culturally competent are described by Spitzberg (1989). Faculty must first begin by being aware of their own self and culture, and then proceed to gain sensitivity and specific knowledge of various cultures. By doing so, faculty can then develop communication competency or the skills necessary to engage in successful interactions with students where both faculty and students feel equally positive about the interactions. Hall (1976) defines the cumulative effect of these three aspects as cultural competency or the ability to establish interpersonal relationships with persons of different cultures by developing an understanding through effective exchange of both verbal and nonverbal levels of behavior.

## Self-Awareness

According to Hall (1976), all aspects of human life are touched and altered by culture. Culture is more than a group of people who share common religious beliefs, customs, values, history and a similar language. It also refers to a group of people who share life experiences together, a common world view and similar patterns of thought, social interaction and communication. Often persons are unaware of the behaviors and customs that are culturally bound.

To understand and fully appreciate the diversity that exists among students, faculty must first appreciate their own culture (Abe and Wiseman, 1983). Cultural self-awareness is the first step toward cultural competency. It serves as a bridge for learning about other cultures. It further provides a means for distinguishing which behaviors, beliefs and attitudes are shaped by one's own culture as opposed to those behaviors that are either universal to all cultures or those that are solely shaped by the individual. It is important to keep in mind that cultural identity is only one variable that guides an individual's lifestyle. Self-awareness can be facilitated by exploring one's own heritage or roots, and then by examining the values, behaviors and beliefs associated with one's heritage in relation to one's cultural identity.

## Understanding Cultural Diversity: Knowledge of Other Cultures

Cultural literacy described by Bjorkland and Bjorkland (1988) includes a broad working knowledge of the traditions, terminology, folklore and history of various cultures. By exploring these aspects, faculty can gain insight into and develop a greater appreciation of how culture affects cross-cultural competency, interpersonal interactions and styles of communication (Storti, 1989). Cultural specific information helps to explain many of the behaviors and attitudes encountered in classroom situations.

It is essential not to assume that cultural specific information applies to all individuals from the same cultural group. This hypothesis leads to stereotyping and decreases the success for achieving cross-cultural competency (Ruben, 1989). Variability exists across and within each culture. Faculty should proceed with caution when applying specific cultural information to an individual student. Making generalizations about an individual from a major cultural group are dangerous because differences are often confounded by other factors such as age and sex. Cultural competency does not imply knowing everything about every culture. Rather it means acknowledging and developing a respect for differences rather than ignoring or minimizing them. Further, cultural differences are viewed as strengths rather than weaknesses. Cultural competency means an eagerness to learn and a willingness to accept that there are many ways to view the world (Lynch, 1991).

Cultural diversity is reflected in languages and linguistic origins, religious, health and educational beliefs and practices, and in learning and communication styles. Central to understanding these aspects is the major dimension of cultural variation: collectivistic versus individualistic orientation (Althen, 1988). American minority groups such as Hispanic/ Latino, Asian/Pacific Islander, American Indian and African/Black Americans share a collectivistic orientation where Anglo Americans share an individualistic orientation. Collectivistic values are rooted in the three teachings or doctrines of Confucianism, Taoism and Buddhism (Triandis, Brislin & Hui, 1988). The corresponding predominant values pertain to family, harmony, health and education. Interdependence and cooperation is maintained among members of the family and society. There is an authoritative structure with respect for elders and ancestors. Harmony and saving face is maintained at all costs. Education is viewed as a formal process continuing throughout a person's life. In individualistic cultures, the individual strives for independence. There is a high regard for personal achievement, competition, hard work and materialism. These basic ideologies are reflected in the behaviors and attitudes displayed by students in academic settings.

The following examples illustrate the diversity that exists within major ethnic groups. Although Hispanics/Latinos share the Spanish language, there exists diverse regional variations in phonology and lexicon that reflect the differences in cultural variation within the Hispanic/Latino population. These populations additionally represent diverse personal backgrounds, in which some are educated and have professional experience in a variety of fields, and where others are illiterate and work mostly in farming. Many Hispanics/Latinos are bilingual and function well in American schools. Others, however, are limited in English proficiency and may even be illiterate in Spanish. Reasons for immigration also reflect diversity. For example, the internal unrest, poverty and dictatorship of some Latin American countries caused many Hispanic/Latinos to immigrate from Mexico, Puerto Rico, Cuba, South and Central Americas.

Southeast Asian refugees, for example, represent intracultural diversity. Their personal backgrounds, range from being clandestine agents for the CIA (Walker, 1985), to highly educated multilingual professionals, to preliterate Hmong. Such diversity is indeed a challenge for faculty. A further example would be the Indian versus Spanish ancestry of Hispanics/Latinos.

Within the Asian/Pacific Island populations religious diversity exists. Some Haitians are believers of voodooism, while about 90 percent of them are Catholic (Ashby, 1983). Further, many Southeast Asians believe in Buddhism and at the same time practice Animism (i.e., the belief that all things possess a spirit) (Gordon, 1987). Even attitudes toward disability vary greatly within major cultural groups. For example, some Asians may view a birth defect as a **karma** which is the result of wrong doing of the individual's ancestors, where others view it as a result of improper diet (Cheng, 1990b, 1991).

The following are some of the questions faculty may address in regard to cultural diversity (Banks, Cortes, Gay, Garcia and Ochoa, 1976; Banks, 1990; Cheng, 1989a; Scarella 1989):

- Have faculty updated their knowledge and skills with regard to issues of diversity?
- Are faculty prepared to teach multicultural students?
- What are the mainstream assumptions about teaching?
- How do various instructional strategies reflect and accommodate the learning styles of diverse students?
- How can faculty accommodate diverse styles of both verbal and nonverbal communication?
- Do faculty provide students with frequent, timely, performance-based feedback that supports improved performance?
- How can faculty encourage positive interaction between themselves and culturally diverse students, as well as between students?
- What teaching methods can faculty utilize to elicit active participation from students?
- How can faculty facilitate the self-development of students with diverse speech and language patterns?
- How should faculty evaluate their teaching effectiveness of diverse students?

## Cross-Cultural Communication Competency

Language and culture are extricably bound (Hall, 1976). Communication, which is a complex process, is the key to achieving effective interpersonal interactions. Interpersonal difficulties are not simply a matter of language differences but are reflective of different thought patterns, different values and different communication styles. Thus, in order to effect successful interpersonal interactions with students, faculty must strive for both verbal and nonverbal cross-cultural communication competency.

### High and Low Context Cultures

Cultures may vary in the amount of information that is explicitly transmitted through verbal channels as opposed to information that is transmitted through the context of the situation, the physical cues present and persons' body and facial language (Hall, 1976; Hecht, Anderson & Ribeau, 1989). High context cultures rely less on verbal communication to send and receive messages. Few words are spoken and verbal interactions are de-emphasized. Rather, individuals formally communicate through shared information, history and implicit or nonverbal messages.

Asian, Native American, Hispanic/Latino and African cultures tend to be high context cultures. Anglo Americans, Germans, Swiss and Scandinavians represent low context cultures where communication is direct, logical and precise. Further, communication interactions tend to be informal, where there is an equal participation or **lots of talking** between communications partners.

In one instance, low context communicators may become impatient with the long pauses, silences and nonverbal, indirect communication modes of high context communicators (Cheng, 1987). In other instances, high context communicators may become dissatisfied when low context communicators fail to process gestures, environmental cues and affective forms of communication. These examples are illustrative of what often results when American mainstream faculty interact within minority students. Faculty and students must be aware and adapt these different forms of communication to foster cross-cultural competency so as to create a maximum learning environment.

Specifically, many of the nonverbal communication behaviors of high and low context cultures easily cause misunderstandings and breakdowns in communication interactions because these behaviors convey different meanings in different cultures (Randall-David, 1989). For example, while an Anglo American will value direct eye contact, Asian Americans may view it as shameful and African Americans may see it as a sign of disrespect. While Asians tend to mask their facial expressions or use a different facial expression to cover other felt emotions (e.g., laughing when embarrassed), Anglo Americans use facial expressions to directly express what they are feeling. Proximity and touch or social distance, is another aspect of nonverbal communication. Anglo Americans tend to converse three feet or an arms length away from the conversational partner. In high context cultures, individuals may either move closer or back away from their conversational partner depending on their relationship with the person. Anglo Americans tend to pat a person's head to show affection, however, Asians consider this behavior as disgraceful since the **head** is the **residence of the soul** (Devine & Braganti, 1989). Body and gestural language can also contribute to misunderstandings. For example, an Anglo American hand and arm gesture for **come here** may mean **to go away** to an Asian American. Anglo Americans nod their heads to show agreement, however to an Asian or Native American this gesture may only mean that **I hear you and not that I agree or understand you** (Lynch and Hanson, 1992).

Cross-culture communication also means a willingness to engage in interactions that explore cultural differences openly and with respect. Thus, it serves to dispel myths and opens doors to understanding between faculty and students of different cultural backgrounds (Giles and Franklyn-Stokes, 1989). In addition to becoming cross-cultural and communicatively competent, students need to understand the mainstream educational process and its practices, **the hidden curriculum.**

## THE HIDDEN CURRICULUM

The concept of the hidden curriculum is not a new one. Jackson (1968), in his book entitled *Life in Classrooms* defined the hidden curriculum as the crowds, the praise, and the power that combine to give a distinctive flavor to classroom life. These aspects collectively form a hidden curriculum which each student must master if he/she is to make his/her way satisfactorily through the academic institution.

Faculty bring to the classroom context a set of values, beliefs and attitudes that they view as being central to the American educational process. Students also bring to classroom context their preconceived notions about the educational process and it's practices. Many of these views stem from their individual cultural beliefs. Most faculty have been socialized in the mainstream society and consider competition, literacy and effective verbal communication to be essential for academic success. More commonly than not, faculty tend to evaluate their students' performances based on their preset conceptions about academic achievement which have been defined by an Eurocentric educational perspective. Kerman (1979) reported that American faculty generally preferred students who were more verbal, asked questions, generated class debate and exhibited a competitive orientation. Students from other cultures, however, may have been taught that reticent behavior is the correct way to show respect for the instructor and the school environment (Tran, 1991). When faculty expectations conflict with those of their students, incongruities often result in academic failure (Trueba, Guthrie & Au, 1981; Trueba, 1987).

The following case study illustrates this point well.

Adwoa Bediako is a twenty-year-old Ghana student who arrived in the U.S. six months ago. She is the first in her family to go to college. On the first day of class, her course instructor entered the classroom, saying, "Good morning," and then introduced himself. Adwoa was surprised, since she expected her classmates to stand when the instructor entered the classroom and for them to say first, "Good morning, professor."

The instructor then asked the students to introduce themselves. When it was Adwoa's turn, the instructor pronounced her name incorrectly and the other students began to giggle. Adwoa, feeling it was rude to correct the teacher, then introduced herself pronouncing her name in the same, incorrect way. She said, "I am from Ghana, and that's it." One student asked, "Is that all?" Another said, "Where is Ghana, anyway?" The other students just laughed it off.

Following the introductions, the instructor gave the class an outline, and put students into groups to discuss and write their reactions to the course require-ments. This shocked Adwoa, since she was accustomed to being told what to do by an instructor without asking questions. Another shock came when the instructor informed the students that all quizzes and examinations would be **open book.**

The next day, Adwoa was shocked again when she saw students drinking coffee in the classroom. During the class discussion, Adwoa did not participate. Neither did she look straight into the eyes of the instructor, as she did not want to appear rude or disrespectful. She was also afraid that her classmates would laugh at her accent. She did not feel confident, but rather uneasy and confused. The instructor then mentioned the final grade would be based not only on written assignments, but also on classroom participation and group work, causing her further discomfort. Adwoa felt hopeless and helpless. (Amkoako, Jie, Low and Neham, 1991).

Adwoa's case provides insight into how many culturally diverse stu-dents with different views of the educational process, and who come with different learning and communication styles actually feel in the classroom. If faculty do not modify traditional teaching styles and reach out to culturally diverse students, they may become discouraged and withdraw from the academic setting.

While students must become culturally literate, faculty need to under-stand which of the students' observed **aberrant** behaviors are appropriate in their home milieu to avoid misinterpretation of such behavior patterns. Faculty who view certain student behaviors as inappropriate to the classroom environment may not understand that such behaviors are culturally appropriate for that student. Lack of classroom participation such as in the case of Adwoa's may be interpreted by the faculty as a lack of interest or motivation, where in reality the behaviors are intended to show respect (Philips, 1983).

Trueba (1989) argues for an understanding of how the classroom is organized, as well as the more abstract social levels of organization, that channel students toward success or failure, and cautions against excessive stereotyping which results from reliance on creating catalogues of cultural patterns, such as learning styles. Effective guidance to students who experience difficulties and ambivalence in the process of acculturating into America's mainstream educational setting can be provided by culturally sensitive faculty.

## CREATING A PARTNERSHIP BETWEEN FACULTY AND STUDENTS

In order to achieve academic success, it is necessary for faculty and students to establish a partnership in the teaching-learning process. The following guidelines for diversity, as suggested by DeRosa (1991), provide excellent insights into the dynamic process of negotiation for meaning, knowledge and understanding between faculty and students:

- Project a feeling of understanding.
- Recognize that it is a long-term struggle to reach mutual understanding.
- Be a role model in multiculturalism.
- Be nonjudgmental but know the bottom line.
- Distinguish between categorical thinking and stereotyping.
- Be aware of one's own attitudes, stereotypes and expectations and critically examine them.
- Be aware of one's own hesitancy to intervene.
- Explain differences and engage in open discourse.
- Do not be afraid of possible conflict.
- Do not ignore possible difficulties and tension.

### Enhancing Students' Learning

The following curricular and interactive suggestions for faculty may help students to achieve cultural literacy and more easily negotiate the higher education environment:

1. Identify differences in students' learning styles, and how these variations may impact on students' academic and later professional success. The Learning Style Inventory (Kolb, 1984) provides a format for students to understand their strengths and weaknesses as learners. Some students learn from observing, some learn by listening, some learn by rote practice and others learn by discovery.

2. Employ a variety of teaching strategies to meet the learning needs of the students. Cooperative learning strategies may be employed for engaging and committing students to the learning process. Instead of direct lecturing, faculty should encourage students to ask questions and facilitate interactions among the students (KuyKendall, 1992). There should be increased attempts to create a classroom climate and interactions that are sensitive to students as nonconfrontational **listeners.** Since some students may feel uncomfortable talking to, or asking questions in front of the whole class, small group assignments may be useful to encourage participation of all students.

Green (1989) provides strategies to enhance individual student's learning potential. Harvard University's New Pathway Program, for example, is a medical student training program that has proven successful in providing students with different ways of learning and problem solving. A patient's case history is presented at the beginning of the class discussion, and students are then placed in groups to work out the diagnosis. The application of this type of approach in which students are placed in small groups to collectively solve problems, and where faculty serve as tutors for the groups, could be applied as a teaching strategy in the various allied health programs.

3. Strengthen writing skills by using **Writing Across the Curriculum** (Scarella, 1989). This approach requires students to complete assignments, or summaries for every class lecture. The assignment is collected at the end of each class so that the faculty can determine what the students have learned.

4. Enhance communication interchanges between faculty and students by having faculty reach out to the less verbal students by making prearranged appointments to talk with them about their concerns and class assignments. This **reaching out** will make the students feel a sense of importance and interest from the faculty (Green, 1989).

5. Nurture students' growth in sensitivity and awareness regarding their faculty and clinical supervisors. When culturally diverse students interact with mainstream American faculty, students have to be sensitive to the educational training and cultural background of their faculty in order to understand their expectations, as well as their styles of interaction (Cheng, 1989b). Developing social and cultural literacy is essential. Clinical supervisors need to provide opportunities for students to receive clinical training with diverse client populations of various ages and disorders.

6. Provide general opportunities for students to learn more about the cultures of various populations. As part of course curricula, students can be assigned to visit ethnic communities, conduct ethnographic interviews and observe interactions at group functions such as going to Chinese funerals, Puerto Rican election campaigns, Jewish weddings, African American Sunday services, Mexican christenings, etc. (Cheng, 1989b). College media departments or professional associations may be able to provide faculty with films or videos that have content appropriate for discussing cultural diversity. For example, ASHA's Office of Minority Concerns provides a list of reading and audiovisual materials for such purposes.

7. Have frequent contacts with students both inside and outside the classroom. For example, sponsor brown bag lunches, go on field trips, make home visits, attend community celebrations or organize picnics (Green, 1989).

8. Provide consistent and continuous mentoring and advisement.

9. Set up a **buddy system** or a **big brother/sister system** with a student peer, or even ask a past graduate or a minority professional to act as a role model (Cheng, 1989a).

10. Include all students' perspectives in classroom discussions about diversity. Solicit students to volunteer expert information about their own cultures with the class while being sensitive not to burden the student with unrealistic demands.

11. Provide study skills including time management, test taking, paper preparation, writing, and oral presentations since minority students typically have different study skills where they primarily concentrate on memorization and perfection of language rules. Students should be encouraged to experiment first with trial writings without jeopardizing their grades. Faculty need to spend time commenting on the specific writings, rather than making general statements such as **rewrite** or **awkward.** Faculty can provide them with written models on how the material needs to be organized. Writing labs are generally helpful. They should be offered opportunities to discuss their ideas in **low-risk** situations.

12. Make sure course requirements are explained explicitly to students.

13. Find student resources for communication enhancement in phonology, morphology, syntax, semantics and pragmatics (Powell and Collier, 1990).

14. Admit several students into the program at the same time from the same minority group so that they will not feel as isolated or alienated.

15. Encourage minority students in your program to complete doctorate degrees in an effort to increase the number of minority faculty in higher education.

## Recruitment Issues

The following suggestion might be useful for recruiting diverse students into the allied health professions (Cheng, 1989):

1. Contact student organizations on campus to inform them about the allied health professions and ask them to help recruit students.

2. Contact local minority community centers, churches and organizations to introduce the allied health professions while informing them of the critical shortages.

3. Contact high school guidance counselors in highly concentrated minority communities, and disseminate information about the allied health disciplines as career options.

4. Contact the media and provide stories about the need for providing health services (e.g., communication and hearing services) to a particular cultural population.

5. Talk to other college departments about the allied health professions, such as education, special education (e.g., hearing handicapped), vocational rehabilitation, psychology, linguistics, sociology, anthropology, journalism and communication, etc. to potentially recruit diverse students.

## CONCLUSION

A primary challenge for faculty as we enter the twenty-first century is that they become intercultural communicators by learning about, understanding and respecting their multiculturally and linguistically diverse students. This quest calls for revisions of our educational ideology practices, as well as our perceptions of minority students. It additionally demands increased awareness and sensitivity to many of the cultural and communication factors discussed in this chapter. This challenge will lay the foundation for a more diverse, pluralistic American classroom.

In order to facilitate embracing diversity, Cheng (1990a) proposes a shift of paradigms that may be applicable in our institutions of higher education. Faculty need to challenge the more traditional modes of teaching that have their roots in a mainstream American orientation. Instead of **tolerating** and **compensating** for students differences in learning and communication styles, faculty can **embrace** and **appreciate** what is already there. Instead of **alienating** students, faculty can **assist** minority students to become acculturated and experience being a **vital member** of the academic community.

Instead of viewing the diverse patterns of writing and speaking as **deficits,** perhaps faculty can be **enriched** by the different modes and **ways with words** (Heath, 1983). When students bring to the educational environment different forms of communication and educational practices, these need to be viewed as **assets,** and to be considered within the context of diversity. Instead of **reducing** a student's accent or another communicative behavior, students can **add** another style of articulation or another style of communication to their repertoire, as well as **code-switch** to meet the communication demands of the educational situation (Grosjean, 1982). Linguistically and culturally diverse students need to **add** to their existing repertoire various forms of academic discourse. Providing all students with the same learning materials is **equality.** However, they may not all learn as equally well. **Equity** means giving students what they need in order to achieve equally as well (Hillard, 1990).

There is a need for the systematic study of the culture of the American higher education system, its self-perceptions, and its operations. Policy makers and educators must redefine themselves as pluralistic as opposed to monolithic (Cheng, 1989b; 1990). "To this end the quality of education and life we enjoy tomorrow depends on how well we educate all of our students today" (San Diego State University, 1991, p. 15).

## REFERENCES

Abe, H. & Wiseman, R.L.: A cross cultural confirmation of the dimensions of intercultural effectiveness. *International Journal of Intercultural Relations, 7:* 53–67, 1983.

Althen, G.: *American Ways: A Guide for Foreigners in the United States.* Yarmouth, Intercultural Press, 1988.

American Speech, Language and Hearing Association: *Directory for Bilingual Speech-Language Pathologists and Audiologists.* Rockville, Author, 1989.

Amoako, S., Jie Gao, Low, F. & Neham, B.: Difficult Dialogues: Achieving the Promise in Diversity. American Association of Higher Education's National Conference. LaGuardia Community College, New York, March 24–27, 1991.

American Speech, Language and Hearing Association: *Urban And Ethnic Perspective.* Rockville, Author, October, 1982, pp. 9–10.

American Speech, Language and Hearing Association: Position paper on social dialect. *Asha, 29:* 1, 1987.

Asby, G.: *Micronesian Customs and Beliefs.* Eugene, Rainy Day, 1983.

Banks, J.A.: *Transforming the Curriculum: Conference on Diversity.* Oakland, California Teacher Credentialing Commission, 1990.

Banks, J.A., Cortes, C.E., Gay, G., Garcia, R. & Ochoa, A.S.: *Curriculum Guidelines For Multiethnic Education.* Washington, National Council for the Social Studies, 1976.

Bjorkland, D. & Bjorkland, B.: Cultural literacy. *Parents,* 144, January, 1988.

Joint Committee for Review of the Master Plan for Higher Education: *California Faces... California Future: Education for Citizenship in a Multicultural Society.* Sacramento, Author, 1989.

Chan, S.Q.: Early intervention with culturally diverse families of infants and toddlers with disabilities. *Infants and Young Children, 3* (2): 78–87, 1990.

Cheng, L.: Cross-cultural and linguistic considerations in working with Asian populations. *Asha, 29:* 33–37, 1987.

Cheng, L.: Service delivery to Asian/Pacific Limited English Proficiency children: A cross-cultural framework. *Topics in Language Disorders, 9* (3): 1–14, 1989a.

Cheng, L.: Ethnic cultural, linguistic diversity: Challenges and opportunities for faculty, students and curriculum. In Ripich, D. (Ed.): *The Graduate Council of Communication Sciences and Disorders 1989 Annual Conference Proceedings.* Tampa, Author, 1989b, pp. 37–61.

Cheng, L.: Recognizing diversity: A need for a paradigm shift. *American Behavioral Scientist, 34* (2): 263–277, 1990a.

Cheng, L.: Asian American cultural perspectives on birth-defects: Focus on cleft palate. *Cleft Palate Journal, 27* (3): 294–300, 1990b.

Cheng, L.: *Assessing Asian Language Performance.* Oceanside, Academic Communication Associates, 1991.

Chu-Chang, M.: Research on Asian and Pacific Americans: The missing link. In Chu-Chang, M. (Ed.): *Asian and Pacific American Perspectives in Bilingual Education: Comparative Research.* New York, Teachers College Press, 1983.

Cole, L.: We're serious. *Asha, 34:* 38–39, 1992.

Current Population Reports: *The Hispanic Population in the United States.* Washington, Bureau of the Census, March 1990.

DeRosa, P.: *Context: Southeast Asians in California.* Cambridge, Bicultural Project for Communication and Education, 1991.

Devine, E. & Briganti, N.L.: *The Travellers' Guide to Asian Customs and Manners.* New York, St. Martin's Press, 1989.

Gardner, R.W., Robey, B. & Smith, P.C.: Asian Americans: Growth, change and diversity. *Population Bulletin, 40:* 1–44, 1985.

Giles, H. & Franklyn-Stokes, A.: Communicator characteristics. In Asante, M.K. & Gudykunst, W.B. (Eds.): *Handbook of International and Intercultural Communication.* Newbury Park, Sage Publications, 1989, pp. 117–144.

Gordon, L.: Southeast Asian refugees migration to United States. In Faucet, J. &

Carino, B. (Eds.): *Pacific Bridges: The New Immigration from Asia and the Pacific Islands.* New York, Center for Migration Studies, 1987, pp. 243–273.

Green, M.F. (Ed.): *Minorities on Campus: A Handbook for Enhancing Diversity.* Washington, American Council on Education, 1989.

Grosjean, F.: *Life With Two Languages: An Introduction to Bilingualism.* Cambridge, Harvard University Press, 1982.

Hall, E.T.: *Beyond Culture.* Garden City, Anchor Books, 1976.

Heath, S.B.: *Ways With Words: Language, Life and Work In Communities and Classrooms.* Cambridge, Cambridge University Press, 1983.

Hecht, M.L., Anderson, P.A. & Ribeau, S.A.: The cultural dimensions of nonverbal communication. In Asante, M.K. & Gudykunst, W.B. (Eds.): *Handbook of International and Intercultural Communication.* Newbury Park, Sage Publications, 1989, pp. 163–185.

Hillard, A.: Validity and Equity in Curriculum and Teaching: Multicultural Lecture Series. San Diego State University, San Diego, February 22, 1990.

Jackson, P.: *Life in Classrooms.* New York, Holt, Rinehart and Winston, 1968.

Kerman, S.: *"Why Did You Call on Me? I Didn't Have My Hand Up." Kappan,* 23–27, June, 1979.

Kolb, D.: *Experiential Learning: Experiences as the Source of Learning Development.* Englewood Cliffs, Prentice Hall, 1984.

KuyKendall, C.: *From Rage to Hope: Strategies for Reclaiming Black and Hispanic Students.* Bloomington, National Education Service, 1992.

Lynch, E.: Developing cross-cultural competence. In Lynch, E. and Hanson, M. (Eds.): *Developing Cross-Cultural Competence: A Guide for Working with Younger Children and their Families.* Baltimore, Brookes, 1991.

Lynch, E. & Hanson, J.: *Developing Cross-Cultural Competence.* Baltimore, Brookes, 1992.

McKenna, B.: Good news and bad on the diversity front. *On Campus, 11* (5): 3, 1992.

Oliver, M.L. & Johnson, J.H., Jr.: The challenge of diversity in higher education. *Urban Review, 20* (3): 139–145, 1988.

Philips, S.: *The Invisible Culture: Communication in Classroom and Community on the Warm Springs Indian Reservation.* New York, Longman, 1983.

Powell, R. & Collier, M.J.: Public speaking instruction and cultural bias: The future of the basic course. *American Behavioral Scientist, 34* (2): 240–250, 1990.

Randall-David, E.: *Strategies for Working with Culturally Diverse Communities and Clients.* Washington, Association for the Care of Children's Health, 1989.

Ruben, B.D.: The study of cross-cultural competence: Traditions and contemporary issues. *International Journal of Intercultural Relations, 13:* 229–240, 1989.

*San Diego State University, College of Health and Human Services Diversity Plan.* San Diego, Author, 1991.

Scarcella, R.C.: Empowering University Students: Providing Language Support Services Across The Curriculum. Speech delivered to the Conference on Celebrating Diversity, Oakland, 1989.

Shewan, C.: ASHA 1988 Omnibus Survey, Rockville, American Speech, Language and Hearing Association, 1988.

Spindler, G., Spindler, L., Trueba, H. & Williams, M.: *The American Cultural Dialogue and Its Transmission.* Philadelphia, the Falmer Press, 1990.

Spitzberg, B.H.: Issues in the development of a theory of interpersonal competence in the cultural context. *International Journal of Intercultural Relations, 13:* 241–268, 1989.

Stanford University: *Stanford University Guidelines.* Author, San Diego, November, 1991, pp. 4–6.

Storti, C.: *The Art of Crossing Cultures.* Yarmouth, Intercultural Press, 1989.

The Commission on Minority Participation in Education and American Life: *One-Third of a Nation.* Washington, American Council on Education, 1988.

Tran, M.: *Hidden Curriculum: An Asian Perspective.* Unpublished manuscript. San Diego, San Diego State University, 1991.

Triandis, H., Brislin, R. & Hui, C.: Cross-cultural training across the individualism-collective divide. *Internal Journal of Intercultural Relations, 12:* 269–289, 1988.

Trueba, H.T.: *Success or Failure?* Cambridge, Newbury House, 1987.

Trueba, H.T.: *Raising Silent Voices: Educating the Linguistic Minorities for the 21st Century.* Cambridge, Newbury House, 1989.

Trueba, H.T., Guthrie, G.P. & Au, K.H.P.: *Culture and the Bilingual Classroom: Studies in Classroom Ethnography.* Cambridge, Newbury House, 1981.

United States Bureau of the Census: *1986 Census of the Population: Asian and Pacific Island Population by State.* Washington, Author, 1987.

United States Bureau of Census: *1990 Census of the Population.* Washington, Author, 1991.

Walker, C.L.: Learning English: The Southeast Asian refugee experience. *Topics in Language Disorders, 5* (3): 53–65, 1985.

# Chapter 2

# ADDRESSING CULTURAL DIVERSITY WITHIN THE ACADEMY

Annette B. Ramírez de Arellano

## INTRODUCTION

*I have been called patriarchal and chauvinistic, because when I describe the discovery of DNA, I mention Francis Crick and James Watson and do not include Rosalind Franklin.*

(A biology professor)

*I fill out students' forms, and I am always surprised by how students describe themselves. One student said that he was Hispanic, but I saw that he was Black and classified him as such.*

(An academic advisor)

*The minute I open my mouth, people can tell my gender, class, race, and ethnicity.*
(A college student, explaining why she chooses to remain silent in class)

Even a casual perusal of the pages of *The Chronicle of Higher Education* and other academic publications reveals the extent to which campuses are grappling with issues of cultural diversity. Whether choosing to ignore the topic or meeting it head-on, institutions of higher education are being confronted with an increasingly varied student population, a changing kaleidoscope of potential clienteles, and the need to extend curriculum content and didactic methods beyond the usual canons and techniques. As Stimpson (1991) has stated, "One change today is social and demographic, the increasing diversity of students, staff, and faculty members . . . A second change is intellectual. We are thinking about and teaching new subjects with new methods . . . " (p. 40).

On many campuses today, the goal of "cultural competence" is not only a moral imperative but a survival tactic. Those who see any change as an attempt to "pander to vocal minorities" ignore the fact that accreditation agencies, boards of trustees, and the public at large are also holding institutions accountable for their commitment to diversity. This is particularly the case in the "helping" professions of education, health, and social welfare, where professionals are expected to understand their clients' needs and interact with persons of different backgrounds. These goals will remain elusive unless professionals can communicate with sensitivity across cultures.

Given the current impact of cultural diversity on campuses, academics have adopted a variety of strategies. Some have championed the changes by recognizing that curricula are tools of power. They then utilize this power to question assumptions and modify beliefs and behaviors. Others have made marginal changes by incorporating a few reading assignments and lectures. They may additionally bring in guest speakers to present an alternative perspective or introduce a new topic. Others, as Scott (1991) has indicated, have remained wedded to "tradition," often ignoring that tradition "is largely invented, always contested, and that what has counted as tradition has changed from generation to generation" (p. 32). Morgan (1991) points out that these faculty members argue that their knowledge is strictly factual, value-neutral, and is therefore not subject to varying interpretations. Each group defends its position with messianic zeal, and the issue of diversity has divided many campuses (Ravitch, 1990; Finn, 1990). Oftentimes the decibel level of the debate has exceeded the level of understanding.

If we are to come to grips with the changing needs of not only the students but the country as a whole, we can no longer afford to ignore the issue of cultural diversity in the classroom. Many well-meaning academicians, however, are fearful of walking into a minefield, being exposed as ignorant, or being called "sexist" or "racist," indelible labels that can tarnish reputations and even destroy careers. As a result, there is a growing need for guidance not only in bringing about curriculum change but in the addressing the day-to-day challenges of a diverse student body.

The "how to's" of acquiring cultural literacy are still in flux. In view of this, the following comments are not offered as prescriptive commandments. They are rather presented as pointers that can serve as buoys as campuses sail into uncharted waters and learn to navigate the subtleties and complexities of dealing with diversity.

1. First, it is necessary to stress that the language of diversity is itself fraught with perils. Cultural designata vary over time and, in times of transition, a variety of labels may be used to self-identify and to identify others (Gates, 1992). The changing use of "Negro," "Black," and "African American" reflects more than a shift in fashion. Each term carries with it

much historical and social baggage. Similarly, persons of Hispanic heritage or from Spanish-speaking countries may refer to themselves as "Hispanic," "Latino," "Chicano," or "raza." Each label has its own nuances, and members of a given group may use different terms to identify themselves. When in doubt, it is best to take your cue from the individual, who has the right to describe himself or herself as he or she sees fit.

Moreover, it is well to recognize that even common, seemingly innocuous terms may be offensive to some. The term "minority," for example, connotes powerlessness and subordination. Furthermore, it makes sense to refer to a group as a minority only vis-a-vis a larger aggregate.

The phrase "people of color" is also problematic: it is overly inclusive as well as inaccurate. By grouping all non-Caucasians as an amorphous "other," it overlooks the differences that exist among and between groups. This "othering" or homogenization of persons into a "collective they" additionally, fails to recognize that everyone's skin has a color (Pratt, 1986).

Rubrics based on language may also be misleading. For example, the label of ESL (English as a Second Language) has been used to describe a broad range of students. Because the rubric includes persons who are proficient in two (or more) languages, as well as those who are proficient in none, the variation among ESL students is likely to be as wide as the distinctions between ESL and non-ESL persons. Unfortunately, the label has at times provided a socially acceptable way to refer to students who are academically disadvantaged (whether linguistically or not). It has thus served to mask the complexities of inadequate academic preparation, whatever its source.

2. Secondly, race and ethnicity are different but not mutually exclusive categories. As Taylor (1991) has indicated, "race is a statement about one's biological attributes. Culture is a statement about one's behavioral attributes in such diverse areas as values, perceptions, world views, cognitive styles, institutions, language and so on. Within all races, there are many cultures" (p. 7). The combinations of race and culture are practically unlimited, a situation that precludes any facile generalization on ethnicity.

3. It is presumptuous and unreasonable to ask one individual to represent or serve as a spokesperson for an entire group, however this is defined. Yet this happens with disturbing frequency. In the words of a student at the University of California at Berkeley, "On the all-female floor of the dormitory where I lived, young White women constantly

bombarded me with questions that they felt I should answer just because I was Black ... " (Daniels, 1991, p. 19). Similarly, Asian Americans, regardless of place of origin, are often taken as representative of persons from countries as diverse as India, the Philippines, and Japan; and Latinos are bracketed together whether they come from the Bolivian *altiplano* or New York City's Washington Heights. This tendency to overgeneralize ignores the idiosyncratic variation based on class, geography, and migration history, to mention only a few distinguishing variables.

A related *faux pas* lies in the unwarranted attribution of expertise to someone merely because of his or her place of birth, or the color of his or her skin. Singling out students to provide background information solely on the basis of their race or ethnicity may be personally embarrassing and uncomfortable. This, however, is often done under the banner of inclusion or multicultural sharing.

Because nonmainstream cultures have often been neglected or devalued in the academy, a person of a particular background may not know much about his or her cultural or ethnic roots. Moreover, unless the person has grown within a culturally homogeneous community, he or she may not be able to distinguish lifelong habits, which may be specific to his or her family, from customs and lifestyles that are culturally-based. In addition, class, education and length of residence in the host country are all confounding variables which may temper or eclipse ethnic identity.

As a faculty member serving on a curriculum committee, I was taken aback to see all eyes focused on me when a proposal for a new course on Puerto Rican history was under discussion. Because I was born in Puerto Rico, I was expected to comment knowledgeably on the proposed topic, the logic of its content and sequence, and the appropriateness of the suggested bibliography. Inwardly, I thought that I had no credentials in the subject and chose to remain silent, an act that could have been interpreted as self-effacement or lack of interest.

4. Another potential trap lies in what has been termed "identity politics," or the assumption that a person's racial or ethnic identity and views are one and the same (Patai, 1991). Thus, African American professors and students are expected to "think black," as if pigmentation determined thought processes and skin color were a necessary and sufficient correlate of ideology. This type of reductionist thinking is at the root of many disagreements in the academy, and permeates much of the debate on who should teach what. The idea that one has to be of a certain

group to understand its mores, care about its history, and transmit its knowledge undermines the power of education, which posits that everyone has the capacity to learn. As Gates (1992) has stated, "Any human being sufficiently curious and motivated can fully possess another culture, no matter how 'alien' it may appear to be" (p. xv).

5. Like cynicism, ethnic and racial jokes have no place in the classroom. Some professors attempt to inject levity into their lectures by lapsing into ethnic jokes, even targeting themselves in the process. Yet much humor is culture bound, and is, therefore, subject to misunderstandings: simply put, one person's witticism is another's wounding comment. Even when the butt of a joke is a stock figure (e.g., the Jewish mother, the Irish cop) and is from the same culture as the speaker, the result may give offense. Not surprisingly, many Jewish women object to the popular image of the Jewish mother because, like any caricature, it distorts and exaggerates, transforming legitimate maternal concern into intrusive overprotection. At the same time, one hears a Latino woman complain that the stereotype of the Jewish mother taints all other mothers by implying that Jewish women have a monopoly on caring. It is, therefore, appropriate to heed the charge that anthropologist Johnetta Cole (1991), President of Spellman College, has given to academicians everywhere: "Whether in the men's room or women's room, in a departmental meeting, or at a departmental picnic, when you hear a racist, sexist, or homophobic joke or comment, don't laugh. Call the person on it" (p. 3).

6. Academicians must also guard against "tracking" students by steering them into particular courses of study on the basis of their race or ethnicity. This process may take subtle forms and is almost always inappropriate. It can occur when placing students in internships or practicums, creating study groups, or assigning projects. To assume that students want to work only with "their own kind" is to reinforce stereotypes and ghettoize students.

Blatant bigotry is relatively easy to combat. In most cases it is illegal, and campuses have internal policies and grievance mechanisms to deal with it. Insensitivity, often unintentional, is more insidious. It takes many guises, and frequently goes undetected by those who are not its victims. The classroom is the perfect arena in which to ferret out prejudice and foster multicultural, multiethnic understanding. Academicians, however, must be aware of their own biases and behaviors, and learn to address issues of race and ethnicity with the same diligence that they keep abreast of their changing disciplines. To do otherwise is to become obsolete, and to condemn a growing proportion of our students to marginality.

# REFERENCES

Cole urges educators to increase efforts to achieve diversity. *Higher Education and National Affairs, ACE,* 3, April 8, 1991.

Daniels, L.A.: Diversity, correctness, and campus life. *Change,* 19, September/October 1991.

Finn, C.E.: Why can't colleges convey our diverse culture's unifying themes? *The Chronicle of Higher Education,* 40, June 13, 1990.

Gates, H.L.: *Loose Canons: Notes on the Culture Wars.* New York, Oxford University Press, 1992.

Morgan, J.: Ohio State pioneers new faculty roles in Black student retention. *Black Issues in Higher Education,* 15, May 24, 1991.

Patai, D.: The struggle for feminist purity threatens the goals of feminism. *The Chronicle of Higher Education,* 10, February 5, 1991.

Pratt, M.L.: Scratches in the face of the country; or, what Mr. Barrow saw in the land of the bushmen. In Gates, H.L. (Ed.): *"Race," Writing and Difference.* Chicago, The University of Chicago Press, 139, 1986.

Ravitch, D.: Multiculturalism yes, particularism no. *The Chronicle of Higher Education,* 44, October 24, 1990.

Scott, J.W.: The campaign against political correctness: What's at stake? *Change,* 32, November/December 1991.

Stimpson, C.R.: New 'politically correct' metaphors insult history and our campuses. *The Chronicle of Higher Education,* 40, May 29, 1991.

Taylor, O.L.: Pragmatic considerations in addressing race, ethnicity and cultural diversity within the academy. In Cole, L. (Ed.): *Institute on Multicultural Professional Education Manual.* Rockville, American Speech, Language and Hearing Association, 1990, pp. 3–12.

# Chapter 3

# UNDERSTANDING ETHNIC IDENTITY AND PREJUDICE

CAROL E. WESTBY

*Future flowers,*
*Now seeds . . .*
*Each unique,*
*And all the same . . .*
*One color.*
*Many shades . . .*
*Our race*
*The human race*
(Vachss, 1991)

## INTRODUCTION

Why discuss ethnic socialization, prejudicial attitudes and discriminatory behavior in a book addressing working with university minority students in speech-language pathology and audiology? Faculty and staff of multicultural programs are generally prepared to address issues of cross-cultural child socialization, dialect variations, assessment and intervention strategies with culturally diverse populations, and types of communicative disorders in multicultural populations. They may also be prepared to provide students with academic support and mentoring. They are, however, seldom prepared to discuss issues of prejudice and discrimination, and are uncomfortable in doing so. These issues cannot be ignored. Prejudice and discrimination are present whether or not they are discussed. University faculty, staff, and students are assumed to be egalitarian and open to diverse ideas and beyond thinking that some groups of people are inferior to other groups. Yet in recent years there have been increasing incidences of racial and ethnic discrimination on college campuses (Beckham, 1987/1988; Carter, Pearson, & Shavlik, 1987/1988; Hood, 1991). Programs in higher education should be alert to students' experiences with and feelings about prejudice and discrimination. They should, in addition, prepare students for dealing with these issues in the workplace once they graduate.

In 1987, I became the Director of the Multicultural Education Program in Communicative Disorders at the University of New Mexico. This program was funded by a grant from the United States Office of Education. The goals of the program were to: (1) acquaint all students in the department with information on communicative disorders in culturally diverse populations and to prepare them to clinically work effectively in this diverse society, and (2) to increase the numbers of professionals from diverse populations in the fields of speech-language pathology and audiology by providing academic and financial support for students from nondominant cultural groups. The need to address ethnic/racial attitudes and prejudice surfaced in the second year of the program.

The first year was a honeymoon phase. The department had not had any special projects or funding for students for several years. Faculty, clinical supervisory staff, and students all expressed interest in the program. Students appeared comfortable with one another and with the faculty and staff. Problems arose, however, during the second year. Instances of racial/ethnic prejudice occurred on campus. A homecoming float depicted the hanging of an American Indian wearing a Buckwheat T-shirt. Letters to the editor of the student newspaper denigrated both minority and majority groups. The multicultural program in the Communicative Disorders Department was also affected by the tensions. Students reported comments by faculty, staff, and other students that they perceived as racist. A Black student reported being told she could not write because she spoke Black English. This particular student was raised in predominantly White and Hispanic communities and evidenced no characteristics of Black dialect. An Hispanic student reported that a faculty member said in class that the coursework was too difficult for Hispanic students. The Hispanic clinical supervisor reported a faculty member saying that minority students were learning disabled. Students within the multicultural program did not feel a sense of unity. Students who were teamed to work together on assignments as part of the academic support system, were not working with the individual to whom they had been assigned. Rather they had regrouped themselves. Hispanic students worked with Hispanic students; Native Americans and Anglos worked with each other, but neither group worked with Hispanic students; a Black student appeared isolated from all of the students.

A similar pattern of self-imposed segregation was observed at the preschool that served as a primary clinical site. The preschool was a grant-funded project to empower Hispanic families. Because the neighborhood was racially mixed, however, the school had become integrated at the request of African American families. The Black children tended to play with other Black children; the Hispanic children played with Hispanic children. The 3, 4, and 5 year olds, representing two different minority cultures did not, however, spontaneously play with each other.

My initial reaction was to ignore the students' comments and behaviors, thinking that the problems would resolve with time. A Hispanic staff member counseled students to dispel derogatory comments regarding their scholastic abilities by "hanging in and achieving." This had been her strategy in graduate school. The incidents and concerns did not, however, dissipate. Since ignoring the situation was nonproductive, my next strategy was, to say, "I really don't think she meant it the way that you're taking it." I felt that perhaps students were seeing prejudice and discrimination where none existed. It quickly became apparent that this was an inappropriate strategy, because it did not acknowledge students' feelings about what they were experiencing, and it made it appear as though I was protecting the status quo. My next strategy was to try to understand what was happening. I talked with faculty at the African American, Hispanic, and Native American Student Centers on campus, and with faculty who specialized in intercultural communication. I came to understand that it is difficult to recognize and identify subtle instances of racism. In order to teach and guide our students, it is necessary to learn about the history of ethnic/racial relations within our particular area. I learned about the history of ethnic/racial relations in New Mexico, and from this I gained insight into minority perspectives on prejudice. Our role as faculty is to teach and impart knowledge. Within our modern society represented by a global village of diverse cultures, teaching about racism and prejudice should be part of the curriculum.

The purpose of this chapter is to provide an understanding of how individuals come to know themselves as part of an ethnic/racial group; how this awareness is related to the development of prejudicial attitudes and discriminatory behaviors; the reasons for and manifestations of prejudice; and ways to foster ethnic self-identity and reduce prejudice. Programs that seek to recruit and retain ethnic/racial minority students often seek to foster the students' identity with their own cultures at the same time as they facilitate students' accommodation to the mainstream university culture. Lynch (1987) has indicated, however, that in the process of acquiring one's own culture, one may also develop attitudes and values that are antipathic to other individuals and groups. Thus, faculty in programs with a multicultural emphasis should seek to assist students in acquiring an understanding and tolerance for students of other backgrounds as they are developing their own positive self-identity. Programs should also be aware of the possibility of prejudice and discrimination occurring on a university campus. Faculty and staff need to be sensitive to the discrimination that students may indeed face within the university environment and must work to assist them in dealing with prejudice. They must also prepare students to understand racial and ethnic identity in their clients and enable them to provide nonbiased services and assist clients in the development of positive ethnic self-identity and tolerance for diversity.

## WHAT IS ETHNICITY?

### Definitions

To understand ethnic socialization, prejudice, and discrimination one must understand what it means to be a member of an ethnic/racial group (Rotheram & Phinney, 1987). There are a number of components involved in the concept of ethnicity. First is the concept of **ethnic socialization.** This refers to the developmental process by which children acquire the behaviors, perceptions, values, and attitudes of an **ethnic group.** An ethnic group is any group of people who consider themselves to be alike by some common virtue such as ancestry, race, religion, or national origin. One may be a member of an ethnic group and have been socialized into its behaviors, but not necessarily be aware that one is a member of that ethnic group.

**Ethnic awareness** is a conscious understanding of one's own group and other groups, and it involves knowledge about the groups' critical attributes, characteristics, customs, and history, as well as differences between oneself and others. Cultures that come into conflict with mainstream values and beliefs generally possess some degree of ethnic/racial awareness. Mainstream students are frequently unaware of the attitudes and behaviors of their mainstream culture. Some students from nondominant cultures who have grown up in fairly homogenous ethnic environments, with minimal contact with mainstream individuals, may also not be aware of how their characteristics differ from mainstream students.

In interviews conducted by multicultural project staff at the University of New Mexico with nondominant culture students, many Hispanic students reported that they were not different in specific ways from Anglo students. They did not think they possessed any behaviors, attitudes, or values that were different from those of Anglo students or that might make their adjustment to the university environment more difficult for them than for Anglos. Analysis of the interviews, however, highlighted several differences that could contribute to their experiencing difficulty adjusting to the university environment. Hispanic students generally had greater responsibilities to immediate and extended family members, and family responsibilities superseded school requirements. Thus, family matters could take precedence over studying for tests or even taking tests. Time at home was to be devoted to the family. Consequently, studying at home could be more difficult for Hispanic students than for Anglo students. Hispanic female students reported being expected to follow traditional gender roles more often than Anglo female students, and as a consequence, reported more instances of their families questioning their decision to pursue a masters degree.

One may or may not have a conscious ethnic awareness yet have an **ethnic identity.** Ethnic identity is one's sense of belonging to a group, and the part of one's thinking and perceptions and feelings that are part of being a member of that group (Rotheram and Phinney, 1987). Although some of the Hispanic students were not consciously aware of their culture, they did consider themselves to be Hispanic, and therefore, had an ethnic identity. The students could seldom describe what made them unique from students of other ethnic/racial background, but they were aware of the history of their families in New Mexico. One might be a member of an ethnic group by birth, but not have an ethnic identity. This has frequently occurred in children adopted by families of different racial/ethnic backgrounds, and in individuals who have sought a rapid acculturation to the mainstream. Some immigrant parents have attempted to shed their own ethnic identity as quickly as possible and have attempted to limit or even discourage their own children's association with ethnic behaviors (Sue & Sue, 1990). **Ethnic self-identification** refers to the use of an accurate and consistent ethnic label based on perceptions of belonging to a group. Thus, the student says, "I'm Puerto Rican, I'm African American, or I'm Vietnamese."

**Ethnic patterns** are attitudes, affects, and behavioral patterns or characteristics that are associated with particular groups. The other chapters in this book address some of the ethnic patterns of nondominant culture students and assist readers in understanding the significance of these patterns to students' success in the university environment. Understanding of ethnic awareness and ethnic identity, however, are also important if faculty and staff are to understand how students feel about their university program and how others feel about them. Attention to academic success alone will not be sufficient to retain nondominant culture students. Students must feel welcomed and valued in the programs, and they must feel that they need not give up who they are.

## Racial/Ethnic Groups in Society

Programs in higher education that are interested in integrating multicultural issues value the concept of a culturally pluralistic society. To contribute to the development of a culturally pluralistic society, faculty, and staff of these programs need some sense of history regarding how diversity has been handled in the United States. Attitudes about racial/ethnic identify determine what happens to racial/ethnic groups in mainstream society (Bennett, 1990). There are three possibilities: cultural suppression, cultural assimilation, and cultural pluralism. Any of these can occur on a university campus. With **cultural suppression** the racial/ethnic minority group is segregated from the mainstream society. Individuals in the group may retain some of their original culture or because of the separation and suppression, they may develop a unique culture to themselves. This has occurred with some African Americans and Native Americans in this country who have become isolated in inner city or rural environments. These groups may attain what is called a **pariah culture** (McDermott, 1987). They are actively rejected by the mainstream population because of behaviors and characteristics that are condemned by society as a whole. The response of the majority culture in this case is to regard the minority group as inferior. The majority do not value the minority group's contributions and they may actually try to hide and repress contributions from that particular racial/ethnic group. Hence, for example, history books seldom report the efforts of Black scientists or Native American statesmen.

Mainstream society in the United States has tended to advocate a **cultural assimilation** model under the guise of the **melting pot** interpretation of society. The minority individual has been told, "Give up your original culture. Become totally one of the mainstream until you are no longer identifiable as a member of a particular ethnic minority group" (Schlesinger, 1991). As long as minority individuals reject their culture, the dominant culture accepts them. (This option of total assimilation is generally not available to people of color who do not have the option of denying who they are). Yet the majority continues to perpetuate the prejudice handed down to them, and to perceive the minority group as inferior. Consequently, there is still a devaluing of the nondominant culture in the cultural assimilation model. Most universities have traditionally operated with the cultural assimilation model. Students from nondominant cultures are welcome as long as they meet the criteria established by the university, and can learn and perform according to the established mainstream patterns.

Ideally, in a **cultural pluralistic** society, each racial/ethnic group can retain many of its traditions. The minority group adopts a number of the mainstream and dominant cultural behaviors, but at the same time maintains a distinct ethnic perspective and contributes that perspective to the welfare of the nation as a whole. In a culturally pluralistic society, the mainstream respects and appreciates racial/ethnic diversity. And, in fact, the mainstream society encourages those groups to maintain their unique characteristics and often incorporates aspects of nondominant cultural groups into their own lifestyles.

## THE DEVELOPMENT OF ETHNIC IDENTITY

If programs with a multicultural focus seek to facilitate the development of a culturally pluralistic society, they must also seek to enable students to maintain their ethnic identity as well as to develop a bicultural identity that enables them to exist in two worlds. Without this bicultural identity, students can become aliens in both their ethnic culture and the mainstream culture. Not infrequently, students discover that they are no longer accepted in their home communities when they complete a university degree. Or, a student may leave the university because, as one of our Native American students said, "I'm losing me; I can't be me and stay at the university."

If faculty are to assist students in being bicultural, they must understand how persons come to identify themselves. There are three components to the development of ethnic identity (Aboud, 1987):

1. Describing oneself in terms of critical ethnic/racial attributes such as religion, country of origin, or physical characteristics;

2. Recognizing that one is different in certain ways from members of other ethnic/racial groups;

3. Recognizing that ethnicity/race remains constant.

The concept of self-identity is not the same in all groups. In the Euro-American world view, the self is that which distinguishes and separates the individual from everyone else (Semaj, 1985). This self is the me, myself, I. In the African world-view, the self is not just me, myself, I, but also a collective, or we orientation. With the African world-view, self identity includes the I of self-perception, which is one's self esteem, one's personality, and how one feels about who one is; the me of self-identity, which develops as a result of incorporating the perceptions of others; and the we identity, or extended self-identity, which represents the feelings and perceptions one has towards one's group. The I and me together are conceptualized as one's personal self-identity. The we or extended self-identity represents one's reference group orientation (Cross, 1985). This distinction between personal identity and extended self-identity (or reference group orientation) is critical for other nondominant cultural groups in addition to African Americans.

Extended self-identity (ESI) may be manifested in three different ways in culturally nondominant students (Semaj, 1985):

1. **Collective ESI.** In children collective ESI is represented by in-group racial preference and identification with their birth culture. In adults collective extended self-identity includes a commitment to the collective survival of their group and efforts to maintain and promote the values, beliefs, and activities of their native culture.

2. **Alien ESI.** Children may show identification with the alien or mainstream culture. Adults with alien ESI exhibit a Eurocentric worldview and are concerned with individual needs over collective needs. They may even deny or reject their native culture. The author of this chapter has encountered school-age children who deny being Hispanic and speaking Spanish. These children have ignored their Spanish-speaking parents when they visited the school.

3. **Diffused ESI.** Children with diffused ESI attempt to balance the values of their birth culture and the mainstream culture by identifying with both sides. Adults intensify this balancing act believing, for example, that "Black is beautiful but knowing that White is powerful" (Simaj, 1985

p. 177). A diffused ESI is a natural consequence for minorities coping in a mainstream world.

To understand the development of ethnic awareness and prejudice it is necessary to acknowledge the distinction between personal and extended self-identity. Self-identity does not develop in exactly the same ways in majority and minority populations. The development of ethnic identity has been explored by a number of researchers (Aboud, 1988; Clark & Clark, 1947; Fox and Jordan, 1973; Ramsey, 1987). Katz (1975) proposed eight overlapping but separable steps in the developmental sequence of ethnic/racial awareness and attitudes.

1. **Observation of Cues.** From the first year, children are observant of characteristics associated with race. Aboud (1988) noted that Chinese infants in a nursery did not react as markedly to Chinese strangers as they did to White strangers.

2. **Formation of Rudimentary Concepts.** By the age of four children begin to perceive perceptual similarities among people and to exhibit differential responses to persons who are perceived as different from themselves. At this level, children's responses tend to be idiosyncratic (Alejandro-Wright, 1985). They do not understand the notion of ethnic/racial labels, and may even have their own personal labels (referring to the color of people as pink, vanilla, chocolate). Skin color is generally not the most salient characteristic for children this age. Sorce (1977) reported that hair and eyes provided more salient cues to children than did skin color.

3. **Conceptual Differentiation.** Once children learn a label for a group of people, they begin to define the characteristics of the group and develop evaluative connotations. Children differentiate Black and White persons by 4 to 5 years of age; Chinese-Americans by 5 to 7 years of age; and Native Americans and Hispanics by 7 to 10 years of age (Fox & Jordan, 1973; Rice, et al, 1974; Weiland & Coughlin, 1979). The distinction between personal and extended self-identity emerges at this stage (Semaj, 1985). At this stage, majority of studies have reported that nearly all White children choose White dolls or pictures of White children as looking most like them (Fox & Jordan, 1973; Morland & Suthers, 1980; Newman, Liss, & Sherman, 1983; Williams & Morland, 1976). Although most Black children choose a Black doll or picture of a Black child as looking most like them, a significantly large number of Black children choose a White doll. Even more Black children in this stage are likely to

indicate a preference for a White doll and to select the Black doll as looking bad (Clark & Clark, 1947; Powell-Hopson & Hopson, 1990).

Cross (1985) maintains that researchers have generally not recognized the distinction between personal and extended self-identity, and hence, have misinterpreted the significance of Black children's selection of White dolls. He proposed that Black children's selection of the White dolls does not represent poor self-esteem or lack of Black self-identity, but rather extended self-identity. The child sees himself as being part of the larger White society, or wants to be part of the larger society.

4. **Recognition of the Irrevocability of Cues.** Preschool children may believe that Black children can become White by washing, that one can become an American Indian by wearing a feathered headdress and moccasins, or that one can become White by wearing a blond wig. Between ages 7 to 10, children become aware that one cannot change one's race or ethnicity (Semaj, 1980; Vaughn, 1963). With development of the awareness of the permanence of ethnic/racial identity, children of color develop an increasing preference for children of their own ethnic/racial identity; and White children, who earlier has strong preferences for White children, begin to exhibit greater acceptance and liking of children of color (Katz, 1987; Vaughn, 1987).

5. **Consolidation of Group Concepts.** Children's perceptual and cognitive components of ethnic identity are interrelated. This may begin as early as the end of the preschool years, but extends for many years. Children begin to demonstrate an awareness that ethnic/racial awareness is based not only on skin color, but also on other physical characteristics (Ramsey, 1987).

6. **Perceptual Elaboration.** Children become increasingly aware of the perceptual characteristics that define or do not define an ethnic/racial group. Hence, skin color or shape of eyes may define a group, but a big smile or the type of shoes one wears do not. Children begin to be aware that the dimensions that distinguish ethnic/racial groups are biological as well as physical (Alejandro-Wright, 1985). Differences among groups may be accentuated for children who hear evaluative (prejudicial) talk, whereas intragroup differences are diminished (Ashmore & Del Boca, 1976).

7. **Cognitive Elaboration.** This is the process by which ethnic identity and racial/ethnic preference become prejudice as a result of school and experiences (or lack of experiences) with other racial/ethnic groups. Children realize that biological properties play a more prominent role

in ethnic/racial identity than perceptual characteristics. In addition, in this stage children begin to recognize the social dimension as a crucial factor in racial/ethnic identity (Alejandro-Wright, 1985). For example, one may belong to a particular racial/ethnic group by birth, but conceal one's identity in certain social settings and **pass** as a majority person. Racial/ethnic identity may vary depending on environmental conditions.

8. **Attitude Crystallization.** This final stage represents the consolation of ethnic/racial attitudes in later grade school as a result of cultural conditioning. Once students reach this stage, they will not rethink attitudes again unless placed in a situation that requires it. Most adults exhibit attitude crystallization (Katz, 1976).

## THE DEVELOPMENT OF PREJUDICE

Prejudice develops as awareness of one's race and ethnicity develops. Prejudice has three components (Aboud, 1988):

1. A negative evaluation;
2. An evaluation elicited by ethnicity/race, not personal qualities;
3. And an organized predisposition to react negatively.

A negative evaluation is the primary component of prejudice. Stereotyping by itself is not prejudicial. A stereotype can be neutral. For example, thinking that all Mexican Americans eat tortillas or that all African Americans can dance is stereotypical. By itself, however, it is not prejudicial because it does not involve a negative judgment. Thinking that all Native Americans are quiet is stereotypical, but it is not prejudicial unless one makes a negative interpretation of the stereotype, such as "Native Americans are quiet because they're not intelligent." In a university setting, attitudes become prejudicial when students are discouraged from entering a field of study because a professor perceives the field to be too difficult for individuals from a particular race/ethnicity; or when a supervisor decides that students from a particular racial/ethnic group will not make good clinicians because their communication styles would not be acceptable to mainstream clients.

Prejudice also involves an organized predisposition. That is, when one is faced with a person from a particular group, one's reaction is to look for negative behaviors. For example, rather than seeing the assets university minority students may bring in terms of expanding cultural awareness, orientations to collaborative and cooperative learning, and sensitivity to the diverse populations served by the clinic, faculty members may question if they will be expected to lower standards for minority students because "they're not as bright" as mainstream students. In evaluations of class presentations and clinic sessions, faculty may focus on the mainstream behaviors that nondominant students lack, rather than noting students' positive contributions and interactions.

## Theories of Prejudice

Three major theories have emerged to explain the development of prejudice: social reflection, inner state, and social cognitive.

## Social Reflection Theory

The social reflection theory has often been used to account for early development of prejudicial attitudes (Allport, 1954). Social reflection theory proposes that persons' attitudes and thoughts about ethnic groups reflect the structure of society. Groups possessing different power and status will be viewed differently. By the time children are 12 years of age, they adopt the attitudes corresponding to the social structures as perceived by their parents. Although this theory can explain why certain groups are targets for prejudice (because they are low in status and power), it does not account for age-related changes in prejudicial attitudes. It assumes that children should exhibit more prejudice as they mature and that their attitudes should reflect the attitudes of their parents. This is not the case, however. Children tend to exhibit prejudice regardless of the families they come from, and younger children can exhibit stronger prejudicial reactions than older children (Aboud, 1988; Davey, 1983; Katz, 1987).

## Inner State Theory

Another approach to understanding the development of prejudice is the inner state theory (Adorno, Frenkel-Brunswick, Levinson, Sanford, 1950). This theory proposes that prejudice reflects internal states, motivations, cognitions, or emotions that predispose a person to dislike those who are different. Individuals reportedly become prejudiced because they haven't resolved certain internal conflicts that they have. In very authoritarian families and in prejudicial families, who tend to be very authoritarian, children are not permitted to exhibit hostility. They are not permitted to say, "I don't wanna do that." The parental response may be, "You're gonna do it, and I don't want to hear about it." It is suggested that in authoritarian families, children do not have a chance to work out their hostility and so when they get older and feel they have power, they act out this hostility on others whom they perceive as not having power. With adults, there may be some truth for this inner state theory. Inner state theory emphasizes the stability of prejudice and does not account for the changes in prejudice that are observed in children.

## Social-Cognitive Development Theory

Although both the social reflection theory and the inner state theory can account for aspects of prejudice in adults, neither adequately explains the development of prejudice. Aboud (1988) suggests a social-cognitive theory to explain the development of prejudice. She maintains that children's prejudice is related to their cognitive level and that prejudice is a natural human behavior in early stages of development. She proposes two social cognitive developmental continua to explain prejudice: a cognitive continuum that moves from affect, to perceptions, to cognitions; and a social continuum that moves from attention on oneself, to attention on groups, to attention on individuals.

Along the cognitive continuum, children's first discriminatory behavior is based on an affective response. A little later, the response is based upon obvious perceptions, that is, the noticing of differences among people. Still later, the response is based upon thinking about those perceptions (Aboud, 1988). Affective responses are more primitive than perceptions and cognitions and can exist independently of them (Zajonc, 1980). Affective responses are immediate and intense, and they are based upon minimal perception and cognition of the stimulus. These emotional responses are easily triggered again by the same object or person. Because these preferences and responses are given little or no cognitive attention, they are rarely examined or changed in the face of contradictory information. Children's early responses are all affective. They are triggered by the fear and attachment that underlie approach and avoidance tendencies.

Young children are typically afraid of what is different and unfamiliar. Aboud (1988) suggested that children have exploratory skills that allow them to explore an unfamiliar object but not a novel person. Young children's preference for persons who look similar to them and prejudice against those who do not is a generalization of their attachment to familiar caregivers and fear toward persons who are less known. This attention to affective responses brings with it a focus on oneself and what is comfortable for oneself. People are liked or disliked to the degree that they satisfy one's needs.

Between ages 4 and 7, perceptual processes provide children with additional information. They begin consciously to note how they are similar to or different from others in terms of physical attributes such as skin color, hair, gender, etc. In this stage, White children show a strong preference toward others who look like them. The literature on Black children and some other ethnic groups indicates that these children are divided in their preferences, with some showing preference for others of their same ethnic/racial group and others showing a preference for the White group (Cross, 1985).

Early studies interpreted minority children's preference for White children as indicative of low self-esteem (Rotheram & Phinney, 1987). Other investigators (Glasberg & Aboud, 1981; Gottfried & Gottfried, 1974; Madge, 1976) have concluded that this preference is related to children's developing awareness of the power structure in mainstream society and to the development of an extended self-identity. Preschool children like to associate with others who are approved of and who receive rewards. Hence, children of color may want to associate themselves more closely to White children whom they perceive as having access to the approval of the teacher. Although they recognize the physical differences between themselves and the White children, their extended self-identity permits them to see themselves as part of a larger group. As their perceptual awareness develops, children shift from a focus on self to a focus on groups. They determine the group they belong to based on physical characteristics, and mainstream White children show a strong preference to their group. At this stage children are likely to show strong prejudicial reactions.

A major cognitive-social shift occurs between 8 and 12 years of age (Aboud, 1988; Flavell, 1977; Katz, 1976). Children develop conservation and perspective-taking skills. They understand that one's race or ethnicity is constant and cannot be changed. They also begin to be aware that there are similarities and differences among persons that are internal and not perceptual. As they are able to consider internal qualities such as emotions, thoughts, and goals, they begin to attend to individual differences among persons rather than difference between groups.

Children who perceive minimal group differences and maximal individual differences exhibit lower levels of prejudice than children who focus on group differences. At this stage children will identify with different social groups for different reasons, regardless of seeming differences. They may identify with one group because of similar ethnic background, but with another group because they hold similar values or interests. At this stage attitudes toward people are based upon their individual characteristics, not their group membership. Theoretically, the cognitive and social skills at this level have the potential to reduce or eliminate prejudice. Although by age 12 children may have the cognitive abilities necessary to develop this stage of ethnic identity and attitude, not all persons reach the stage (Kohlberg, 1976). Many adults continue to function at the affective/attention to self or perceptual/attention to groups stages, making judgments based on emotional responses or perceptual cues.

## THE LANGUAGE OF PREJUDICE

In principle, the majority of mainstream adults maintain egalitarian attitudes toward racial/ethnic groups and condemn prejudice and discrimination. They acknowledge that there is discrimination against minority groups, but they tend to minimize the extent of the discrimination and to assume that instances of discrimination occur more frequently somewhere else (compared to their own community or university) (Rothbart, 1976). Because mainstream culture is pro-White and Eurocentric, mainstream White individuals find it difficult to recognize the pervasiveness of racism. Minority individuals are alert to incidences of prejudices. When they attempt to explain their frustration to instances of prejudice and discrimination, however, they are accused of "having their antennae up," "being too sensitive," or "misinterpreting" (Essed, 1991). These attitudes of mainstream persons prevent them from hearing the minority persons' concerns, and consequently, they are prevented from being actively involved in reducing prejudice.

## Themes of Prejudice

How do persons recognize instances of prejudice when they encounter it? Prejudicial beliefs are transmitted through social discourse (van Dijk, 1987). To recognize and understand prejudice, then one must understand the structure of the discourse, its form and content. Prejudicial talk in adults has fairly regular macrostructures or organizational patterns and microstructures or themes. A study by van Dijk (1987) in both the United States and Amsterdam reported that similar attitudes triggered prejudicial talk. The ethnic/racial minority groups talked about in the two countries differed, but the nature of the conversation was the same. Thematically, prejudicial talk centers on three notions:

**Difference:**   They are different (in culture, mentality, norms).
**Deviance:**     They are involved in negative acts.
**Threat:**       They threaten out socioeconomic and cultural interests.

In fact, all of these themes center on perceived threats. The first represents a threat to norms, rules, habits, and cultural order ("We'll have to change admission standards"). The second can be interpreted as a threat to safety or well being or, in general, a threat to social order ("Collaborating on class projects is cheating"). And the last is a perceived threat to socioeconomic interests ("They get all the financial assistance and scholarships"). These dimensions of difference, deviance, and threat may be further organized by the well-known dimension of superiority. The differences or competition involved are not perceived to divide equal groups. Minority groups are seen as inferior and therefore, denied the same privileges as the majority.

In the workplace these themes are reflected by remarks such as, "They take our jobs;" "They don't adapt;" "They don't have good values;" "They are lazy, less intelligent, unmotivated." Variations of these comments are readily heard on college campuses. In departments with limited enrollments, students and faculty may feel threatened that minorities may be taking slots that could be taken by "better qualified Whites." Minority students may hear, "You got in just because there was grant money for you." Admissions committees may say, "We'll have to lower our standards. We only take students with GRE scores over 1000 and GPAs of 3.5 or better. There are no minorities with those qualifications." Even though it may not be explicitly stated, the underlying assumption is that this is an indication that minorities are not as capable (or that capable minorities threaten prejudicial dogma). The nondominant culture students may not be given consideration for having different educational experiences, or that they are learning in a language that is not their first language. In addition, the effects of the demands of extended families and jobs on students' GPAs may be ignored.

## Structure of the Discourse of Prejudice

Prejudicial talk generally takes the form of an argumentative macrostructure with the following elements (van Dijk, 1987):

(1) **Position statement** (opinion): I do not like X of group Y. For example, "I do not like the lack of initiative of Native American students. You have to hold their hands through everything."

(2) **Inference principle** (mostly implicit): If Y has/does X, then Y is bad. For example, students should be independent and require minimal guidance from professors.

(3) **General fact:** Y always have/do X. For example, "Native American students never show initiative."

(4) **Particular fact:** I have experienced that X1 did/have Y1. For example, "If I do not tell Alicia (student) exactly what to do, she does not do it. She should have known that I wanted references for the paper."

(5) **Supporting** ("objective") **evidence** for truth of (3) or (4). For example, "In their culture it is not considered appropriate to do something for oneself and one should not do anything that makes one stand out or look better than the group."

Argumentative structure is a common form used for the expression of delicate opinions. People who explicitly state prejudicial opinions about minorities will, implicitly or explicitly, state such opinions with supporting evidence. Such arguments may involve general principles and general facts, as well as particular facts, such as personal experiences. Because it is generally considered inappropriate to express a racist opinion about minorities, speakers must provide supporting evidence and evaluations in accordance with accepted norms, and they must use a positive self-presentation strategy when stating the opinions. Concrete stories of personal experiences have an important persuasive function because they are in principle true and not just opinion. One is not generally criticized for giving a personal story, although it might carry prejudicial information.

A frequent move in such prejudicial argumentation is to emphasize cultural differences to explain the perceived cultural conflict. For example, "It's not appropriate in their culture to stand out." Such explanations presuppose, that the minority group indeed have the cultural properties as stated (lack of initiative) and then attribute such cultural behavior (and hence conflict) to such cultural differences. Thus, the others are blamed and, at the same time, speakers contribute to their own positive self-presentation by showing understanding for such cultural differences. Because arguments of this are based on real experiences and premises that are generally known to be true, the arguments appear plausible and hence can be persuasive. It is, therefore, difficult for persons to produce counter arguments because they often lack the information to challenge the wrong (prejudiced) presuppositions.

The overall goal of persons using prejudicial arguments is to present others in a negative manner, while at the same time preserving a positive image of themselves. Because social norms do not allow negative talk about minority groups, speakers must use strategies to reconcile these inconsistencies. Van Dijk (1987) calls these strategies **semantic moves.** A statement such as "they are always slow" may be interpreted as an expression of a racist opinion. At the global or macrostructure level of conversation, therefore, the speaker will make sure to provide arguments and stories that are taken as evidence for the opinion that "they are slow." In this case, then, the proposition will no longer be a subjective, prejudiced opinion, but taken as a statement of fact.

At the local or microstructure level speakers make strategic moves that may inhibit negative inferences about the opinions or personality of the speakers. For instance, after saying, "They're not motivated to work hard," the speaker may add "but that's true of a lot of students today," or "They haven't had a good model." By extending the negative characteristic to most students, the speaker cannot be accused of ethnic/racial prejudice, and by adding an explanation for the negative characterization to others, the speaker cannot be accused of ethnic prejudice and by adding an explanation that specifies one of the causes, a possible excuse is formulated. Several types of semantic moves are available to speakers as a means of mitigating prejudicial statements.

1. **Example.** Personal examples are provided as evidence for supporting generalized statements (e.g., "They don't have the ability to handle this

information. I've had four of them in my classes and they have always gotten the lowest grade").

2. **Generalization.** Generalization is a complementary move to giving personal examples. After a specific example, the speaker generalizes to an entire group. "Kim can't organize her ideas in writing." "Most faculty report the same difficulties with Asian students."

3. **Apparent denial and negation.** This is an especially common move in prejudicial discourse. The speaker denies having negative opinions and then gives a negative opinion (e.g., "I really would like to have more minorities in the department, but I don't want to lower the quality of the program").

4. **Explanation.** Statements about controversial topics usually need explanation. As persons learn about cultural differences in communication and behaviors patterns, they may use this knowledge to mitigate their negative feelings (e.g., "They just can't do well in my class. They have been socialized to learn by watching, not by processing language. By this age their brain functioning has been established, and they can't easily learn the material in my class").

5. **Apparent concession.** This move begins with a positive statement, but concludes with a negative opinion. Speakers are attempting to show that they are not prejudiced because they are aware of positive characteristics of the group. For example, "I admire their attentiveness to their families, but they won't be able to advance in a job if they always put their family first."

6. **Mitigation.** This move avoids saying very negative things. Instead of saying, "Her behavior is strange and I can't tolerate her interaction style," the speaker says, "Her behavior is a little unusual," and "Her interactions aren't quite what we would like."

7. **Contrast.** These statements often focus on "what is done for them versus what is done for us." For example, "The government provides all kinds of help for minorities, and the qualified Anglos can't get anything."

## Style

The same underlying prejudicial opinions may be expressed in different ways. The lexical and syntactic variation is referred to as style. Stylistic variation in discourse is usually a function of contextual properties such as (in)formality of the social situation and social dimensions such as power, status, position, or gender of the speech participants.

Speakers generally use indirect rather than direct forms when talking
about minorities. One is not likely to hear, "I hate them," regardless of
how strong the feelings might be. The tendency is to express negative
feelings in rather soft language (e.g., "I'm not comfortable around them").
Because of strong official norms about racism, persons will downplay or
understate racial/ethnic feelings.

Speakers may also use second person pronouns and demonstrative
pronouns (e.g., those) to convey their social distance from the ethnic/racial
group under discussion. Persons tend to avoid naming people they do
not like, using instead words like "those people," "you" or "that man."
These pronouns are associated with power and group relationships among
speakers (Brown & Gilman, 1960). This pronominal use may be so much
a part of mainstream discourse that speakers are not fully aware of the
message they are conveying to listeners. This was highlighted in the 1992
Presidential Campaign when Ross Perot, addressing the National Association for the Advancement of Colored People, made frequent reference
to "you people" and "your people."

## STRATEGIES FOR REDUCING PREJUDICE

According to Samuel Johnson, "Prejudice not being founded on reason cannot be removed by argument" (cited in Peters, 1977, p.420).
Although prejudicial opinions are generally presented in an argumentative structure, counter arguments alone will not reduce prejudice. In
programs with a multicultural focus, faculty, clinical supervisory staff,
and students from culturally diverse backgrounds should be able to work
together to achieve common goals. Such goals include not only recruiting
and retaining minority students and providing all students with information about cultural diversity, but also striving to produce students and
faculty who model a philosophy of cultural pluralism. To accomplish
this, programs must seek to have faculty and students recognize instances
of prejudice and know how to handle prejudicial attitudes and discriminatory behavior.

### Components of Prejudice Reduction

Reduction in prejudicial attitudes requires a curriculum that addresses
three crucial aspects: cognition, affect, and behavior (Lynch, 1987). Cognitive components can include:

1. Providing demographic information on society;
2. Correcting misinformation about racial/ethnic groups;
3. Extending information and understanding about values, beliefs, and achievements of various cultural groups;
4. Enabling individuals to recognize instances of discrimination and prejudice and their social and personal effects;
5. Providing guidelines for acceptable and unacceptable values, attitudes, and behaviors;
6. And providing intellectual skills to counter prejudice.

Cognitive goals can be addressed in formal coursework and faculty meetings. Cognitive goals are essential but not sufficient, however, to reduce prejudice. Affective or attitudinal goals must also be addressed:

1. Enabling students to explore feelings of comfort and discomfort with their own identity and culture;
2. Encouraging the appreciation of the unique value of each person;
3. Expecting high academic standards of all students;
4. And developing a moral commitment against prejudice and discrimination by addressing issues of discrimination, rather than ignoring them.

These components all involve developing positive attitudes and feelings about minority individuals. Faculty and staff must model these affective components. They must be willing to spend time outside of classes with students to hear their experiences and listen to them talk about their feelings. Rather than making excuses for the prejudice and discrimination on campus or rather than telling students they should ignore the prejudicial attitudes and discrimination and "hang in there to show the persons they are wrong about minorities", faculty and staff need to make clear their own values and beliefs, and openly address instances of prejudice and discrimination. It is especially critical that faculty and staff exhibit a willingness to understand students' cultures and exhibit confidence in the students' abilities to succeed academically.

This cognitive information and affective attitudes must be united in experiences to develop behaviors that:

1. Nurture nonprejudiced verbal and nonverbal behavior;
2. Encourage perception, analysis, and interpretation of social situations for prejudice and discrimination;
3. Develop a repertoire of strategies for coping with prejudice.

Faculty and staff must learn to monitor their own communication. Statements such as, "I'm in a black mood today," or "I know this assignment is low on your totem pole," are not meant to disparage groups of people but can have that effect. Clinical experiences can provide excellent opportunities for students to monitor and discuss their own and others' attitudes, language, and behaviors that are or may appear to be prejudicial. The use of ethnographic observation and interviews can assist faculty/staff in understanding the perspectives of students and students in understanding the perspectives of clients.

## Theories of Prejudice Reduction in Groups

Programs that provide specific financial and academic assistance for minority students have the potential for arousing prejudicial feelings in majority students. Ideally, to reduce opportunities for prejudicial feelings, programs should also seek funding for majority students and make academic support available to all students. Admittance of culturally nondominant students into programs does not, however, assure that they will feel comfortable with or be accepted by majority students. The literature suggests that neither multicultural education programs nor behavior modification technique have been especially successful in fostering positive attitudes and behaviors that endure and generalize (Miller & Harrington, 1990).

Approaches that teach students to individuate members of another race seem to offer more promise for reducing prejudice. This is in accord with Aboud's cognitive-social theories of prejudice. Cooperative learning strategies have become a popular mechanism for facilitating both students' academic development and their ability to work effectively with culturally diverse students. The goal of such activities is to move students beyond affective or perceptual responding to racial/ethnic groups and to enable students to understand and appreciate members of these groups as individuals. Cooperative learning strategies are becoming popular in elementary and secondary schools, but have not received widespread acceptance in higher education. Four hypotheses or theories have been proposed to explained why cooperative activities have the potential to foster positive racial/ethnic attitudes.

### The Realistic Conflict Theory

The realistic conflict theory proposes that the struggle between ethnic groups lies in the struggle for scarce resources (e.g., number of openings in a program, recognition from an instructor, number of high grades).

This competition produces feelings of contempt for others. In this case, bias can be reduced by not limiting resources when possible (e.g., using criterion reference assessment rather than "grading on the curve") and when using group activities, structuring the groups so that they are racially/ethnically diverse and all students must cooperate to attain superordinate goals.

## Reinforcement Theory

This theory maintains that people like those who reward them (Lott & Lott, 1968). Groups can provide social approval for their members. In a classroom, membership in the group that wins instructor approval can result in an individual seeking to adopt the values of the approved group. If students do not believe they have access to this approved group, or if they feel they are rejecting their own identity by joining the approved group, they may form their own group with others experiencing similar feelings and find their approval within that group. In such instances the group perceives its failures as attributable to the external system. Again, strategies for intervention focus on cooperation to achieve a common goal that is rewarding to all students.

## Expectation Theory

Society has traditionally given status to certain characteristics such as sex, race, ethnicity, socioeconomic level, and attractiveness and has differentially evaluated these characteristics in terms of esteem and desirability (Berger, Cohen, & Zelditch, 1972). Status characteristics serve as a basis for expectations that persons have for themselves and others in social interaction. Both high and low status students will hold expectations. High status students expect to have the necessary information and to perform well; low status students are more likely to question their abilities. Status expectations create a halo effect. Faculty are likely to look for the positive aspects of the performance of high status students, and the negative or weak aspects of the performance of low status students. Minority students have reported being told, "Do you really think you can do a paper on this topic?" or "You'll be doing fine if you can get a B." In group situations, high status students are likely to dominate the interactions and provide all the ideas, thus reinforcing expectations. Cohen (1982) suggested that "it is easier to modify the expectations for low status members' performance held by high status members than it is to change the expectations low status members hold for themselves" (p.

216). Miller and Harrington (1990) suggested that low-status students need advance preparation for group activities to compensate for this social disadvantage. Staff of the University of New Mexico Multicultural Program have reviewed with students the information necessary to participate in classroom group activities, discussed the nature of the interactions, and role-played group interactions. We have practiced ways to enter conversations and how to present well-organized ideas positively and authoritatively.

**Social Identity Theory**

The three theories discussed so far may be sufficient to explain prejudice and why collaborative group activities reduce prejudice, but they are not necessary to account for prejudice. Miller and Harrington (1990) maintain that the social identity theory is both necessary and sufficient to account for prejudice in groups. This theory assumes that people have a basic need to establish and maintain a positive self-identity and that one's identity includes both social and personal components (Tajfel & Turner, 1979). Social identity includes the social categories to which one belongs, such as gender, race, age, physical/mental condition, religion, politics, etc. Personal identity refers to those aspects of the self that are unique and idiosyncratic, the interests, skills, and values.

Perceptual and cognitive processes account for intergroup behavior in social identity theory. The perceptual component involves a categorization process. The categorization exaggerates both the similarities among persons within a category and the dissimilarities of persons in different categories. Persons who are similar on salient perceptual characteristics are assumed to be similar on unobservable characteristics such as interests, abilities, and values. And those persons who are perceived to differ on perceptual characteristics are also assumed to differ on nonobservable characteristics. Differences can more readily be seen among persons in the ingroup (majority group), but less readily seen in persons in the outgroup (minority group). Members of the outgroup are depersonalized because of this undifferentiation (the "they all look alike phenomenon"). They are not perceived as individuals but as representatives of the outgroup. This categorization process has an affective component because comparisons between groups are usually made along dimensions involving liking and disliking of attributes and behavior, and the comparisons are always favorable to the ingroup.

According to the social identity theory, approaches to prejudice reduction must counteract the effects of this social categorization and competitive social comparison processes (Brewer & Miller, 1984). Elimination of categorization requires differentiation and personalization. **Differentiation** involves perceiving distinctiveness of individuals within the outgroup, i.e., realizing that **they** don't all think, act, or feel alike. This weakens the assumption of homogeneity and facilitates the development of personalization. **Personalization** involves the perception of the uniqueness of an outgroup member. This may result in seeing similarities with the self in terms of common interests and shared beliefs. Prejudice is reduced by experiences that encourage a decategorization process in which outgroup members are perceived and responded to as individuals rather than as representatives of a social category.

Collaborative group activities can facilitate this decategorization and personalization. To accomplish this, groups must be racially/ethnically diverse, reward structures must be collaborative and individualistic but not competitive (either within or between teams), and students must be prepared to carry out their roles on the team. Within these activities, students can begin to share something of themselves. Self-disclosure, the verbal presentation of oneself to others, is helpful because persons tend to like others who disclose to them more than those who do not. Persons also tend to like others as a result of having disclosed to them, and they tend to perceive that they are liked by others who disclose to them (Chelune, 1979; Derlega & Berg, 1987). In early stages of encounters, self-disclosure seems to be a function of similarity of demographic or social identity characteristics; at later stages, the motivation to self-disclose is based on the discovered similarities in intimate areas of personal characteristics.

## CONCLUSION

I am convinced that when the intellectual history of our times comes to be written, the idea of race, both the popular and the taxonomic, will be viewed for what it is: a confused and dangerous idea which happened to fit the social requirements of a thoroughly exploitive period in the development of Western man (Ashley Montague, as cited in Peters, 1977, p.441).

Universities are preparing professionals for the 21st century. Because these professionals are to advocate for and join a pluralistic society, universities need to model the principles of a pluralistic society. Presently, many of the practices of universities promote rather than reduce prejudice.

If universities are to facilitate pluralism, they will need to understand and reduce prejudice. There must be changes in attitudes toward students from nondominant cultures, as well as changes in class organization and attitudes toward student performance. Businesses and early childhood intervention programs are giving increasing attention to team building, team decision making, and team product development. Universities have traditionally trained students to work independently and competitively, a strategy that can promote prejudicial attitudes. To fulfill the vision of a pluralistic society, attention must be given to facilitating persons' abilities to relate to individuals as individuals rather than as members of groups, and to develop the communication skills essential for team functioning. Persons must be able to look at the knowledge, attitudes, and skills each individual brings to the classroom and work setting rather than making judgements about these matters on the basis of a person's race or ethnicity.

## REFERENCES

Aboud, F.: The development of ethnic self-identification and attitudes. In Phinney, J.S., & Rotheram, M.J. (Eds.): *Children's Ethnic Socialization.* Beverly Hills, Sage, 1987, pp.32–55.

Aboud, F.: *Children and Prejudice.* New York, Basil Blackwell, 1988.

Adorno, T.W., Frenkel-Brunswick, E., Levinson, D.J. & Sanford, R.N.: *The Authoritarian Personality.* New York, Harper & Row, 1950.

Alejandro-Wright, M.N.: The child's conceptualization of racial classification: A socio-cognitive developmental model. In Spencer, M.B., Brookins, G.K. & Allen, W.R. (Eds.): *Beginnings: The Social and Affective Development of Black Children.* Hillsdale, Erlbaum, 1985, pp.185–200.

Allport, G.W.: *The Nature of Prejudice.* Cambridge, Addison-Wesley, 1954.

Ashmore, R.D. & Del Boca, F.K.: Psychological approaches to understanding intergroup conflicts. In Katz, P.A. (Ed.): *Towards the Elimination of Racism.* New York, Pergamon, 1976, pp.73–123.

Beckham, B.: Strangers in a strange land: Blacks on White campuses. *Educational Record, 68/69:* 74–78, 1987/1988.

Bennett, C.I.: *Comprehensive Multicultural Education.* Boston, Allyn & Bacon, 1990.

Berger, J., Coehn, B.P. & Zelditch, M.: Status characteristics and social interaction. *American Sociological Review, 37:* 241–255, 1975.

Brewer, M.B. & Miller, N.: Beyond the contact hypothesis: Theoretical perspectives on desegregation. In Miller, N. & Brewer, M.B. (Eds.): *Groups in Contact: The Psychology of Desegregation.* New York, Academic Press, 1984.

Brown, R. & Gilman, A.: The pronouns of power and solidarity. In Sebeok, T.A. (Ed.): *Style in Language.* Cambridge University Press, 1960, pp.253–277.

Carter, D., Pearson, C. & Shavlik, D.: Double jeopardy: Women of color in higher education. *Educational Record, 68/69:* 98–103, 1988/1989.

Chelune, C.J.: *Self-Disclosure: Origins, Patterns and Implications of Openness in Interpersonal Relationships.* San Francisco, Jossey-Bass, 1979.

Clark, K.B. & Clark, M.P.: Racial identification and preference in Negro children. In Newcomb, T.M. & Hartley, E.L. (Eds.): *Readings in Social Psychology.* New York, Holt, 1947, pp.169–178.

Cohen, E.G.: Expectation states and interracial interaction in school settings. *Annual Review of Sociology, 8:* 209–235, 1982.

Cross, W.E.: Black identity: Rediscovering the distinction between personal identity and reference group orientation. In Spencer, M.B., Brookins, G.K. & Allen, W.R. (Eds.): *Beginnings: The Social and Affective Development of Black Children.* Hillsdale, Erlbaum, 1985, pp.155–183.

Davey, A.G.: *Learning to be Prejudiced: Growing Up in Multi-Ethnic Britain.* London, 1983.

Derlega, V.J. & Berg, J.H.: *Self-Disclosure: Theory, Research, and Therapy.* New York, Plenum, 1987.

Essed, P.: *Understanding Everyday Racism.* Newbury Park, Sage, 1991.

Flavell, J.H.: *Cognitive Development,* Englewood Cliffs, Prentice Hall, 1977.

Fox, D.J. & Jordan, V.D.: Racial preference and identification of Black, American Chinese, and White children. *Genetic Psychology Monographs, 88:* 229–286, 1973.

Glasberg, R. & Aboud, F.E.: A developmental perspective on the study of depression: Children's evaluative reactions to sadness. *Developmental Psychology, 17:* 195–202, 1981.

Gottfried, A.W. & Gottfried, A.E.: Influence of social power versus status envy modeled behaviors on children's preferences for models. *Psychological Reports, 34:* 1147–1150, 1974.

Hood, J.: University of New Mexico must work to create a climate for diversity. *New Mexico Daily Lobo.* Wednesday, February 20, 1991.

Katz, P.A.: The acquisition of racial attitudes in children. In Katz, P.A. (Ed.): *Towards the Elimination of Racism.* New York, Pergamon, 1975, pp.125–154.

Katz, P.A.: Development and social processes in ethnic attitudes and self-identification. In Phinney, J.S. & Rotheram, M.J. (Eds.): *Children's Ethnic Socialization.* Beverly Hills, Sage, 1987, pp.92–99.

Kolhberg, L.: Moral stages and moralization: The cognitive-developmental approach. In Lickona, T. (Eds.): *Moral Development and Behavior.* New York, 1976.

Lott, A.J. & Lott, B.E.: A learning theory approach to interpersonal attitudes. In Greenwald, A., Brock, T. & Ostrom, T. (Eds.): *Psychological Foundations of Attitudes.* New York, Academic Press, 1968.

Lynch, J.: *Prejudice Reduction and the Schools.* New York, Nichols Publishing, 1987.

Madge, N.J.H.: Context and the expressed ethnic preference of infant school children. *Journal of Child Psychology and Psychiatry, 17:* 337–344, 1976.

McDermott, R.: Achieving school failure: An anthropological approach to illiteracy and social stratification. In Spinder, G.D. (Ed.): *Education and Cultural Process.* Prospect Heights, Waveland Press, 1987, pp.173–209.

Miller, N. & Harrington, H.J.: A situational identity perspective on cultural diversity and teamwork in the classroom. In Sharon, S. (Ed.): *Cooperative Learning*. New York, Praeger, 1990, pp.39–75.

Morland, J.K. & Suthers, E.: Racial attitudes of children: Perspectives on the structural-normative theory of prejudice. *Phylon,* 267–277, 1980.

Newman, M.A., Liss, M.B. & Sherman, F.: Ethnic awareness in children: Not a unitary concept. *Journal of Genetic Psychology, 143:* 103–112, 1983.

Peter, L.J.: *Peter's Quotations.* Toronto, Bantam, 1977.

Phinney, J.S. & Rotheram, M.J.: *Children's Ethnic Socialization.* Newbury Park, Sage, 1987.

Powell-Hopson, D. & Hopson, D.S.: *Different and Wonderful: Raising Black Children in a Race-Conscious Society.* New York, Simon & Schuster, 1990.

Ramsey, P.G.: Young children's thinking about ethnic differences. In Phinney, J.S. & Rotheram, M.J. (Eds.): *Children's Ethnic Socialization.* Newbury Park, Sage, 1987, pp.56–72.

Rice, A.S., Ruiz, R.A. & Padilla, A.M.: Personal perception, self-identity, and ethnic group preference in Anglo, Black, and Chicana preschool self-identity of young Black girls. *Journal of Cross-Cultural Psychology, 5:* 100–108, 1974.

Rothbart, M.: Achieving racial equality: An analysis of resistance to social reform. In Katz, P.A. (Ed.): *Towards the Elimination of Racism.* New York, Pergamon, 1976, pp.341–375.

Rotheram, M.J. & Phinney, J.S.: Introduction: Definitions and perspectives in the study of children's ethnic socialization. In Phinney, J.S. & Rotheram, M.J. (Eds.): *Children's Ethnic Socialization: Pluralism and Development.* Newbury Park, Sage, 1987, pp.10–31.

Schlesinger, A.M.: *The Disuniting of America.* Knoxville, Whittle Books, 1991.

Semaj, L.T.: The development of racial evaluation and preference: A cognitive approach. *Journal of Black Psychology, 6:* 59–79, 1980.

Semaj, L.T.: Afrikanity, cognition, and extended self-identity. In Spencer, M.B., Brookins, G.K. & Allen, W.R. (Eds.): *Beginnings: The Social and Affective Development of Black Children.* Hillsdale, Erlbaum, 1985, pp.173–183.

Sorce, A.: The role of physiognomy in the development of racial awareness. Paper presented at the biennial meetings of the Society for Research in Child Development, New Orleans, 1977.

Sue, D.W.: *Counseling the Culturally Different: Theory & Practice.* New York, Wiley.

Tajfel, H.: Differentiation between Social Groups: Studies in the Social Psychology of Intergroup Relations. London, Academic Press, 1979.

Vachss, A.: If you could listen to a child's soul. *Parade Magazine, 45:* June 16, 1991.

van Dijk, T.A.: *Communicating Racism: Ethnic Prejudice in Thought and Talk.* Newbury Park, Sage, 1987.

Vaughn, G.M.: Concept formation and the development of ethnic awareness. *Journal of Genetic Psychology, 103:* 93–103, 1964.

Vaughn, G.M.: A social psychological model of ethnic identity development. In Phinney, J.S. & Rotheram, M.J. (Eds.): *Children's Ethnic Socialization.* Beverly Hills, Sage, 1987, pp.73–91.

Weiland, A. & Coughlin, R.: Self-identification and preferences: A comparison of White and Mexican-American first and third graders. *Journal of Cross-Cultural Psychology, 10:* 356–365, 1979.

Williams, J.E. & Morland, J.K.: *Race, Color, and the Young Child.* Chapel Hill, The University of North Carolina Press, 1976.

Zajonc, R.B.: Feeling and thinking: Preferences need no inferences. *American Psychologist, 35:* 151–175, 1980.

# PART TWO
# DIVERSE STUDENT GROUPS: PREREQUISITE KNOWLEDGE FOR ACHIEVING EFFECTIVE RECRUITMENT AND RETENTION

## Chapter 4

# PROFILE OF AFRICAN AMERICAN STUDENTS

GLORIAJEAN L. WALLACE

## INTRODUCTION

African Americans comprise approximately 12 percent of the United States population and have the greatest representation of all groups from the multicultural community (U.S. Bureau of Census, 1990; Cole, 1989). African American representation in academia, however, is proportionately low given the representation of African Americans within the population at large. There is a paucity of African Americans at all levels of academia, extending from undergraduate and graduate student representation, to faculty and administrators (*The Chronicle of Higher Education Almanac,* 1992).

Recent data concerning university and college enrollment for African Americans at the undergraduate, graduate and profession levels, indicate that enrollment has remained consistently low for African American students over the last ten years (National Center for Education Statistics, 1992a). Where enrollment of African American students increased to 117,000 between 1980 to 1990, Anglo American students' enrollment increased to 840,000. Equally as alarming is the fact that only a small portion of African Americans enrolled in colleges and universities actually graduate. According to statistics recently published by the U.S. Department of Education (National Center for Education Statistics, 1992b), only 5 percent of all college and university degrees were conferred to African Americans in 1991, whereas 82 percent were awarded to Anglo Americans. This data suggests that critical problems exists with the recruitment and retention of African American students in higher education.

One possible reason why African American student enrollment and retention remain low, may be related to the small number of African American role models and mentors in academic positions (*The Chronicle of Higher Education Almanac,* 1992). A number of institutions of higher

63

education have demonstrated an interest in enhancing the minority representation in academia. With this goal in mind, the chapter provides information about how the cultural beliefs, attitudes and values of many African American students have been influenced and shaped by their history and unique circumstances of early forced migration to America. Specifically, the chapter will address how history and culture influence the basic aspects of language patterns, communication interactions and attitudes toward health care, as well as cognitive learning styles and academic achievement. It is hoped that such information will serve faculty to better understand, appreciate, accept and facilitate African American students to achieve in higher education. In addition, specific suggestions for facilitating the integration of African Americans into all levels of academic are presented. The reader should note that the terms "Black" and "African American" are both intentionally used in different sections of the chapter as preferred designation varies among individuals representing specific subgroups.

## AFRICAN AMERICAN HISTORY

Immigration to the United States by ethnic groups has generally been to escape from political or religious oppression, poverty, or to improve the quality of life (Moynihan, 1989; Myers, 1991). For those of African ancestry, however, the early relocation to this country was not guided by a conscious decision, but occurred under the forced and inhumane conditions of slavery (Palmer, 1992). It has been estimated that the transatlantic slave trade brought an estimated twelve to fifteen million Africans to the United States (Palmer, 1992; Smead, 1989). The slave traffic was so pervasive that by 1850 a third of the people of African descent lived outside of the continent of Africa (Curtin, 1969).

### Before the Transatlantic Slave Trade

Before being brought to America, African people shared a copious existence characterized by unique intratribal cultures, customs, languages, and religious practices. The Africans were, and are described as deeply spiritual people at peace with their environment and one with the universe (Idowu, 1973). Scientific, scholarly, and aesthetic contributions of African people were, and continue to be, numerous. Early Africans made great contributions ranging from the development of modern medicine to the design and construction of the great pyramids (Corbin, 1986; Sertima, 1989).

Many of the tribes in the Western part of Africa, just south of the Sahara, were united into empires. The most prominent of these were Ghana, Mali, and Songhai, which became powerful mainly because of their location on the caravan routes across the Sahara that allowed them to exchange wheat, sugar and salt from the north for gold and cattle from the south. Trade with the Arabs of North Africa brought the people of the African empires into contact with the written Arabic language and the religious teachings of Islam. As a result, their cities became the centers of Muslim learning and culture. Racial intermixing also took place as a result of increased contact between West Africans and Arabs. Africans, like other people of the world, participated in the practice of slavery (Palmer, 1992; Redding, 1958; Smead, 1989). Unlike the institutional slavery that occurred later in America, this enslavement was generally a result of tribal war or as a means of survival through self-enslavement to more prosperous tribes when crops failed or cattle died.

## Slavery in America

Holloway (1990) reviews the beginning of slavery in America. In the 1400s, Portuguese were the first group involved in the trade of African slaves, followed by the Spanish, the Dutch, and the English. The 1600s marked the beginning of the slavery era in which African slaves were brought primarily from the central and west coast regions of Africa, between modern Senegal and Angola, to what is now the United States (Holloway, 1990). The major areas from which these slaves were taken include: Senegal, Mozambique, Madagascar, Senegal, Gambia, Sierra Leone, the Ivory Coast, Togo, Benin, Nigeria, Cameroon, the Congo, and Angola.

Slavery in America evolved from a practice of indentured servitude (Palmer, 1992; Smead, 1989). Indentureship, however, was gradually discontinued for the Africans, so that by the late 1600s most Africans in the American Colonies were slaves for life. Palmer (1992) reported that by the end of the 1700's, there were over 640,000 slaves in Maryland, Virginia, the Carolinas and Georgia. As agricultural products became increasingly more important, such as tobacco, rice, indigo, cotton, and sugarcane, greater numbers of slaves were enlisted to provide the agricultural manpower. By the 1800's, an estimated half-million African slaves had been forced to work in the fields, plantations and mines of America.

During this period, Africans were stripped of their culture, customs, language, first and last names, family roots, traditional forms of religious practice and their dignity. They were, in fact, viewed as animals, not humans (Frazier, 1966). The view of Africans as subhuman provided slave traders and owners with the justification for slavery, and contributed to their lack of concern for the sanity, safety, health, and comfort of the slaves during their transportation to and life in America (Frazier, 1966).

In order to economically transport as many slaves as possible, slaves were brought to America under intensely cruel and inhumane conditions. Palmer (1992) describes that the human cargo was arranged on wooden platforms in a holding area that was highly constricted with rarely enough space for an adult to stand erect or to lie down. Because of the slave trader's fear of rebellion, the slaves were usually chained together in pairs at the ankles. The highly unsanitary and confining conditions were a breeding ground for disease. On some ships, it was reported that as many as half of the slaves died en route to America.

It was not until the 18th Century that European countries set space standards for the allocation of slaves on the slave ships. Additionally, faster ships with portholes for ventilation were constructed. Although mortality rates dropped, many of the slaves who survived the trip, arrived in America in states of malnutrition, starvation, and with severe illnesses (Palmer, 1992).

Once in America, slaves were sold under humiliating conditions. They were often forced to wear harnesses around their necks, arms, and legs, similar to animals. They were, additionally, displayed naked on the public auction blocks, where potential buyers poked, prodded, and inspected their bodies, including genital areas (Harrison, 1975; Palmer, 1992). Resistance to any treatment imposed by the slave trader would have generally resulted in severe public thrashings, torture, and even death.

Slave owners residing in the northern regions of America were primarily interested in purchasing slaves to serve as domestic workers and artisans while southern slave owners sought plantation field workers (Holloway, 1990). Holloway (1990) reports that slave owners of the North and South held the stereotyped belief that intellectual capacity and physical prowess varied across the African ethnic groups. Thus, the more northern colonies were most heavily populated by West African slaves. Northern slave owners regarded the West African slaves as being more intelligent because of their mixed Arabian blood, and therefore, thought of them as being more capable of training for higher level domestic service and handicraft work than the other "pure" Africans. Additionally, West African slaves were judged to be less physically able to perform the fieldwork labor.

The southern colonies had a greater number of slaves from the central parts of Africa (Holloway, 1990). These individuals became field workers because they were viewed as being large and robust in physical stature, and therefore, of greater value in providing a labor force for the plantations. The plantation system was wholly supported by field slaves, including children from the ages of eight or nine years old.

Those slaves who were domestic servants and artisans, were forced to give up their own cultural identities in order to reflect their master's control and capacity to "civilize" the Africans. Rape of African females by slave owners was a fairly common, although not an openly spoken of practice (Brent, 1973; Davis, Gardner & Gardner, 1988; Jacobs, 1987). This violation resulted in a caste system with light skinned house slaves, who were the children of the slave masters, and darker skinned field slaves. These authors discuss that special privileges were sometimes afforded to the lighter skinned house slaves who were also acculturated to the White mores. This proved to be a source of contention among the slaves.

Whitehead (1990) describes the life of slaves as including their being forced to work from dawn to dark. Their food consisted of cornmeal, salt pork, salad greens, salt fish, and leftover parts of meat which their owners viewed as undesirable. Slaves developed creative methods for seasoning. Many aspects of southern cooking and food spicing techniques originate from attempts to make these undesirable foods palatable.

The slaves were subjected to harsh laws which permitted them to be whipped, branded, or have a body part cut off for stealing. Slaves were not permitted to strike White persons, even in self-defense. Some slave owners hired brutal overseers and plantation managers known as slave drivers, who whipped slaves as a way of forcing them to work harder (Genovese, 1976). Survival required compliance. As an outlet for venting anger, the slaves resorted to the traditional African practice of witchcraft (Pluckett, 1926).

Harrison (1975) reports that slave owners provided health care for slaves often as a means of protecting their financial investment in their slave "property." For this reason, pregnant females and their newborn children received particularly good care. The death rate of African Americans during that time was not appreciably higher than that of Whites. Some reports state, however, that slaves were used to test new surgical procedures and other medical treatments before they were attempted on Whites (Fisher, 1968). While slaves had access to contemporary medicine, they often used herbal cures behind the backs of their slave owners (Harrison and Harrison, 1971; Harrison, 1975). In addition to providing medical care when a slave became ill, slave owners attempted to protect their "property" by prohibiting or mediating violent disputes that might result in physical injury.

Besides the physical hardship, anguish, and humiliation, the institution of slavery was designed to de-Africanize Africans (Hale-Benson, 1986) by isolating them from their family and tribal group members. This was done in order to discourage communication which might have led to insurrection. The African slaves developed and relied on tightly knit extended family networks and adapted systems for communicating across tribal groups (Willis, 1992). This resulted in the development of a Pidgin/Creole language system, which combined the elements of the African languages with those English elements spoken by American Southerners. For the slaves, the African element of the pidgin/creole language was influenced by their keener association with the "pure" African languages (Dalby, 1972). The Africans who were in close contact with Whites, such as house slaves, however, used a language system that was influenced to a larger extent by the English language. When slavery ended and the slave caste system began dissolving, the overall language system of African Americans moved closer to that of the mainstream English patterns which were most characteristic of the region where African Americans resided. This process continued to such an extent so that the present day language systems known as African American English, Ebonics or Black English, used by African Americans is quite diverse (Asante, 1985, 1990). Structural aspects of African American English will be discussed in a later section.

The Christian religion was promoted by slave owners to encourage a passive attitude and the self-acceptance by slaves of their lowly status and maltreatment. Many slaves owners felt that "religious slaves" were more obedient and hardworking (Boles, 1943). African slaves participated in the Christian religious ceremonies, which differed from their own traditional religious ceremonies, because such ceremonies provided support and fellowship as a source of strength for enduring the stressful slavery conditions. Slaves made up spiritual songs that contrasted their hard life on earth to the happiness they expected to find in heaven. These spiritual songs were among some of the first songs composed in America (Fisher, 1990).

The slave preacher enjoyed a special position within the slave community as role model and moral leader. The slave preacher provided the inspiration for slaves to attempt to triumph over their situation so as not to become enslaved psychologically or consumed with bitterness. In part, this may account for why pastors traditionally hold great leadership roles, and are held in high esteem by the African American community today. During the early 1800s, many insurrections were planned during church meeting fellowships (Boles, 1943; Cone, 1969). This may be an additional reason for why the political power of the African American community is based in the church today.

Blacks were generally denied education as a means of discouraging self-empowerment (Smead, 1989). The slave preacher was often the only member of the slave community who could read or write, skills acquired during study of the Bible. While some slaves in the North were allowed to learn to read and write, it was highly unusual for a slave to obtain schooling past the first or second reader. Not until 1826, did Blacks graduate from American colleges.

## The Beginnings of Freedom

By 1860, there were nearly 500,000 free Blacks in the United States. While technically free, Blacks were unable to enjoy the full benefits of freedom that were taken for granted by the White citizens of the United States. Free Blacks in the South had to carry passes or certificates of freedom. If they were caught without passes, they could be sold into slavery. For fear of insurrection, Blacks were prohibited from forming clubs or discussion groups and from holding large meetings. Free Blacks were not allowed to own guns. Thus, they could not protect themselves against the kidnapping attempts to sell them into slavery. Because the barriers that the freed slaves faced were insurmountable, some free slaves returned on their own volition to Africa (Smead, 1989).

During the early and mid 1800s, many free Blacks who were light enough in color to be mistaken for White, "passed" into the world of

White people in order to escape the handicap of race. However, for the vast majority of Blacks, it was impossible to avoid the barriers imposed by the White world. Even though their life was modeled after that of White people, Blacks who had been stripped of their own culture, were not accepted into the White world. Therefore, Blacks began organizing their own churches, building their own schools and establishing their own newspapers, theaters and clubs. The mid 1800s marked the period of the abolitionist movement (Bennett, 1989; Igus, 1991). Frederick Douglas, Sojourner Truth and Harriet Tubman, fought for the freedom of slaves through their involvement in the Underground Railroad (Bennett, 1989; Igus, 1991).

The moral, political, and economic debates between the northern and the southern states on the issue of slavery ultimately contributed to the beginning of the Civil War in 1861. On September 23, 1862, President Abraham Lincoln issued the Emancipation Proclamation. Contrary to what is often thought, the main purpose of the Emancipation Proclamation was to save the political union of the States rather than to emancipate Black slaves. In fact, as of January 1, 1863, the Proclamation freed only Black slaves in those states that were in rebellion (Smead, 1989). The Proclamation served to harden the South's determination to maintain the institution of slavery. At the beginning of the Civil War, Black Americans were denied from entering military service, however, they later served in segregated regiments often under the direction of White officers (Smead, 1989). In December 1865, Congress abolished slavery throughout the country with the passing of the Thirteenth Amendment to the Constitution of the United States.

The southern states passed special laws, called Black Codes, in an attempt to keep freed slaves, known as freedmen, in an inferior position. Under the direction of the War Department, President Lincoln established the Freedmen's Bureau for the purpose of helping some 4,000,000 newly freed slaves find jobs and obtain adequate health care. More than 4,000 schools were supported by the Freedmen's Bureau. Other schools and colleges were established by gifts from religious groups and wealthy northerners. From 1865–69, the following Black institutions of higher education were established: Clark College in Georgia, Fisk University in Tennessee, Hampton Institute in Virginia, Howard University in Washington, D.C., Morehouse College in Georgia, Shaw University in North Carolina and Talladega College in Alabama.

Discrimination, however, continued until 1885. Slaves could not receive patents for their own inventions nor could they assign an invention to their master. For example, Jo Anderson, who was a slave of Cyrus McCormick, is said to have made a major contribution of the reaper for harvesting grain in 1834. This ruling did not apply to free persons of color. Many of the inventions by African Americans prior to and after 1885 contributed to the growth of this country.

During the mid 1800s, universal suffrage was adopted, Black Codes were abolished, and a public school system was established for children of all races. These accomplishments were achieved as a result of the Fourteenth Amendment of the Constitution, the Civil Rights Acts of 1866 and 1875 which granted all citizens of the United States unrestricted access to public places, and the Fifteenth Amendment of 1870 which guaranteed people of all races the right to vote.

African Americans began participating in the political process during the Reconstruction Period, where they even served in the House of Representatives. At this time, discriminatory voting practices called Jim Crow Laws, were passed, requiring voters to pay a $2.00 poll tax, to pass a literacy test and/or to own a certain value of land or property. Since many poor Whites were also excluded from voting because of the Jim Crow Laws, a "grandfather clause" was established where voters could forgo the poll tax if they had an ancestor who voted in the 1860 election. Again, many African Americans were excluded from voting because their ancestors had been slaves during the 1860 election.

Smead (1989) reports that while a number of laws were passed to establish separate, "but equal" schooling, transportation, housing, and health care services for African Americans, these services were viewed by African Americans as inequitable. For instance, schools for White students received twice as much funding as those for African Americans. Similarly at the university level, African American colleges had difficulty obtaining financial support unless their curriculum emphasized manual and vocational training (Smead, 1989). During the mid 1890s, segregated facilities became even more widespread, leading the way for segregated waiting rooms, bathrooms, drinking fountains, lunch counters and restaurants, public parks, cemeteries, and even the use of "Jim Crow" Bibles in some states' courtrooms (Smead, 1989).

African Americans remained in a politically powerless position in the late 1890s (Moynihan, 1989; Tucker, 1991). At this time, three contemporaries came to the forefront to motivate African Americans to fight for a freer existence. Booker T. Washington, promoted economic independence and self-respect for African Americans (Donovan, 1990). Dr. W.E.B. DuBois strived for African Americans to embrace their African heritage and to take a more militant stance in striving for equality. Monroe Trotter provided the impetus for African Americans to assert their rights as U.S. citizens.

## The 1900s

In the early 1900s, many Blacks migrated North because of the promise of better wages. By 1950, three fourths of the African American population or more than 15 million, dwelled in cities with slightly more than half residing outside of the South (Smead, 1989). This marked the beginning of urban ghetto life for African Americans in this country. Among the earliest established communities was Harlem, which was considered to be a city within New York City where some 200,000 African Americans lived within an area of 2 square miles (Smead, 1989). Jazz, the art form which can be traced to the American spiritual and to the rhythm, melody and harmony of West African music, was born during this era.

Discrimination toward Blacks continued throughout U.S. history. It is reflected in the segregation of the military, as well as the limited distribution of food and clothing during the Great Depression. African American and White troops were not integrated until 1945. As a result of political pressure, executive orders signed on June 25, 1941 banned employment discrimination practices in the war defense industry. On May 17, 1954, Thurgood Marshall won his famous Brown versus Board of Education Case, where school segregation was no longer outlawed.

During The Civil Rights Movement of the 1960s, African Americans engaged in sit-in's, freedom rides, boycotts and peaceful demonstrations under the leadership of Martin Luther King. Malcolm X, another great leader of the African American community, promoted equal rights for African Americans (Perry, 1990). Perry (1900) discusses that The Civil Rights Act of 1964 and the Voting Rights Act of 1965 were passed to insure African Americans' protection against discrimination by providing stronger avenues for enforcement of the existing laws. The year 1965 was marked by race riots resulting from the persistence of racial inequality and the frustration experienced by African Americans with regard to the slowness of change and the need for continual efforts to achieve freedom in those areas already protected by law.

Since the 1960s, a number of political leaders, such as the Reverend Jessie Jackson, have led the African American community. Others have been in the forefront in the arts, medicine, and sports such as Gwendolyn Brooks, Jon Wallace, Wilma Rudolph and Meredith Gourdine, respectively (Corbin, 1986; Igus, 1991; Sertima, 1989). African Americans continue to participate at all levels of the U.S. armed forces with large representation in both Vietnam and Desert Storm (Terry, 1992).

Today disparities continue for Black Americans in: health care services and opportunities, high mortality rates, housing inequalities, increased problems of substance abuse, law enforcement, the disproportionate number of incarcerated African American males, the inequality in the quality of education in inner city elementary and secondary schools, and the current court rulings pertaining to ongoing desegregation at the college level. These highlight the fact that racial discrimination and racial disparity are still a reality in this country in the 1990s (Brooks, 1990; Clancy, 1990; Cole, 1990; Conyers, 1992; Eccles, 1990; Hare, 1981; Jaschik, 1992).

Bell (1992) and Carter (1991) discuss how the history of this country has marred the experience of African Americans, and the perceptions of Whites towards African Americans in a way that makes it difficult for parity to be achieved. During the period of slavery, Whites developed a deep disrespect and disregard for the humanity of African people. Individuals of African ancestry, on the other hand, developed a deep distrust for Whites. More than any other factor, the historical reality of slavery has led to the present day prejudice and disparity in academic opportunity for African Americans (Bell, 1992; Carter, 1991). Long-standing racial prejudice towards those of African ancestry, whether unconscious or conscious, is an unpleasant reality which must not be overlooked when addressing issues of recruitment and retention of African Americans in higher education (Jackson, 1977; McFadden, 1976). Further, many present day African American students represent the first generation of their families to attend college. Thus, like many other minority students, African American students have had no role models to provide them with guidance for negotiating the college admission process or for learning how to adapt and successfully achieve once in higher education. Similarly, African American faculty have had few role models for mentoring through the ranks of tenure and promotion.

Barriers related to the history of racial prejudice in this country are as significant as those imposed by cultural diversity. History has shaped both African Americans' and Whites' perceptions. For this reason, history and cultural factors need to be considered during interactions among all persons so that a better understanding of one's own perceptual views and those of others, can be achieved.

## CULTURE, COMMUNICATION PATTERNS AND COGNITIVE STYLES OF AFRICAN AMERICAN STUDENTS

### Cultural Diversity and Core Elements Among African Americans

While African Americans are a heterogeneous group, they demonstrate a core set of cultural values which stem from their African beginnings. These cultural values are embedded within the context of their history and the American mainstream cultural framework in which they now reside. The core elements of African American culture include: a common history, strong group identity, a connectedness to family and the extended family, a deep level of spirituality, a great respect for elders, a high-esteem for pastors who are often the political leaders in the African American community, common styles of dress and methods of hair grooming, similarities in preferences for food and music, similarities in styles of discipline and conflict management, and commonalities in communication patterns and cognitive styles. These aspects may affect how African American students perceive, negotiate, adapt and achieve in the higher education environment.

The influence of "Americanization" has resulted in a range of diversity among African Americans with regard to the cultural practices adopted, their physical appearance, interactive styles, linguistic patterns, socioeconomic and educational levels, exposure to vocational role models, and overall social status. Much of this diversity can be attributed to the extent of forced (such as during slavery), as well as to voluntary blending with other cultures. Because of the range of diversity among African American people, it is important to avoid overgeneralizing and stereotyping. This can be achieved through face-to-face personal interactions with a variety of members of the group that one is interested in learning about so as to obtain an accurate understanding and interpretation of various cultural and individual practices.

## Communication Patterns

Asante (1991) discussed that most allied health professional education programs generally do not admit students into their programs until the junior year in college. By this time, most African American students are well acculturated into the many aspects of mainstream culture of the higher educational system, while still employing culturally appropriate African American elements in their private lives. Thus, some of the cross-cultural communication differences discussed in this section may not be readily apparent to faculty and students in the academic environment. However, for those African American students who may not be entirely proficient in speaking and writing Standard English, it may be helpful for the faculty to become acquainted with the major structural features of African American English (Turner, 1949). It should also be noted that not all African American students have been raised to learn African American English.

Whether students who are speakers of African American English should be required to demonstrate proficiency in speaking and writing of Standard English is a controversial topic (Adler, 1985, 1987, 1992; Cole, 1985). However, the issue of cross-cultural code-switching becomes important when the clinical emphasis is on providing assessment and management. The controversies surrounding this topic will vary for each specific allied health discipline.

### African American English: Sound and Grammatical Structure

African American English does not contain fricatives and, therefore, "th" is pronounced as "d," "t," or "f" (e.g., dis/this hat), nor does it contain the intervocalic or postvocalic [r] (e.g., pat/parrot). The nasal consonants, [m] and [n], do not always appear in the final position, and [ng] is substituted by [n] in the medial and final positions (e.g., walkin/ walking). The voiced plosive sounds [b, d and g], tend to be devoiced in the final position (e.g., rip/rib). The [r] sound is omitted in initial consonant clusters (e.g., staight/straight). Final consonant clusters, particularly those involving [t, d, s] and [z] are reduced (e.g., stan/stand) (Dillard, 1972; Turner, 1949).

The copula verb is absent in the present tense (e.g., "She comin" instead of "She is coming"). Some linguists (e.g., Dillard, 1972; Dalby, 1972) speculate that this indicates different verb conjugations with the absent copula denoting both aspect, as well as tense. For example, "She talking" means "She is talking now," while "She be talking" means "She talks continually".

Other grammatical features of African American English include (Dillard, 1972; Turner, 1949): the absence of the possessive "s" (e.g., "Mary baby" for "Mary's baby"); the absence of the plural "s" (e.g., "ten cent" for "ten cents"); multiple negation (e.g., "He ain't never goin' " for "He is not going"); subject reiteration (e.g., "Mary, she work hard" for "Mary works hard"); failure to mark the past tense (e.g., "Yesterday, Mary walk home" for "Yesterday, Mary walked home"); lack of subject-verb agreement (e.g., "She run" for "She ran"); and undifferentiation of third person pronouns (e.g., "He a woman doctor" for "She is a woman/female doctor") (Dillard, 1972; Turner, 1949).

### Nonverbal Styles of Communication Interaction

Similar to other high context cultures, African Americans rely more heavily on nonverbal than verbal forms of communication (Sue & Sue, 1990). Refer to Chapters 5, 6, and 7 for further elaboration of high context cultures. A few of the major nonverbal styles of communication which have been identified with African Americans include:

1. Head position and eye contact. As signs of respect, African Americans assume a downward head position, and nondirective eye gaze, especially when interacting with persons of authority.

2. Rolling the eyes to express disapproval and hostility. During "rolling of the eyes," the eye lids are slightly lowered as the eyeballs are moved in a low arc from one side of the eye socket to the other. The eyeball movement, which is very quick, is always in a direction away from the other individual.

3. Limp stance during perceived intimidating interactions with those seen as holding an authority position. This posture slowly evolves such that the head is lowered, then the total body becomes very relaxed. The person appears to be in a trance, giving the appearance that they are no longer receiving the message. This posture provides an outlet for anger and protest, without requiring any overt verbal rebuttal. It is as if the individual is nonverbally communicating the fact that they have the real control of the situation, because they can choose to receive or reject the message as they see fit.

4. Nonverbal body posturing of African American audiences. African American audiences assume an interactive role when listening to a speaker, such as a teacher or preacher. The audience will often shift

positions in their seats such that their backs are turned slightly to the speaker, so as to nonverbally communicate their confirmation and agreement of the speaker's remarks. Additionally, before this posturing, members will sometimes bend slightly forward in their seats to nonverbally communicate that they are concerned about, or unsure of what the speaker is saying. As soon as they understand or decide that they are in agreement with the speaker, a shifting movement is again noted. It is thought that this shift in posture to expose the back (which is a vulnerable part of the body) to the view of the speaker, may be done to communicate a level of approval, comfort, and trust.

## Cognitive Style

Grammar, pronunciation and interactive style are patterns that one can readily learn to change as is contextually appropriate. However, learning style which cuts to the core of the individual's essence is highly resistant to change. The cognitive style of learning that has been identified with African American students may significantly impact on their ability to gain entry into the higher educational system, as well as to achieve once involved in the system.

African Americans are sometimes described as possessing a field-dependent cognitive style of learning, which serves to guide and define how they view the world (Hale-Benson, 1986). While further research is needed to learn more about African American's cognitive style, Hillard (as cited in Hale-Benson, 1986) describes the following field-dependent cognitive styles of many African Americans.

1. African Americans respond to things in terms of the overall gestalt rather than to the individual parts of a whole. By contrast, mainstream Americans tend to respond analytically to the parts.
2. African Americans tend to prefer inferential reasoning strategies over deductive or inductive reasoning strategies.
3. African Americans tend to approximate space, numbers, and time rather than utilize exact figures for more precise accuracy.
4. African Americans tend to be people oriented, placing great value on individuals and activities rather than on things. Hillard notes that this tendency is demonstrated by the fact that many African Americans choose careers in the helping professions, such as teaching, psychology or social work.

5. African Americans have a keen sense of justice, and are quick to detect and analyze injustice.
6. African Americans tend to have a strong sense of concern for their fellow man.
7. African Americans tend to be innovative, autonomous, and unique in terms of their personal style. This is demonstrated by the improvisational music forms and creative styles of dress observed in the African American community.
8. African American people tend to be highly proficient in nonverbal communication rather than dependent on the spoken "word".

Some educators have related that the field-dependent cognitive style may account for why African American students perform poorly on college entrance examinations such as the GRE's and SAT's, and on objective academic course examinations. Anderson (1985) and Payne (1988) suggest that differences in learning styles may account for the low performance by African Americans on the National Examinations in Speech-Language Pathology and Audiology (NESPA) acquired for professional certification, as compared to their demonstrated outstanding performance in academic coursework. As an outgrowth of their observations, Payne and Anderson (1991) have developed a training program including a manual, where African American students and other students are taught how to prepare for the NESPA. The program provides instruction in how to develop analytical test-taking skills. Cognitive learning style also has implications for classroom learning and clinical training. Students may learn best when course and clinical materials are related to contextual information.

Anderson (1988) emphasizes the value of interpersonal relationships and the social-affective orientation among African Americans. The development of a close sense of comradery with others in same social network results in a close identity with and loyalty to the individual's immediate ("extended family") network as opposed to the secular identity of the mainstream culture. Thus, cooperative learning activities may facilitate learning in the classroom environment.

Attitudes towards time and the use of time among African American students may differ from mainstream American students. While Western cultures clearly define time concepts for the past, present and future, African American people fail to judge time as a constant variable that can be measured in a quantifiable fashion (Pennington, 1985). According to the African culture, "the future" is not a part of time because it is viewed as absent, not having taken place. Events pertaining to the "rhythm of nature" which extend beyond the present into the immediate future (e.g., pregnancy or the harvest of crops), constitute "potential time" rather than actual time (Pennington, 1985). Actual time is what is present and what is past. The daily focus of African American students, therefore, is on issues pertaining to the present in relation to the past, rather than on the present in relation to the future.

Because of the difference in time concepts, African American students may not manage time in the same manner as mainstream American students. In Western cultures, most of life's activities are geared towards a striving to leave an imprint on the future (Smith, 1952). According to African American culture, "Man is not a slave to time but takes as much time as he wants" (Mbiti, 1970, p. 24). Because the Western time concept is at variance with the African time concept, African American students may need to adapt to the rituals of punctuality and time management of the mainstream educational setting.

## AFRICAN AMERICAN STUDENT ISSUES

African American high school, junior high school and even elementary school children should be made aware of and exposed to the allied health professions (Carey, 1992). Exposure to these professions can be gained through participation in professional career presentations at schools, as well as reviewing printed career and recruitment materials available from national professional allied health associations. Recruitment materials can be disseminated through African American national and student organizations, and their news letters. For example, the professions of Audiology and Speech-Language Pathology have The National Black Association for Speech-Language and Hearing (NBASLH). Identification of potential students for recruitment can also come from faculty at the traditional African American universities and colleges (see *Black American Information Directory 1990–91,* 1990 in the reference section). Additionally, the establishment of student exchange programs between predominately African American and White institutions, may assist in identifying potential applicants.

As mentioned, many African American students have a field-dependent cognitive style, and thus do not perform well on college entrance examinations, such as the SAT's and GRE's. This places African American students at a disadvantage when competing for college acceptance and financial scholarship support. Thus, it may be helpful for institutions to explore alternative methods for evaluating students for admission, such as weighing of students' academic performance over time, coupled with their letters of recommendation (Klitgaard, 1985). For the vast majority of students, the availability of financial support is often the first and foremost consideration in selecting a particular university. For this reason, time should be spent by a recruiter or a faculty member in apprising potential applicants of the types of scholarships and financial support sources available to them.

Issues of student support will vary depending on whether students attend a predominately African American or White institution of higher learning. Many African American students select a predominately African American institution because of a cultural tie that fosters a feeling of understanding, caring and a willingness to individualize attention. Blair (1992) emphasizes the importance of a warm, friendly and supportive social climate within the academic program where African American students feel welcomed and appreciated for their achievements, and feel a sense of inclusion from faculty and their peers both inside and outside the classroom. Social networking is an important aspect of the African American culture.

In order for students not feel abandoned and isolated once they have been admitted into a program, faculty can demonstrate their interest and support by periodically meeting with students to discuss their academic progress, and at the same time suggest ways for students to develop networks with other students. Some institutions have formally developed student cultural exchange programs for: assisting students to more easily acclimate into the academic environment, mentoring, reducing students' stresses, and for providing opportunities for networking and social interactions among students and faculty (Blair, 1992). While programs like these are laudable, care must be taken to insure that the special mentoring and support efforts do not further isolate African American students from the mainstream student body. Depending on the needs of a given academic program/department, it might be more productive to offer similar opportunities to small interracial groups of students who are selected merely on the basis of being assigned to an undergraduate/ graduate advisor. Small group cooperative learning experiences in class may help develop relationships, as well as promote learning among students.

Students who are not exposed to the African American culture, often innocently but wrongly ask inquisitive questions of African American students such as questions pertaining to hair grooming or style of dress. However, African American students perceive these types of questions as invasive and even offensive (Cole, 1989; Taylor, 1992). Similarly, faculty may pose culturally probing questions in the classroom which can be disconcerting to African American students. It is important for faculty to recognize that students may not be the "real" information experts with regard to their culture.

Some African American students tend to be overachievers and forfeit a balanced social life by spending excessive amounts of time on academic assignments. In order to prevent this from happening or resulting in academic burnout, faculty and student advisors should facilitate development of self-recognition of ones' achievements.

Clinical supervisors should be sensitive to cultural differences in communication patterns and styles of interaction among students by becoming more flexible and accepting of "reasonable" variations, particularly in the professional programs of Speech-Language and Audiology. While recent research delineates the generally acceptable communication styles of clinicians in the professions of Speech-Language Pathology (Sorensen, 1992), research is currently being conducted to determine the boundaries for acceptable cross-cultural variations in communication patterns and interactive styles within the clinical setting (Champion & Mercaitis, in personal communication; Farmer & Farmer, 1989). Until such information is available, decisions regarding acceptable differences will continue to be supervisor-directed.

## ISSUES RELATING TO AFRICAN AMERICAN ACADEMICIANS AND RESEARCHERS

A paucity of African American representation exists in higher education, particularly with tenured faculty and administrative positions (U.S. Equal Employment Opportunity Commission, 1989). The professional education programs of allied health serve to provide students with the necessary academic and clinical foundations for assuming their later professional roles as effective health care providers of diverse client populations. One effort toward achieving this goal is to increase and strengthen the multicultural professional education base in the allied health professional programs.

Many of the challenges facing African American faculty in higher education are similar to those faced by students. When African Americans and other minority individuals apply for faculty positions in higher education, some administrators and even faculty members, assume that these individuals are being hired to fill a minority quota rather than being hired for their expertise in a particular academic, professional and research area (Carter, 1991; Jackson, 1977). This assumption may lead faculty peers (and even students) to question the African American faculty member's expertise, and the level of their academic knowledge for which they have been hired (Carter, 1991; Steele, 1990). In order to combat these misperceptions, African American faculty like other minority faculty, feel under undue stress to perform so as to eradicate such perceptions. For instance, African American faculty members commonly state that they feel the need to be twice as prepared as other faculty members in the classroom setting and to be twice as demanding of students in terms of course requirements, in order to achieve the same level of respect and recognition by their faculty peers (Bell, 1992). To ensure a racially healthy environment where African American and other minority faculty members feel a sense of unity with their peers, a sense of importance and are equally recognized for their achievements, administrators should be involved in the daily operation of their departments.

Further, an African American faculty member may be hired by the administration with the expectation and assumption that he/she will serve as the multicultural spokesperson and "expert" for the department. Thus, they may be given the responsibility of recruiting African American students and teaching the multicultural coursework. While it is important to recognize that most African American faculty like other minority faculty share a personal commitment to enhancing multicultural issues, this may not be their preferred or educationally prepared area of teaching. Rather, the educational preparation and research interests of many African American faculty have been in highly specialized allied health areas that are outside the realm of multicultural issues.

When a faculty member is designated to serve as a multicultural spokesperson for the department, every effort should be taken to insure that the "expert" merely serves as a facilitator for the development and planning of infusing multicultural information in the department's course offerings by all faculty. If the total faculty do not take part in this effort, multicultural issues may not be viewed by faculty and students as an important professional and research area for the allied health discipline. While African American faculty often serve effectively as minority student recruiters, recruiting is time-consuming. Thus, the faculty member's responsibilities must be prioritized.

Administrators, as well as faculty, who are serious about the retention and promotion of African American and other minority faculty, would benefit from implementing well-monitored mentoring and support systems within their department. Department administrators and a senior faculty mentor assigned from the department (from a related department or "sister/brother" institution) and preferably with expertise in areas related to that of the junior faculty member, can assist by monitoring the faculty member's progress towards obtaining the teaching, research and scholarly writing goals necessary for tenure and promotion. In addition, the faculty mentor can help the junior faculty member to network with other researchers and professionals in their specific allied health discipline.

Even in the most supportive academic environments, African American faculty report challenges with time management. Their research and scholarly writing time is often consumed by assigned and self-imposed non-academic obligations. For instance, African American faculty often feel obliged to serve on university, professional and community committees, which have "minority" under-representation. Additionally, because of the personal challenges encountered during their own academic experiences, many African American faculty members may assume the serious and extensive role as mentor and advisor to all students where it turns into a 24 hour responsibility.

While acceptance of research and sources of research funding in multicultural areas has improved (NIDCD, 1992), this area still has not received the widespread recognition it deserves as a viable and important area of research and scholarly pursuit. Given the changing demographics of this nation, more research will be needed in this area to build a solid foundation for the effective delivery of health care and education services to linguistically and culturally diverse client populations.

## CONCLUDING REMARKS

Solid grounding in the history, culture, and communication and cognitive styles of African American people, by both faculty and students should serve as a basis for the effective delivery of health care and educational services to African American clients. Additionally, such information should serve to enhance cross-cultural communication among students and faculty, and to help faculty effectively teach African American students so that they can achieve their full learning potentials. While the information in this chapter focused primarily on the recruitment and retention needs of African American students in higher education, there also exists a critical need for the retention and successful career laddering of African American faculty.

## REFERENCES

Adler, S.: Comment on social dialects, *ASHA, 27* (4): 46, 1985.

Adler, S.: Bidialectalism? Mandatory or elective. *ASHA, 29* (1): 41–44, 1987.

Adler, S.: *Multicultural Communication Skills in the Classroom: An Enterprise Between Speech-Language Specialists and Educators.* Needham Heights, Allyn and Bacon, 1992.

Anderson, N.: Cultural considerations within the national examination for speech-language pathology and audiology (NESPA). In Payne, K., Anderson, N. & Cole, P. (Eds.): *Howard University NESPA Project Plenary Meeting Proceedings.* Washington, Howard University, 1988, pp. 1–39.

Asante, M.K.: The African essence in African-American language. In Asante, M.K. and Asante, K.W.: *African Culture: The Rhythms of Unity.* Westport, Greenwood, 1985, pp. 233–252.

Asante, M.K.: African elements in African-American English. In Holloway, J. (Ed.): *Africanisms in American Culture.* Bloomington, Indiana University, 1990, pp. 19–33.

Asante, M.K.: Afrocentric curriculum. *Educational Leadership, 19:* 29, 1991.

Bell, D.: *Faces at the Bottom of the Well: The Permanence of Racism.* New York, Basic Books, 1992.

Bennett, L.: *Before the Mayflower: A History of Black Americans.* New York, Penguin, 1987.

*Black American Information Directory 1990–91.* Detroit, Gale Research, 1990.

Blair, C.: Our multicultural agenda: Student perspective. *ASHA, 34:* 43–44, 1992.

Boles, J.B.: *Black Southerners 1619–1869.* Lexington, University Press of Kentucky, 1943.

Brent, L.: *Incidents in the Life of a Slave Girl.* San Diego, Harcourt Brace Jovanovich, 1973.

Brooks, R.L.: *Rethinking the American Race Problem.* Berkeley, University of California, 1990.

Carter, S.: *Reflections of an Affirmative Action Baby.* New York, Harper Collins, 1991.

Carey, A.: Get involved multiculturally. *ASHA, 18:* 3, 1992.

Champion, T. and Mercaitis, P.A.: In personal communication. Amherst, University of Massachusetts, 1992.

Clancy, F.: Healing the delta. *American Health,* 43–55, November, 1990.

Cole, L.: Response to Adler. *ASHA, 27* (4): 47–48, 1985.

Cole, L.: E pluribus pluribus: Multicultural imperatives for the 1990s and beyond, *ASHA, 20:* 66–70, 1989.

Cole, J.: The south in United States and United States in the south. In Baer, H.A. and Jones, Y. (Eds.): *African Americans in the South: Issues of Race, Class and Gender.* Athens, University of Georgia, 1990, pp. i–xiii.

Cone, J.H.: *Black Theology and Black Power.* San Francisco, Harper, 1969.

Conyers, J.: The Urgency of Health Care Reform. Keynote presentation at the Fifth National Conference on Health Care for the Poor and Underserved: Targeting the Needs of the Underserved. Nashville, Meharry Medical College, October 5–6, 1992.

Corbin, R.M.: *1999 Facts About Blacks: A Sourcebook of African-American Accomplishment.* Los Angeles, Beckham House, 1986.

Curtin, P.D.: *The Atlantic Slave Trade: A Census.* Madison, University of Wisconsin, 1969.

Dalby, D.: The African element in American English. In Kochman, L. (Ed.): *Rappin and Stylin Out: Communication in Urban Black America.* Urbana, University of Illinois, 1972, pp. 23–40.

Davis, A., Gardner, B.B. & Gardner, M.R.: *Deep South.* Los Angeles, The Center for Afro-American Studies at U.C.L.A., 1988.

Dillard, J.L.: *Black English: It's History and Usage in the United States.* New York, Random House, 1972.

Donovan, R.X.: *Black Scientists of America.* Portland, National Book Company, 1990.

Eccles, A.: Forgotten Americans. *American Health,* 41–42, November, 1990.

Farmer, S. & Farmer, J. (Ed.): *Supervision in Communication Disorders.* Columbus, Merrill Publishing Company, 1989, pp. 126–127.

Fisher, U.: Physicians and slavery in the Antebellum Southern Medical Journals. *Journal of the History of Medicine and Allied Science, 23:* 41, 1968.

Fisher, M.M.: *Negro Slave Songs in the United States.* New York, Carol Publishing Group, 1990.

Frazier, E.F.: *The Negro Family in the United States.* Chicago, University of Chicago, 1966.

Genovese, E.D.: *Roll Jordon, Roll: The World the Slaves Made.* New York, Vintage Books, 1976.

Hale-Benson, J.: *Black Children: Their Roots, Culture and Learning Styles.* Baltimore, Johns Hopkins University, 1986.

Hare, N.: Black Ecology. In Dana, R.H. (Ed.): *Human Services for Cultural Minorities.* Baltimore, University Park Press, 1981, pp. 103.

Harrison, I. & Harrison, D.S.: The Black family experience and health behavior. In Crawford, C.O. (Ed.): *Health and the Family: A Medical-Sociological Analysis.* New York, MacMillan, 1971, pp. 175–199.

Harrison, I.: Healing status and healing practices: Continuations from an African past. *Journal of African Studies, 2:* (4) 547–560, 1975.

Holloway, J.: The Origins of African-American culture. In Holloway, J.E. (Ed.):

*Africanisms in American Culture.* Bloomington, Indiana University Press, 1990, pp. ix–xxi.

Idowu, E.B.: *African Traditional Religion.* Maryknoll, Orbis Books, 1973.

Igus, T.: *Book of Black Heroes: Great Women in the Struggle.* New Jersey, Just Us Books, 1991, Vol. 2.

Jackson, G.G.: The emergence of a Black perspective in counseling. *Journal of Negro Education, 24:* 230–253, 1977.

Jacobs, H.A.: *Incidents in the Life of A Slave Girl Written By Herself.* Cambridge, Harvard, 1987.

Jaschik, S.: High-Court ruling transforms battles over desegregation at colleges in 19 states. *The Chronicle of Higher Education,* A16–A18, July 8, 1992.

Klitgaard, R.: *Choosing Elites.* New York, Basic Books, 1985.

Mbiti, J.S.: *African Religions and Philosophy.* New York, Doubleday, 1970.

McFadden, J.: Stylistic dimensions of counseling Blacks. *Journal of Non-white Concerns, 5:* 23–28, 1976.

Moynihan, D.P.: A nation of nations. In Smead, H. (Ed.): *The Afro-Americans.* New York, Chelsea House, 1989, pp. 7–11.

Myers, W.D.: *Now is Your Time! The African American Struggle for Freedom.* New York, Harpertrophy, 1991.

National Center for Education Statistics: *Trends in Racial/Ethnic Enrollment in Higher Education: Fall 1980–Fall 1990.* Washington, U.S. Department of Education, June, 1992a.

National Center for Education Statistics: *Race/Ethnicity Trends in Degrees Conferred by Institutions of Higher Education: 1980–81 through 1989–90.* Washington, U.S. Department of Education, May, 1992b.

National Institute on Deafness and Communication Disorders: Research and Research Training Needs of Minority Persons and Minority Health Issues Working Group. Bethesda, National Institute of Health, April, 1992.

Palmer, C.: African slave trade: The cruelest commerce. *National Geographic,* 64–91, September, 1992.

Payne, K.: Dimensions of difficulty: Black students' performance on the NESPA. In Payne, K., Anderson, N. & Cole, P. (Eds.): *Howard University NESPA Project Plenary Meeting Proceedings.* Washington, Howard University, 1988, pp. 1–44.

Payne, K. & Anderson, N.: *How to Prepare for the NESPA.* San Diego, Singular Publishing Group, 1991.

Pennington, D.L.: Time in African culture. In Asante, M.K. & Asante, K.W. (Eds.): *African Culture: The Rhythms of Unity.* Westport, Greenwood Press, 1985.

Perry, B.: *Malcolm: The Life of a Man Who Changed Black America.* New York, Station Hill, 1991.

Pluckett, N.N.: *Folk Beliefs of the Southern Negro.* Chapel Hill, University of North Carolina Press, 1926.

Redding, J.: *The Story of the Negro in America.* New York, Doubleday, 1958.

Sertima, I.V. (Ed.): *Blacks in Science.* New Brunswick, Transaction Books, 1989.

Smead, H.: *The Afro-Americans.* New York, Chelsea House, 1989.

Smith, M.: Different cultural concepts of past, present, and future. *Psychiatry, 15* (4): 24–25, 1952.

Sorensen, D.N.: Communicator style characteristics of speech-language pathology students. *ASHA,* 67–71, 1992.

Steele, S.: *The Content of Our Character: A New Vision of Race in America.* New York, Harper Perennial, 1990.

Stowe, H.B.: *Uncle Tom's Cabin.* Boston, Houghton Mifflin, 1918.

Sue, D.W. & Sue, D.: *Counseling the Culturally Different: Theory and Practice.* New York, John Wiley and Sons, 1990.

Taylor, O.: Clinical practice as a social occasion. In Cole, L. & Deal, V.R. (Eds.): *Communication Disorders in Multicultural Populations.* Rockville, American Speech-Language-Hearing Association, 1992.

Terry, W.: *Bloods: An Oral History of the Vietnam War by Black Veterans.* New York, Ballantine, 1992.

*The Chronicle of Higher Education Almanac.* Washington, Author, August 26, 1992.

Tucker, R.K.: *The Dragon and the Cross: The Rise and Fall of the Ku Klux Klan in Middle America.* Hamden, Shoe String, 1991.

Turner, L.D.: *Africanisms in the Gullah Dialect.* Chicago, University of Chicago, 1949.

United States Equal Employment Opportunity Commission: *Higher Education Staff Information Report Covering the 89–90 Academic Year,* EEO-6 Report, Washington, Author, 1989.

United States Department of Commerce, Economics and Statistics Administration, Bureau of the Census: *1990 Census of Population and Housing.* Washington, Summary Population and Housing Characteristics United States, CPH-1-1, 1990.

Whitehead, T.L.: In search of soul food and meaning: Culture and food and health. In Baer, H.A. & Jones, Y. (Eds.): *African Americans in the South: Issues of Race, Class and Gender.* Athens, University of Georgia, 1990, pp. 95–110.

Willis, W.: Families with African American roots. In Lynch, E.W. & Hanson, M.T. (Eds.): *Developing Cross-Cultural Competence.* Baltimore, Paul H. Brooks, 1992, pp. 147–149.

# Chapter 5

# PROFILE OF HISPANIC/ LATINO AMERICAN STUDENTS

HENRIETTE W. LANGDON AND LYNNE W. CLARK

## DEMOGRAPHICS OF HISPANIC/LATINO POPULATIONS

The Hispanic/Latino population has increased from 14.6 to 23.4 million during the past decade. This factor contributes considerably to the current linguistic and cultural diversity in the United States. At the present time, Hispanic/Latino population is the second largest and fastest growing minority group in the United States. Hispanic/Latino population may be even larger if one were to include those undocumented persons who are not counted in the census (Current Population Reports, 1990). By the year 2020, it is projected that they will become the largest of the minority groups (Davis, Haub & Willette, 1983). In fact, the United States has the seventh largest number of Hispanics/Latinos in the World, only being exceeded by Mexico, Spain, Argentina, Colombia, Peru, and Venezuela (United States Bureau of the Census, 1990).

Hispanic/Latino population is comprised of diverse ethnic subgroups. The term **Hispanic** is generally defined as having a Spanish surname, being Spanish, or having a birth place in a Spanish-speaking country, such as Mexico, Puerto Rico, Cuba, El Salvador, Dominican Republic, and other Central and South American countries (Cuellar, 1991). Where the designation of Hispanic is accepted by some individuals, others prefer to be referred to as **Latino.** These designations, however, remain problematic since they obscure "the salient national, ethnic and racial variations of a highly heterogenous population with significantly different histories and perspectives" (Cuellar, 1991, p. 369). For the purposes of this chapter, the combined terms Hispanic/Latino will be used, as well as reference to specific subgroups where appropriate.

The largest Hispanic/Latino group within the United States is that of Mexican origin constituting 12.1 million, or 63 percent of the total U.S. Hispanic/Latino population. Puerto Ricans are the second largest comprising 2.5 million, or 12 percent of the population. Hispanic/Latino Americans from South and Central America constitute 2.2 million, or 11.5 percent of all Hispanic/Latino Americans. Persons originating from Spain, or those who refer to themselves as Hispanic in a generic sense constitute 1.6 million, or 8.1 percent of the Hispanic/Latino population in the United States. Cubans comprise 1.0 million, or 5.3 percent of the Hispanic/Latino American population (United States Bureau of the Census, 1990).

Mexican Americans tend to live in the Southwest, whereas Central and South Americans reside in large metropolitan areas of the Midwest, West, and East. As a result of the Cuban Revolution in the late 1950s, large numbers of Cubans settled in Florida and New York (Rogg & Cooney, 1980). In fact, 11 percent of Florida's population is Hispanic/Latino. With the development of manufacturing in the Northeast, along with free access to U.S. mainland, Puerto Ricans settled in New Jersey and New York (Davis, Haub & Willette, 1983). The states primarily populated by Hispanics/Latinos, and in particular Mexican Americans, include: California, Texas, Arizona, New Mexico, and Colorado.

According to the Current Population Reports (1990), there is an overrepresentation of Hispanic/Latino Americans among the poor and unemployed. About 26 percent of Hispanics/Latinos live below the poverty level, as compared to 12 percent of the rest of the U.S. population. Americans of Puerto Rican heritage have the highest percentage of persons living below the poverty level (40%), followed by Mexican Americans (28%). Sue and Sue (1990) discuss employment among Hispanic/Latino groups. Hispanics/Latinos are generally employed as blue collar, semi-skilled and unskilled workers. Mexican Americans are employed in farming, forestry, and fishing. As compared to other Hispanic/Latino subgroups, more Cuban Americans hold technical, sales, managerial, and professional positions.

The proportion of Hispanics/Latinos entering college is significantly below that of other minority and Anglo student groups (Center for Budget Policy Priorities, 1988; Current Population Reports, 1990). Quintana, Vogel & Ybarra (1991) report that as of 1988, only 5.2 percent of all college students were Hispanics/Latinos. Unfortunately, this trend continues today (Valencia, 1991). Only 8.4 percent of the 27 percent of Hispanic/Latino students enrolled in the California public school system are presently represented in the state's university system (Pearl, 1991). Despite affirmative action policies (D'Souza, 1992), Sánchez with

Marder, Berry and Ross (1992) report that in 1980 only 48 percent of Hispanic/Latino high school seniors applied to one or more colleges in contrast to 63 percent African Americans and 65 percent Anglo-American applicants. Only 58 percent of Hispanic/Latino Americans, particularly Puerto Ricans and more recently immigrated Cubans, completed high school, and only 10 percent of Hispanics/Latinos completed a college education in contrast with 22 percent for the rest of the American population.

About 30 percent of all Hispanic/Latino students drop out of college before the end of their freshman year. Barry (1991) notes that now more Hispanic/Latino women than men, are enrolled in college. Many of the Hispanic/Latino college-bound students represent the first generation of their families to pursue a college education. Of those Hispanic/Latino American students who do pursue studies in higher education, a large proportion enter two-year, nondegree programs (Chacón, Cohen & Strover, 1986; Nora & Rendón, 1990; Quintana, Vogel & Ybarra, 1991). Additionally, more Hispanic/Latino students attend these programs as compared to Anglo-American students (46% and 23%, respectively) (Olivas, 1986).

Given the low number of Hispanic/Latino students entering and completing college, it is critical that faculty examine the possible factors impacting on these students' academic achievement. Additionally, given the present and projected general growth of the Hispanic/Latino American population, and the fact that shortages of Spanish-speaking health care professionals exist, there is a critical need to recruit and retain more Hispanic/Latino American bilingual students into the professional education programs of allied health. For instance, in the professions of speech-language pathology and audiology, only 0.1 percent of the total membership of the American Speech, Language and Hearing Association is Hispanic/Latino. Further, only a small number of these members report being bilingual speakers of English and Spanish (ASHA, 1992). Within the allied health professional education programs, there is also a critical need to educate and clinically prepare all students to professionally serve with competence Spanish-speaking, Hispanic/Latino clients.

With these issues in mind, this chapter is intended to provide important information that university faculty will need to consider for effectively teaching Hispanic/Latino students, and for assisting these students in their adjustment into the mainstream American higher educational environment. Faculty, in addressing these considerations, can empower Hispanic/Latino students in the academic setting, and can promote cross-communication and understanding among all students. This chapter also describes cultural styles of social interaction, communication and learning specific to Hispanic/Latino individuals, that may affect how Hispanic/Latino students interact in the classroom environment. Further, the chapter describes how the heterogeneous nature of the Hispanic/Latino subgroups must be taken into account if students are to achieve and easily adjust to the academic environment. Such information can serve as basic content information for teaching and clinically training non-Hispanic/Latino students in the allied health professions so as to provide effective health care services to Hispanic/Latino clients. The content of this chapter is supplemented by information from interviews with Hispanic/Latino and Anglo graduate students, as well as from the personal perspective and experience of the first author which extend some twenty years.

## HETEROGENEITY AMONG THE HISPANIC/LATINO POPULATION

### Factors of Heterogeneity

Heterogeneity exists between and within the different subgroups of the Hispanic/Latino population. Even within some Hispanic/Latino families, members use different terms for self-identity as related to generational and political issues. For example, parents and older generation Mexican Americans may use **Mexicano**, whereas sons and daughters may choose to identify themselves as **Mexican Americans.** Further, grandchildren may select the term **Chicano** to politicize their identity and pride in their Indian and Spanish ancestry (Lampe, 1984; Valle, 1990). Hispanic/Latino individuals of the older generation consider this later term insulting (Muñoz, 1982).

Hispanics/Latinos share unifying cultural themes, beliefs, and values that differ from Anglo American traditions. One might, however, appreciate these generalizations without stereotyping all members of the same ethnic group into rigid preconceptions. The heterogeneity of the Hispanic/Latino population is related to several factors: (1) geographic location of country of origin and its political history; (2) reason for and patterns of immigration which may be voluntary, economical or political; (3) length of time in United States and stability of residence for some persons, such as Mexicans who migrate back and forth to their country of origin; (4) biogenetic heritage with its physiological traits; (5) degree of acculturation coupled with intergenerational differences; (6) primary language use and English language proficiency; (7) socioeconomic level and class status (Davis, Haub, Willette, 1983; Sue and Sue, 1990; Valle, 1990; Veltman, 1988).

These factors make broad cultural generalizations about the Hispanic/Latino population difficult. Cultural variations, in fact, are sometimes misinterpreted as socioeconomic class variations. Cultural norms tend to refer to the public reality of how relationships and behaviors "ought to be." However, because of the above factors, the private realities of "how things really are" tend not to coincide with the public reality.

## Biogenetic Heritage

Biogenetic heritage of the Hispanic/Latino population is highly diverse. Their Indian and African heritages contribute to both the diverse physical characteristics and cultural traditions among Hispanic/Latino individuals. These biogenetic aspects have partially contributed to the racial prejudice felt by Hispanics/Latinos in the United States (García-Preto, 1982; Mizio, 1979; Valle, 1990).

Some Hispanics/Latinos are descendants of the **indios** (Indians) who lived in North America prior to Spanish colonalization. In fact, over 200 Indian tribes exist in Mexico today who are descendants of the great Myan and Aztec empires (Dostert, 1989). Other Hispanics/Latinos consider themselves **negros,** descendants of the Africans brought over as slaves to New Spain. Still, others identify themselves as **mesitzo** (e.g., a mixture of hispano-indios), as **mulattos** (e.g., a mixture of hispano-negros), or as **pochos** (e.g., a mixture of hispano-gringo).

Cubans have cultural traditions similar to Puerto Ricans, Dominican Republicans, and other Caribbean Americans whose ethnic ancestry and cultural foundations are rooted in Afro-Hispano-Mulatto traditions. These Hispanic/Latino cultures are significantly different from those of Mexico, South and Central America where ethnic and cultural traditions stem more from Mesitzo-Indio-Hispano traditions (Valle, 1990).

## Immigration and Acculturation Patterns

Hispanic/Latino individuals represent different immigration patterns to the mainland of the United States, as well as variation in the degree of acculturation into the mainstream American society. As a result of the Cuban Revolution, the first group of Cubans immigrated to the United States between 1959–1961 (Zuniga, 1992). Because this group consisted of upper and middle class highly educated professionals with their own financial resources, they found acculturation easy in comparison to the subsequent groups of Cuban immigrants. During the period of the Bay of Pigs (1965–1973), middle and low class Cubans, including those owning small businesses and skilled labors, immigrated to the United States for economic and family reasons. The third and largest Cuban group to immigrate, consisted of marginal and sociopolitical dissident populations of the young, female, and non-White with low socioeconomic and educational levels (Casal, Prohias, Carrasco & Prieto, 1979). These latter two groups of Cuban immigrants found acculturation more difficult, experiencing racial, educational, and socioeconomic class barriers (Guillermo, 1982; Perez-Stable, 1981).

Mexican Americans began immigrating as early as the 1900s, fleeing from violence of the Mexican Revolution. However, with severe unemployment in the United States during the Great Depression of 1910, many Mexicans were deported, or forced by the U.S. government to return to Mexico. During World War II, a new wave of Mexicans immigrated to United States. Because of language barriers, discrimination in housing, education, and unemployment, Mexican Americans found acculturation difficult. This resulted in high rates of unemployment and children not finishing their schooling. Many Mexican Americans still remain in cultural transition today (Falicov, 1982).

Early in the 1900s, Puerto Rican's came to the United States' mainland to seek jobs, education, political refuge, adventure, and to help family members already living in the mainland to care for their children and sick relatives (García-Preto, 1982). The majority of Puerto Ricans immigrated to the mainland after World War II, with immigration peaking in 1952 (García-Preto, 1986). Of all Hispanic/Latino American subgroups, Puerto Ricans have remained less acculturated, particularly those who immigrated after World War II. Lack of educational and employment opportunities, coupled with cultural insensitivity and racism have, contributed to their social problems, particularly with regard to the structure and functioning of the Puerto Rican family (Fernandez-Marina, 1961). For instance, when many non-White Puerto Rican families first arrived to the United States mainland, their families were perceived by others as interracial (Zuniga, 1992). The family's exposure to racial prejudice led to the resentment, rejection and even to eventual splits within the family. Because of low socioeconomic levels, and more employment opportunities for women, divorce and separation increased. Gender role changed between husbands and wives where wives and not husbands, were employed (Mizio, 1974).

Within the past ten years, due to wars in Central America, political refugees from such countries as El Salvador and Nicaragua have immigrated to the United States (Zuniga, 1992). The experiences of war and conflict burden of their emotional well being, have lead to cultural shock for many Central Americans.

## PREREQUISITE KNOWLEDGE OF HISPANIC/LATINO STUDENTS: FAMILY, COMMUNICATION, LEARNING, ACCULTURATION AND HEALTH

Collectively, a survey of the literature (e.g., Keller, Deneen & Megallán, 1991; Olivas, 1986), as well as interviews with graduate Hispanic/Latino and Anglo students in the allied health professional programs of speech-language pathology and audiology, identifies four major challenges faced by Hispanic/Latino students in higher education. In many instances, these challenges prevent students from completing their studies and from easily negotiating the higher education environment. These include: (1) the degree of acculturation into the mainstream American educational system; (2) limited family support and guidance in pursuing higher education; (3) insufficient or inadequate prior academic preparation to enter and succeed in postsecondary education; and (4) financial constraints.

Many of these factors are directly related to a collectivistic cultural orientation of **familismo** which permeates Hispanic/Latino students' styles of social interaction, learning and communication in the academic environment. Further, socioeconomic level and class factors also impact on Hispanic/Latino students' ability to successfully achieve in higher education.

## Familismo

Hispanics/Latinos place great value on the family (Sue and Sue, 1991; Vega, Hough & Romero, 1983; Szapocznik, Kurtines & Hanna, 1979). Family pride, dignity, and obligation begin early, and are nurtured throughout an individual's lifetime. With a collectivistic or humanistic orientation, the needs and welfare of the family take precedence over the individual's needs (Kluckholm & Strodtbeck, 1961; Sue & Sue, 1990). Instead of asking "How are you today?", a Hispanic/Latino might ask "How is your family today?". Children are expected to financially contribute to the family, and older children are expected to care for younger siblings, especially when parents work. Within the family, a patriarchical structure exists with regard to age, sex, and authority. Male domination exists with the female assuming a submissive role of nurturing and supporting the children. Children are characterized as dependent, as well as dutiful to their parents. Zuniga (1992) discusses strong sibling and extended family systems. Siblings assume various roles in terms of responsibility to one another and a division of labor. Because siblings emotionally support, advise, provide practical help and companionship among themselves, few Hispanic/Latino children feel the need to seek friendships outside the family. Close relationships exist between cousins, aunts, uncles, godparents, and godchildren. Godparents act as a second set of parents, providing security and guardianship to their godchildren.

Hispanic/Latino family values remain the last and most resilient to change. Those from lower socioeconomic backgrounds, those residing for a long time in the United States, and those in close geographical proximity to country of origin where maintenance and renewing of ties can be made, often retain their ethnic family identify (McGoldrich, Pearce & Giodano, 1982).

Hispanic/Latino family structure is directly influenced by the marked differences that exist between lower and upper/middle class socioeconomic levels. For instance, generalizations about the Mexican culture and its family values which are in transition, apply more to the poor and working class families, and to those families from rural and semirural areas. Upper and middle class Mexican American families function more like mainstream American families (Falicov, 1982; Zuniga, 1992). The same values hold true for Puerto Rican American families. Low socioeconomic Hispanic/Latino classes' view of passiveness or fatalism also affects how Hispanic/Latino families view education and achievement. Those who are poor and less educated, have a limited sense of educational and future occupational options.

The traditional family structure within some Hispanic/Latino American subgroups is undergoing a transition. For example, in some Mexican American families, joint decisions are made by the husband and wife. There exists a greater equality between males and females because of females working and/or males being unemployed and thereby losing their self-respect and esteem (Alvirez, Bean & Williams, 1981; Cromwell & Ruiz, 1979). Language barriers have also created a strain on the Hispanic/Latino family structure with regard to parent and child relationships. Hispanic/Latino children learn English in school. Thus, parents who are often non-English speakers must rely on their children as interpreters. This places a great strain on family relations by placing parents in an inferior position, particularly in front of strangers. The collectivistic orientation and traditional family values of Hispanic/Latino population, permeate styles of social interaction, communication, and learning for Hispanic/Latino students.

## Communication and Social Interaction Styles

Race, cultural ethnicity, age, gender, and even socioeconomic status, may affect Hispanic/Latino students' styles of communication and interaction within the classroom environment. Similar to other minority groups, Hispanics/Latinos are high context communicators (Hall, 1976). As such, they rely heavily on nonverbal communication cues and the group's identification or understanding shared by those communicating. The communicated message is, therefore, anchored in the physical context or situation, or is internalized in the person. As opposed to low context communicators, such as Anglo Americans, Hispanics/Latinos rely less on the explicit code in the message content (Sue and Sue, 1990). While these characteristics are observed, styles of communication and social interaction of all Hispanic/Latino students should not be generalized. Socioeconomic status and geographic origins also contribute to variation in styles. Students from upper, and even middle classes, may demonstrate styles that are more similar to that of Anglo American students.

In traditional Hispanic/Latino cultures, children are taught to listen, obey and not to challenge older persons or persons of authority, such as parents or teachers (Gallegos & Gallegos, 1988; Stein, 1983). Students will, therefore, tend not seek clarification or contradict the teacher. As one graduate student stated: "When I was a child, I was suppose to listen to my parents' dialogue. I was never invited to verbalize my preferences or opinions." The student went on to identify her learning and interactive styles as one of listening in class throughout high school and college, seldom venturing to partake in class discussions. Although, it is necessary to avoid generalizations, it is important to consider that certain Hispanic/Latino families may not ask their children to voice their opinions (Heath, 1986). This behavior is further reinforced for Hispanic/Latino students in those educational settings that foster a learning style of listening and minimal participation in class discussions. While some of the literature describing communication patterns among Hispanic/Latino families tends to support this observation (Heath, 1986), other observations indicate that Hispanic/Latino children from upper and middle socioeconomic classes, are often given opportunities to verbalize their preferences and to negotiate with adults (Delgado-Gaitán & Trueba, 1991).

Some Hispanic/Latino students may find the mainstream American environment incongruent with the behaviors they were taught and learned from early childhood. They are generally raised to control and suppress aggressive and assertive behaviors, and to maintain preserving facial/body appearance of outward dignity and calm. While Hispanic/Latino women are taught that they can display positive emotions, it is unacceptable for them to display negative emotions, such as assertiveness and anger (Torres-Matrullo, 1982). The influence of the Catholic religion has affected the way Hispanics/Latinos behave and raise their children with regard to aggressive behavior (Sue and Sue, 1982). Hispanics/Latinos hold beliefs that sacrifice in this world is helpful to salvation, being charitable to others is a virtue and enduring wrongs against one as a consequence of these beliefs is unheard of. Thus, it is wrong to behave assertively for beliefs and events are meant to be, and cannot be challenged. This may be one of the reasons why students fail to ask questions. Additionally, Hispanic/Latino students may not ask questions of professors, or seek their advise and assistance for they have been raised not to ask questions for which they already know the answer and not to speak until spoken to (Crago, 1992). Further, parents, such as Puerto Ricans, tend to provide answers to the questions they posed to their children before giving their children a chance to answer (García-Preto, 1982). Where American mainstream emphasizes "getting to the point," Hispanic/Latino students view this behavior as immature, rude, and lacking finesse. Only Cubans characteristically use **choeto** (or humor) and an exaggerated form of self-criticism as a defensive mechanism, where they ridicule or make fun of people, situations, or things by exaggerating them out of proportion (Rubenstein, 1976).

Some Hispanic/Latino students, like Mexican American students, may find it difficult to be open and self-disclosing with faculty and peers. They are taught from an early age not to discuss personal matters with individuals outside of the family, since such matters reflect on the whole family and not just on the individual (Falicov, 1982). Thus, when a professor asks a Hispanic/Latino student during class to comment about something that represents their cultural background, the student may experience discomfort.

Hispanic/Latino students tend to speak softly, and use mild delays of silence and polite forms of discourse. They may be less verbal, avoiding direct eye contact when listening or speaking to professors and other persons of high status. Touching, hugging and kissing in public are common between familiar persons in Hispanic/Latino cultures. Robinson (1985) even notes that Hispanic/Latino grade school teachers tend to couple their verbal praise with touching of their students' shoulders more frequently than do Anglo teachers. In terms of physical and social proximity, Hispanics/Latinos prefer closer proximity while speaking than do Anglo Americans (Hall, 1976). However, some Hispanics/Latinos like Mexican Americans, prefer more physical distance from strangers and less familiar persons. Anglo Americans often perceive the closer proximity of Hispanic/Latinos as reflecting haughtiness or superiority. On the other hand, Hispanics/Latinos perceive the Anglo American's behavior of a more distant proximity as aloof, cold, lacking a desire to communicate, intimidating and even as aggressiveness (Wolfgang, 1985). In not appearing rude, Hispanics/Latinos prefer casual talk to proceed the topic of interaction.

Many Hispanic/Latino students are field-dependent sensitive to interpersonal relationships where they are highly sensitive in assessing the nonverbal communication indicators of feelings and interactions with others (KuyKendal, 1992). They value interpersonal relationships and social interactions in which individuals deal with each other with caring, trusting, warm, and respectful behaviors (Zuniga, 1992). Thus, faculty can advise and assist in making students feel more comfortable in the academic setting by making direct personal contact with students, and by providing warm individualized attention and responsiveness to each student. In fact, the educational literature reveals that Hispanic/Latino students adjust better to mainstream American setting when teachers and peers extensively interact and support, provide assurances, and avoid intrusive behaviors (KuyKendal, 1992).

The presence of an accent for Hispanic/Latino students may compound their ability to easily adjust to the mainstream American education setting. It may additionally affect how clinical supervisors perceive the students' ability to clinically interact with a variety of clients. Valencia & Aburto (1991) report that Chicanos and Mexican Americans often receive negative reactions from other nondominant and dominant groups because of their accents. Cheng (1990) suggests that people may be more tolerant of those accents that are not based on the ethnic origin of that person's accent. However, further research is needed to accurately document the degree to which a professional's accent may interfere in the effective health and educational management of American Spanish-speaking clients.

A student's accent should only become an issue when it interferes with speech intelligibility. To be an effective healthcare professional (particularly a speech-language pathologist or audiologist), students with English as a Second Language (ESL) need to understand and learn the standard pronunciation of vowels and consonants of American English, as well as understand the difference between what constitutes "different" versus "deviant" phonological patterns. A professional's bilingual proficiency should be viewed as an asset. Therefore, faculty in the professional education programs of allied health should make every effort to recruit and retain more bilingual students. In this way, the provision of more effective clinical services for the growing American linguistic minority populations, which have been projected as becoming the majority population by the year 2100, can be realized.

## Academic Preparation and Learning Style

### Academic Preparation

Lack of sufficient academic preparation, coupled with culturally different learning styles for acquiring new material and for test taking, are the third and fourth most frequently encountered challenges faced by Hispanic/Latino students in higher education. Chacón, Cohen, and Strover (1986) found that 36 percent of their sample of 668 Hispanic/Latino college-bound students surveyed, considered their high school preparation as poor, whereas only 16 percent considered it to be excellent. The remainder of the student sample rated their educational preparation as average. Although the majority of the student sample had received their secondary education in the United States, students reported their oral and written English skills as inadequate to ensure academic success in college. Further, inadequate secondary school preparation for Hispanic/Latino students enrolled in technical colleges, influenced their low performances in algebra, language skills, and problem-solving skills. They had difficulty following the necessary steps to solve a mathematics problem (Mestre, 1986). Inadequate educational preparation, as well as culturally different study habits, prevented these students from academically succeeding. For example, Mestre (1988) found that Hispanic/Latino American students learning algebra relied on the teacher's lectures, rather than supplementing the class lecture material with material from the textbook. Additionally, because many students came from families with modest incomes, they experienced difficulty comprehending many of the mainstream American concepts and words used in mathematical problems such as "shares of stock, monthly payments," and "interest."

Faculty should offer graduate Hispanic/Latino students meaningful alternative learning strategies for acquiring information that may not have been stressed or adequately presented in their earlier educational experiences. Hands-on laboratory experiences may be required to make science courses in anatomy, physiology, and neurology more meaningful in allied health professional programs.

**Learning Style**

A large percentage of Hispanic/Latino students may be field-dependent learners or field-sensitive learners "where they tend to be aware of the social and personal relevance of the learning experience" (Howard, 1987; KuyKendal, 1992, p. 37). Field-dependent learning style is partially attributed to traditional Hispanic/Latino family childrearing practices (Zuniga, 1991), that adhere to family values of cooperation as opposed to competition; mutual assistance as opposed to individual problem solving; sharing as opposed to withholding resources, and respect for authority. For Hispanic/Latino families, teaching respect for authority should result in a child who is "well educated," or rather one who is taught human relationships and understands the importance of interacting and relating to others, such as professors with respect and dignity (Romero, 1983).

**Table 5-1.**
**Students Learning Preferences**

| *Field Independent Students* | *Field Dependent Students* |
|---|---|
| Independent learning projects, working alone | Group learning projects, sharing, discussions |
| Hypothesis-testing approaches | Personal examples, anecdotes, stories |
| Solving problems | Relating learning to own experiences |
| A focus on details, moving from specific to general concept/topic | A focus on the main concept/topic, an overview moving from the general to the specific details |
| Clear grading criteria with specific feedback | Praise, assurance, working to please others, frequent interaction with faculty |
| Teacher-centered environment | Student-centered environment |

Adapted from Howard, B.C.: *Learning to Persist/Persisting to Learn.* Courtesy of Mid-Atlantic Equity Center, The American University, revised and reprinted, 1989.

Students who are field-dependent learners tend to prefer small cooperative group learning experiences where the group works together for the benefit of the group, as opposed to the individual styles and competitive modes as seen in Anglo American learners. With group learning, the pace of learning is set by the group rather than by time constraints. Table 5-1 highlights the major preferences in learning style between mainstream American field-independent students and field-dependent students such as Hispanic/Latino students. Further, Hispanic/Latino students may wait for the teachers directions rather than attempting to initiate independent work. Thus, Hispanic/Latino students prefer a teaching style that displays physical and verbal expression of approval and warmth, and encourages learning from modeling rather than from discovery, trial and error, or task orientation (Delgado-Gaitán, 1987; Ramirez & Price-Williams, 1974).

Some research on optimal "process-oriented" learning conditions for younger Hispanic/Latino students includes the use of cognitive, meta-cognitive, and social-affective strategies (Chamot & O'Malley, 1986). Several of these strategies can be applied to students enrolled in higher education. For example, visual organizers, such as charts and flow diagrams, can facilitate the assimilation of newly presented material. Advanced organization might be helpful in previewing the main ideas or concepts for unfamiliar material. Self-monitoring can then be used to check student's comprehension during listening and reading, and with self-evaluation students can judge how well they have learned a certain activity. Some cognitive strategies include how to use reference materials and textbooks (See Westby's Chapter 10 for further elaboration and resources). Other specific strategies include using visual imagery to understand new concepts, or elaboration by relating new information to what is already known. To enhance the learning process, it is important that Hispanic/Latino students learn to ask their professors and peers for clarification of the material presented in class, as well as in the text.

Another factor preventing Hispanic/Latino students from gaining access to higher education or succeeding in higher education courses, is the lack of understanding mainstream American test-taking strategies. Many Hispanic/Latino students score low on the SAT's and GRE's, because they lack familiarity with the vocabulary, cultural content of the test, and how the test directions and questions are organized and designed. Directions may become culturally biased when they involve linguistic complexities unfamiliar to the student, and when test procedures and requirements are inconsistent with the students' cognitive learning style, for example, "Select the best answer to the following" (Taylor, 1986). As based on data provided by the Educational Testing Service, Laosa & Henderson (1991) report a 65 point advantage for non-Hispanic Whites over Mexican Americans on the verbal section of the SAT, and a 61 point advantage in mathematics.

Students in general, and more specifically minority students, should be taught test-taking strategies to improve their performance on both entrance examinations like SAT's or GRE's, and academic course examinations (Keller, 1991). For example, students should be aware that in answering multiple-choice questions, correct guessing might be the preferable strategy over leaving the answer blank. In addition, further research needs to be conducted to determine if increasing time limits to complete a test might positively influence students' performances. Some research indicates that bilingual individuals may process information somewhat slower, and in a different manner in a second language (Bialystok, 1991; Dornic, 1980; Merino, 1991). For example, Holley & King (1971) found that additional wait-time increases second language learner's performance. Because of this, a professor might consider giving a student additional time in oral and written language tasks. This could apply to completing a course examination, as well as when responding to a question in class (Llabre, 1991). Other suggestions include: speaking more slowly, increasing the stress or volume of key words, repeating and elaborating on main topics so that bilingual students can more readily comprehend a professor's lecture (Terrell, 1981).

Last, Hispanic/Latino students' orientation to time may affect their class attendance, and whether they complete class assignments on schedule. The Spanish word **mañana** does not necessarily mean **tomorrow,** but may mean "sometime in the future." Culturally, Hispanic/Latino students do not follow rigid time schedules as Anglo students. Rather, value is given to the present time, "the here and now" as opposed to mainstream American value with emphasis on the past and planning for the future (Valle, 1990).

## Acculturation into Mainstream American Educational System

Hispanic/Latino students who have been able "to learn the mainstream American educational system," and those students that are already "a part of the system," are more likely to succeed in college and graduate school. Olivas (1986) reports that those Hispanic/Latino students who are involved in both mainstream and ethnic activities on campus succeed in college. However, Hispanic/Latino students tend to mingle within their own ethnic group, thus reducing their contact with the mainstream students (D'Souza, 1992). Oliver, Rodríguez and Mickelson (1985) state: "those students who have an early opportunity to learn the types of social and cultural skills and attitudes are more likely to do well in the university and adjust better" (p. 16).

Knowing how to approach and become a part of the mainstream American educational system, is seen by Hispanic/Latino students as a key factor for ensuring greater academic success. Faculty are critical in facilitating this process for Hispanic/Latino students by directly approaching students to offer assistance. Pairing new students with more "seasoned" students will also help students in their adjustment to the college environment. Some Hispanic/Latino students may need to take additional coursework, or learn specific strategies on how to succeed in their courses (see Chapter 10). With the additional time invested by faculty and other students, more Hispanic/Latino students may graduate and become successful professionals.

Ethnicity of the professor has been described as a key factor for developing more comfortable relationships between student and faculty (Pearl, 1991). Pearl (1991) and Sánchez and colleagues (1992) argue that lack of representation of Hispanic/Latino faculty on campuses often prevents students from having an ethnic role model with whom they can identify. For instance, Hispanic/Latino students use counseling services more readily when they have access to a Hispanic/Latino counselor (Mussenden & Bingham, 1985). Valencia and Aburto (1991) propose that if educational institutions had more Hispanic/Latino faculty representation, it would help students in "passing on cultural heritage, instilling minority pride, and promoting racial understanding among all students" (p. 231).

## Variable of Socioeconomic Level and Status

The degree of Hispanic/Latino family support and guidance in their children's pursuits of higher education is directly related to socioeconomic level and class status. While Mestre and Royer (1991) and Valencia (1991) report that Anglo and Hispanic/Latino Americans do not differ in their views on the importance of an education, Arbona and Novy (1991) discuss social class as a factor in distinguishing which Hispanic/Latino students will pursue studies in higher education. The more successful students belong to middle and upper middle class families. These tend to include Cubans, and recent legal immigrants from Central and South America, who are generally better prepared both socially and educationally for the challenges of college. The less educationally successful group of Hispanic/Latino students belong to poorer working class families of primarily Puerto Rican or Mexican descent, who were born in the United States or who immigrated at an early age. Parental, financial, and educational support are not as available to these latter students.

Hispanic/Latino American girls, especially Mexican American girls, are culturally discouraged from choosing careers which might interfere with their family life. However, those Hispanic/Latino women who have been successful in post-secondary education, come from families where their mothers encouraged and fostered academic aspirations (Gándara, 1982). Laosa and Henderson (1991) report that a mother's level of education is directly related to a child's success in school. Educated mothers tend to use a more inquiring conversational style than modeling style (i.e., motoric demonstrations) and to give much verbal reinforcement.

These authors hypothesize that "the children of the more highly schooled parents learn to master in their homes the form and dynamics of teaching and learning processes that take after those of the school (mainstream) classroom" (p. 171). While many Hispanic/Latino parents encourage their children to pursue an education, they are unable to assist in their childrens' learning because they, themselves, have had limited schooling (Laosa & Henderson, 1991; Oliver, Rodríguez & Michelson, 1985). As Ortíz (1986) describes, this situation improves with each new generation. " . . . first-generation Hispanic youths are educationally disadvantaged. However, second-generation Hispanic youths have significantly higher achievements after controlling for family background, while third-generation youths do not differ significantly from non-Hispanic White youth" (p. 43).

Arbona and Novy (1991) suggest that this generational factor might explain the greater success achieved by some of the Hispanic/Latino American subgroups, such as Cubans and those Hispanic/Latinos, who have resided longer in the United States. In fact, many of these Hispanic/Latino Americans are the second or third generation of their family to complete college and even graduate school. This contrasts with those Hispanic/Latinos who are newcomers, or who are children of parents with a limited educational background.

**Financial Constraints**

Financial aid and resources are some of the major challenges that Hispanic/Latino students face in entering and completing a degree in higher education (Sánchez et al., 1992). Stress from lack of personal funds results when students must take additional jobs which interfere with their available time for studying (Muñoz, 1982; Oliver, Rodríguez & Michelson, 1985; Quintana, Vogel & Ybarra, 1991). As part of students' obligations to their families, many Hispanic/Latino students may be required to financially support their family's modest incomes by assuming full-time jobs, or by caring for their siblings when parents work. As mentioned, the needs of the Hispanic/Latino family take precedence over school and job obligations (Sue and Sue, 1990). Consequently, students may drop out of school, or pursue their studies at a slower pace in order to support their families.

Faculty might encourage and mentor students in seeking financial assistance. Providing student loans or stipends may enhance the likelihood that more Hispanic/Latino students will complete their college degree, and even pursue a graduate education.

## Health Practices and Views of Disability

Health practices and views of disability stem in part from religious practices. Views and practices may initially impact on how students in the allied health professional education programs initially view and function in the clinical training process.

While a majority of Hispanics/Latinos are Roman Catholic, some groups living in more remote rural areas practice spiritualism, witchcraft, and black magic (Ruiz and Langrod, 1981). There is also a growing number of followers of the various Protestant sects. Roman Catholic practices of the Hispanic/Latino population are described as different from those practiced by Catholics in the United States (McGoldrich, Pearce & Giodano, 1982). Hispanic/Latino Catholics distrust organized religion, the Church, the Priest, and believe they can make contact with God and the supernatural without the help of the clergy. Hispanics/Latinos personalize their relationship with God by creating special relationships with the Saints who act as their personal emissaries to God.

Spiritualism practiced by Hispanics/Latinos is the belief that the visible world is surrounded by an invisible world inhabited by good and evil spirits that influence human behavior (Delgado, 1978; Delgado, 1988; Ruiz and Langrod, 1981). Since spirits are believed to protect and harm, or prevent and cause illness, incense, candles, and magical powders are used to cure illness or to ward off the "evil eye." The Puerto Ricans and Cubans practicing spiritualism may believe that illness and disability result from the presence of evil in the person's environment, or from a curse placed by someone (Morales-Porta, 1976). Additionally, nonphysical conditions, such as mental health conditions, are categorized as spiritual (Delgado, 1978). In some Hispanic/Latino cultures, evil spirits are exorcised. Puerto Ricans seek spiritualists for healing practices, for dispelling evil spirits and for spiritual protection.

Cubans practice a combination of African folk healing traditions (e.g., herbalist, faith healer, pharmacist, chiropractor), combined with Spanish Catholic medical practices (García-Preto, 1982). Puerto Ricans and Cubans often practice Santeria, which is a syncretism of Catholic saints and African orishas or saints (Gonzales-Whippier, 1989).

Mexicans practice a dual system of health beliefs and practices (i.e.,

Western and folk medicine) (Gonzalez, 1976). It is not unusual for certain Hispanic/Latino groups to refer to **curanderos** or Mexican healers and **espiritistas** or Puerto Rican spiritualists. In some Indian villages, Mexicans, Caribbeans, Central and South Americans conduct ancient practices including sorcery and witchcraft. Mexicans practice folk beliefs, such as **mal ojo** (evil eye), where illness or disability results from excessive admiration or desire on the part of another; **susto** (fright), where a physical syndrome such as cleft palate or heart defect results from an emotionally traumatic experience; and **mal puesto** (an evil hex). Therefore, Mexican parents may take a child with a disability to a curandero(a) to seek a cura (cure), or a sobador (i.e., the person who heals through massages). In cases where there is no traceable etiology for the health condition or disability, the problem may be attributed to something that happened during pregnancy. Our Lady of Guadalupe, who is the patron saint and Virgin Mother of Mexico, is implored to intercede to cure a child of disease or disability (Zuniga, 1992). For example, if the mother does not take care with using knives and scissors during pregnancy, it is believed that the child will be born with a cleft palate (Padilla, Ruiz & Alvarez, 1975). Meyerson (1990) reports that mothers of children with craniofacial anomalies may also attribute their children's problems to an eclipse of the moon, to a **susto** (a frightening situation), to **mal puesto** (witchcraft), or to **mal ojo** (evil eye).

No clear distinction is made between physical and mental health and disability in the Hispanic/Latino culture (Padilla, Ruiz & Alvarez, 1975). Cubans may attribute their child's physical or mental problem to an **empacho** (i.e., indigestion), **decaimiento** (i.e., lack of energy), or **barrenillo** (i.e., obsessive thinking) which occurred during pregnancy (Queralt, 1984).

Socioeconomic class and educational level impact on how Hispanics/Latinos view a person with a disability. Educated families of higher socioeconomic status tend to keep those with a disability, such as mental retardation, hidden. On the other hand, families of lower socioeconomic status who practice folk beliefs, more readily care for and accept persons with disability.

## CONCLUSION

This chapter provides a detailed review of the heterogenous composition of Hispanic/Latino population. It includes population demographics and descriptions. It emphasizes that while the Hispanic/Latino population differs markedly from other groups, it represents a vast diversity within itself. To understand and appreciate the Mexican culture does not insure an appreciation of the Puerto Rican or Cuban cultures. Through the issues presented, it emphasizes the dangers of over generalizing and stereotyping.

Through the chapter's presentation of factual information, it prepares faculty with a nonbiased approach to the education of Hispanic/Latino students in higher education by describing some of the strategies that faculty can implement for recruiting and retaining Hispanic/Latino students in the allied health professional education programs. It is hoped that the information and suggestions will serve as a starting place for empowering Hispanic/Latino students to succeed in higher education. Additionally, it is hoped that the information will be beneficial in fostering better communications between all students. Finally, it is hoped that the information will serve faculty as a source for effectively preparing all students as health care professionals to competently serve Hispanic/Latino clients. The reader, who is interested in information specifically pertaining to the communication assessment and management of Hispanic/Latino children and adults, should refer to Langdon (1992) in the reference section.

## REFERENCES

Alvirez, D., Bean, F. & Williams, D.: The Mexican American Family. In Mindel, C. & Habenstein, R. (Eds.): *Ethnic Families in America.* New York, Elsevier Press, 1981, pp.269–292.

American Speech, Language and Hearing Association: Our multicultural agenda: We're serious. *ASHA, 34:* 38–39, 1992.

Arbona, A. & Novy, D.M.: Hispanic students: Are there within-group differences? *Journal of College Student Development, 32:* 335–341, 1991.

Barry, P.: Interview: A new voice for Hispanics in higher education: A conversation with Antonio Rigual. *The College Board Review, 160:* 2–7 and 16, 1991.

Bialystok, E.: Metalinguistic dimensions of bilingual language proficiency. In Bialystok, E., (Ed.): *Language Processing in Bilingual Children.* New York, Cambridge University Press, 1991, pp.113–140.

Casal, L., Prohias, R., Carrasco, J. & Prieto, Y.: The Cuban migration of the sixties in its historical context. In Casal, L., Prohias, R. & Carrasco, S. (Eds.): *Black Cubans in the United States.* Washington, Project Sponsored by the Ford Foundation, Office of Latin America and the Caribbean, 1979.

Center on Budget and Policy Priorities. *Shortchanged: Recent Developments in Hispanic Poverty, Income and Employment.* Washington, Author, 1988.

Chacón, M.A., Cohen, E.G. & Strover, S.: Chicanas and Chicanos: Barriers to progress in higher education. In Olivas, M.A., (Ed.): *Latino College Students.* New York, Teachers College, Columbia University, 1986, pp.296–324.

Chamot, A.U. & O'Malley, M.: *A Cognitive Academic Language Learning Approach: An English as a Second Language Content-Based Curriculum.* Wheaton, The National Clearinghouse for Bilingual Education, 1986.

Cheng, L.L.: Recognizing diversity. *American Behavioral Scientist, 34.* (2): 263–278, 1990.

Crago, M.B.: Ethnography and language socialization: A cross-cultural perspective. *Topics in Language Disorders, 12.* (3): 28–39, 1992.

Cromwell, R. & Ruiz, R.A.: The myth of macho dominance in decision-making within Mexican and Chicano families. *Hispanic Journal of Behavioral Sciences, 1:* 355–373, 1979.

Cuellar, J.: Hispanic American Aging. In *Minority Aging: Essential Curriculum Content for Selected Health and Allied Health Professions.* Publication No. HRS (P–SV-90-4), Washington, Health Resources and Service Administration, Department of Health and Human Services, Government Printing Office, 1990, pp.363–381.

Current Population Reports: *The Hispanic Population in the United States.* Washington, Bureau of the Census, March, 1990.

Davis, C., Haub, C. & Willette, J.: U.S. Hispanics: Changing the face of America. *Population Bulletin, 38:* 1–44, 1983.

Delgado, M.: Folk Medicine in Puerto Rican culture. *International Social Work, 21,* (2): 46–54, 1978.

Delgado, M.: Groups in Puerto Rican spiritism: Implications for clinicians. In Jacobs, C. & Bowels, D. (Eds.): *Ethnicity and Race: Critical Concepts in Social Work.* Silver Spring, 1988, pp.71–83.

Delgado-Gaitán, C.: Traditions and transitions in the learning process of Mexican children: An ethnographic view. In Spindler, G. & Spindler, L., (Eds.): *Interpretive Ethnography of Education: At Home and Abroad.* Hillsdale, Lawrence Erlbaum, 1987, pp.333–359.

Delgado-Gaitán, C. & Trueba, H.T.: *Crossing Cultural Borders.* New York, The Falmer Press, 1991.

Dornic, S.: Information processing and language dominance. *International Review of Applied Psychology, 74:* 224–229, 1980.

D'Souza, D.: *Liberal Education: The Politics of Race and Sex on Campus.* New York, Vintage Books, 1992.

Falicov, C.: Mexican families. In McGoldrich, M., Pearce, J. & Giodano, J. (Eds.): *Ethnicity and Family Therapy.* New York, The Guildford Press, 1982, pp.134–161.

Fernandez-Marina, R.: The Puerto Rican Syndrome: Its Dynamics and Cultural Determinants. *Psychiatry, 24:* 79–82, 1961.

Gallegos, A. & Gallegos, R.: The Interaction between families of culturally diverse handicapped children and the school. In García, S., Chávez, R.C., (Eds.):

*Ethnolinguistic Issues in Education.* Lubbock, College of Education, Texas Technical University, 1988, pp.125–132.

Gándara, P.: Passing through the eye of the needle: High-achieving Chicanas. *Hispanic Journal of Behavioral Science, 4:* 167–179, 1982.

García, G.E.: Ethnography and classroom communication: Taking an "emic" perspective. *Topics in Language Disorders, 12.* (3): 54–66, 1992.

García-Preto, N.: Puerto Rican families. In McGoldrich, M., Pearce, J. & Giodano, J. (Eds.): *Ethnicity and Family Therapy.* New York, The Guildford Press, 1982, pp.165–186.

Gonzalez-Whippier, M.: *Santeria, The Religion.* New York, Harmony, 1989.

Guillermo, B.: Cuban families. In McGoldrich, M., Pearce, J. & Giodano, J. (Eds.): *Ethnicity and Family Therapy.* New York, The Guildford Press, 1982, pp.187–207.

Hall, E.T.: *Beyond Culture.* Garden City, Anchor, 1976.

Heath, S.B.: Sociocultural contests of language development. In California State Department of Education (Ed.): *Beyond Language: Social and Cultural Factors in Schooling Language Minority Students.* Los Angeles, Evaluation, Dissemination and Assessment Center of California State University, 1986, pp.143–186.

Holley, F. & King, J.: Imitation and correction in foreign language learning. *Modern Language Journal, 55:* 494–498, 1971.

Howard, B.: *Learning to Persist/Persist to Learn.* Washington, Mid-Atlantic Center for Race Equity, The American University, 1987.

Keller, G.D.: Introduction: Advances in assessment and the potential for increasing the number of Hispanics in higher education. In Keller, G.D., Deneen, J.R. & Megallán, R.J., (Eds.): *Assessment and Access: Hispanics in Higher Education.* Albany, State University of New York Press, 1991, pp.1–35.

Keller, G.D., Deneen, J.R. & Magallán, R.J., (Eds.): *Assessment and Access: Hispanics in Higher Education.* Albany, State University of New York Press, 1991.

Kluckholm, F. & Strodtbeck, F.: *Variations in Value Orientations.* Evanston, Row and Peterson, 1961.

KuyKendal, C.: From Rage to Hope: *Strategies for Reclaiming Black and Hispanic Students.* Bloomington, National Education Service, 1992.

Lampe, P.E.: Mexican Americans: Labeling and mislabeling. *Hispanic Journal of Behavioral Sciences, 6:* 77–85, 1984.

Langdon, H.W.: In Langdon, H.W. with Cheng, L.L., (Eds.): *Hispanic Children and Adults with Communication Disorders: Assessment and Intervention.* Gaithersburg, Aspen, 1992 a,b,c pp.20–56, 99–131, 201–271.

Laosa, L.M. & Henderson, R.W.: Cognitive socialization and competence: The academic development of Chicanos. In Valencia, R.R., (Ed.): *Chicano School Failure and Success: Research and Policy Agendas for the 1990's.* New York, The Falmer Press, 1991, pp.164–199.

Llabre, M.M.: Time as a factor in the cognitive test performance of Latino college students. In Keller, G.D., Deneen, J.R. & Magallán, R.J., (Eds.): *Assessment and Access: Hispanics in Higher Education.* Albany, State University of New York Press, 1991, pp.95–104.

McGoldrich, M., Pearce, J. & Giodano, J. (Eds.): *Ethnicity and Family Therapy.* New York, The Guildford Press, 1982.

Merino, B.J.: Promoting school success for Chicanos: The view from inside the bilingual classroom. In Valencia, R.R., (Ed.): *Chicano School Failure and Success: Research and Policy Agendas for the 1990's.* New York, The Falmer Press, 1991, pp.119–148.

Mestre, J.P.: The Latino science and engineering student: Recent research findings. In Olivas, M.A., (Ed.): *Latino College Students.* New York, Teachers College, Columbia University, 1986, pp.157–192.

Mestre, J.P.: The role of language comprehension in mathematics and problem solving. In Cocking, R. & Mestre, J., (Eds.): *Linguistic and Cultural Influences on Learning Mathematics.* Hillsdale, Lawrence Erlbaum, 1988, pp.201–220.

Mestre, J.P. & Royer, J.M.: Cultural and linguistic influences on Latino testing. In Keller, G.D., Deneen, J.R. & Magallán, R.J., (Eds.): *Assessment and Access: Hispanics in Higher Education.* Albany, State University of New York, 1991, pp.39–66.

Meyerson, M.D.: Cultural considerations in the treatment of Latinos with craniofacial malformations. *The Cleft Palate Journal, 27:* 279–288, 1990.

Mizio, E.: Impact of external systems on the Puerto Rican family. *Social Casework, 55* (1): 76–83, 1974.

Mizio, E.: *Puerto Rican Task Report — Project on Ethnicity.* New York, Family Service Association, 1979.

Morales-Dorta, S.: *Puerto Rican Espiritismo: Religion and Psychotherapy.* New York, Vantage, 1976.

Muñoz, J.A.: The Spanish-speaking consumer and the community mental health center. In Jones, E.E. & Korchin, S.J., (Eds.): *Minority Mental Health.* New York, Praeger, 1982, pp.362–398.

Mussenden, M.E. & Bingham, R.: Hispanic academic enrichment group: An outreach strategy for counseling academically underachieving Hispanics. *Journal of College Student Personnel, 26:* 356–358, 1985.

Nora, A. & Rendón, L.: Differences in mathematics and science preparation and participation among community college minority and non-minority students. *Community College Review, 18:* 29–40, 1990.

Olivas, M.A.: Introduction: Financial aid for Hispanics: Access, ideology, and packaging policies. In Olivas, M.A., (Ed.): *Latino College Students.* New York, Teachers College, Columbia University, 1986, pp.281–295.

Oliver, M.L., Rodríguez, C.J. & Mickelson, R.A.: Brown and Black in White: The social adjustment and academic performance of Chicano and Black students in a predominantly White university. *The Urban Review, 17:* 3–23, 1985.

Ortíz, V.: Generational, status, family background, and educational attainment among Hispanic youth and non-Hispanic white youth. In Olivas, M.A., (Ed.): *Latino College Students.* New York, Teachers College, Columbia University, 1989, pp.29–46.

Padilla, A.M., Ruiz, R.A. & Alvarez, R.: Community mental health services for the Spanish-speaking/surnamed population. *American Psychologist, 30:* 892–905, 1975.

Papajohn, J. & Spiegel, J.: *Transactions in Families.* San Francisco, Jossey-Bass, 1975.

Pearl, A.: Systemic and institutional factors in Chicano school failure. In Valencia, R.R., (Ed.): *Chicano School Failure and Success: Research and Policy Agendas for the 1900's.* New York, The Falmer Press, 1991, pp.273–320.

Perez-Stable, E.J.: Cuban Immigration: A Socio-Historical Analysis. Presentation at the Bicultural Association of Spanish Speaking Therapists and Advocates. San Francisco, February 1981.

Queralt, M.: Understanding Cuban immigration: A cultural perspective. *Social Work, 29:* 115–121, 1984.

Quintana, S.T., Vogel, M.C. & Ybarra, V.C.: Meta-analysis of Latino students' adjustment in higher education. *Hispanic Journal of Behavioral Sciences, 13:* 155–168, 1991.

Ramirez, M. & Price-Williams, D.: Cognitive styles in children: Two Mexican communities. *InterAmerican Journal of Psychology, 8:* 93–101, 1974.

Robinson, G.L.N.: *Cross Cultural Understanding: Processes and Approaches for Foreign Language. English as a Second Language and Bilingual Educators.* New York, Pergamon Press, 1985.

Rogg, E.M. & Cooney, R.S.: *Adaptation and Adjustment of Cubans: West New York, New Jersey.* New York, Hispanic Research Center, 1980.

Rubenstein, D.: Beyond the cultural barriers: Observations of emotional disorders among Cuban immigrants. *International Journal of Mental Health, 5* (2): 69–79, 1976.

Ruiz, P. & Langrod, J.: The role of folk healers in community mental health services. In Dana, R.H., (Ed.): *Human Services for Cultural Minorities.* Baltimore, University Park Press, 1981, pp.217–224.

Sánchez, J.E. with Marder, F., Berry, R. & Ross, H.: Dropping out: Hispanic students, attrition, and the family. *College and University, 67:* 145–150, 1992.

Stein, R.C.: Hispanic parents' perspective and participation in their children's special education programs: Comparisons by program and race. *Learning Disability Quarterly, 6:* 432–438, 1983.

Sue, D.W. & Sue, D.: *Counseling the Culturally Different: Theory and Practice.* New York, John Wiley and Sons, 1990.

Szapocznik, J., Kurtines, W. & Hanna, N.: Comparison of Cuban and Anglo-American cultural values in a clinical population. *Journal of Consulting and Clinical Psychology, 47* (3): 623–624, 1979.

Taylor, O.L. (Ed.): *Nature of Communication Disorders in Culturally and Linguistically Diverse Populations.* San Diego, College-Hill Press, 1986.

Terrell, T.D.: The natural approach in bilingual education. In Office of Bilingual Bicultural Education, California State Department of Education (Ed.): *Schooling and Language Minority Students: A Theoretical Framework.* Los Angeles, Evaluation, Dissemination and Assessment Center, California State University, 1981, pp.117–146.

Torres-Matrullo, C.: Cognitive therapy of depression in the Puerto Rican female. In Becerra, R.M., Karno, M. & Escobar, J. (Eds.): *Mental Health and Hispanic Americans: Clinical Perspectives.* New York, Grune & Stratton, 1982, pp.101–113.

U.S. Bureau of the Census: Statistical Abstract of the United States, 1990, 110th ed. Washington, U.S. Department of Commerce, 1990.

Valencia, R.R.: The plight of Chicano students: An overview of schooling conditions and outcomes. In Valencia, R.R., (Ed.): *Chicano School Failure and Success: Research and Policy Agendas for the 1990's.* New York, The Falmer Press, 1991, pp.3–26.

Valencia, R.R. & Aburto, S.: Research directions and practical strategies in teacher testing and assessment: Implications for improving Latino access to teaching. In Keller, G.D., Deneen, J.R. & Magallán, R.J., (Eds.): *Assessment and Access: Hispanics in Higher Education.* Albany, State University of New York Press, 1991, pp.195–234.

Valle, R.: The Latino/Hispanic family and the elderly: Approaches to cross-cultural curriculum design in the health professions. In *Minority Aging: Essential Curriculum Content for Selected Health and Allied Health Professions.* Publication No. HRS (P–SV-90-4), Washington, Health Resources and Service Administration, Department of Health and Human Services, Government Printing Office, 1990, pp.433–444.

Vega, W., Hough, R. & Romero, A.: Family life patterns of Mexican Americans. In Powell, G., Yamamoto, J., Romero, A. & Morales, A. (Eds.): *The Psychosocial Development of Minority Group Children.* New York, Brunner/Mazel, 1983, pp.194–215.

Veltman, C.J.: *The Future of the Spanish Language in the United States.* Washington, Population Reference Bureau, 1988.

Wolfgang, A.: The function and importance of nonverbal behavior in intercultural counseling. In Pedersen, P.B. (Ed.): *Handbook of Cross-Cultural Counseling and Therapy.* Westport, Greenwood, 1985, pp.23–25.

Zuniga, M.: Families with Latino roots. In Lynch, E. & Hanson, J. (Eds.): *Developing Cross-Cultural Competence: A Guide for Working with Young Children and Their Families.* Baltimore, Brookes, 1992, pp.151–179.

# Chapter 6

# PROFILE OF ASIAN AND PACIFIC ISLAND STUDENTS

Li–Rong Lilly Cheng and Lynne W. Clark

## INTRODUCTION

Political unrest and economic opportunity have served as two major factors for the increase in Asian and Pacific Island populations in the United States. The current and projected future demographic explosion of Asian and Pacific Islanders (API) will yield increasing numbers of Asian and Pacific Island American students seeking higher education, including professional programs in allied health. In a biennial survey report on the racial and ethnic characteristics of American college students, the American Council on Education, as cited in *On Campus* (McKenna, 1992), stated that the college enrollment of minority group members rose 10 percent from 1988 to 1990. Asians' and Pacific Islanders' enrollment climbed 11.7 percent, representing one of the largest increases.

Because these increases in Asian and Pacific Island enrollment in higher education, this chapter addresses important information about these student groups as a means of facilitating intercultural understanding that is necessary for productive faculty and student interactions. Specific issues include: patterns of immigration; the complexity of acculturation patterns; how philosophical and religious beliefs permeate cultural attitudes regarding the educational process and its practices; how the orientation to education is different from a Eurocentric mainstream American orientation; how styles of learning and communication may create learning and communication barriers in the academic setting; how the diversity in languages and linguistic origins may create difficulty in learning English, and how the orientation to health care and

Some of the information in this chapter is abstracted from previous works by the first author including Cheng, L.: *Assessing Asian Language Performance.* Oceanside, Academic Communication Associates, 1991.

practices may impact on the philosophy behind clinical practices and the delivery of other health care and educational services.

## ASIAN AND PACIFIC ISLAND IMMIGRATION PATTERNS

Considerable ethnic variation exists among API groups. Therefore, it is important to identify and define the API population and how immigration patterns may impact upon students adaptation to American educational systems of higher education. Asian students and/or their family have primarily immigrated the Philippine Islands, China, Japan, Vietnam, Korea, India, Cambodia, Laos, Pakistan and Thailand (U.S. General Accounting Office, 1991). The three major Asian regions or countries include: East Asia (China, Japan, and Korea); Southeast Asia (Vietnam, Cambodia, Laos, Thailand, Burma, Philippines, Malaysia, Singapore and Indonesia); South Asia (India, Pakistan and Sri Lanka) (Ruhlen, 1976). Students from the Pacific Islands may come from: Melanesia (Solomons, New Caledonia, Fiji, New Hebrides); Micronesia (the Mariana, Marshall, Caroline, Gilbert and Elluce Islands); Polynesia (New Zealand, Tonga, Tahiti, Samoa and Hawaii).

Asian and Pacific Island immigrants and refugees have been one of the fastest growing populations in the United States (U.S. General Accounting Office, 1991). This occurred after the Second World War, when there was a major shift in United States immigration patterns from Europe to Asia, Mexico, and South and Central Americas. From a total of 1.5 million API's enumerated in the 1970 Census, the number grew to 3.5 million in the 1980 Census and to 7 million in the 1990 Census (U.S. Bureau of Census, 1988a). By the year 2000, the Asian and Pacific Island populations are expected to collectively reach 10 million (U.S. Bureau of Census, 1988b). Filipinos, Chinese, Vietnamese, Japanese, and Koreans are currently the most widely represented of the ASI groups in the United States. With the exception of the Vietnamese, these groups have maintained a steady pattern of immigration. The earliest and first group to immigrate to the United States in 1785 were the Chinese. The largest and most recent influx has been the Vietnamese who came in waves following the fall of Saigon in 1975. Some left immediately, others left following detainment in resettlement camps, and many left as soon as they could find sponsors or sources to assist them (U.S. General Accounting Office, 1991).

The major reasons the API groups left their countries of origin were varied and multiple. Primary motivation, however, included escape from war and political trauma, and the promise of better educational and socioeconomic status (Gardner, Robey & Smith, 1985). While these groups are scattered throughout the United States, more dense concentrations can be found in the following areas. The Chinese mainly reside in West and Northwest states and in the cities of San Francisco, Oakland, Los Angeles, Houston, Chicago, and New York. Southeast Asians mainly reside in California, Texas, and Washington state, as well as Minnesota, Massachusetts, Rhode Island, and Wisconsin. The Koreans who are the most widely dispersed of all groups, mainly reside in California, New York and Illinois, and in the cities of New York, Los Angeles, and Chicago. Filipinos reside in California and Hawaii (U.S. Bureau of Census, 1990).

## PATTERNS OF ACCULTURATION

Asian and Pacific Island students differ in patterns of acculturation or adaptation to American lifestyle, and more specifically to the American educational system. The experience of Asian and Pacific Island students is markedly varied with respect to their education, socioeconomic status and degree of exposure to the English language. There has generally been a noted variation in the ability of API immigrants to adapt to the American lifestyle following immigration to the United States (Cheng, Trueba & Ima, 1992). Scholars in the social sciences have examined the reasons why some Asian families successfully adapt to the American mainstream way of life, while other families adapt slowly in their integration into mainstream society.

Spindler, Spindler, and Trueba (1987; 1990) have argued that the adaptation of immigrant groups follows six stages that occur in response to cultural conflict. The first stage, **Reaffirmation** is characterized by a nativistic orientation and efforts to revive native cultural traditions, accompanied by rejection of the mainstream culture. The **Synthesis** stage is characterized by selective combination of various cultural aspects of one group combined with those of another culture in certain domains of life, especially with respect to religious rituals and beliefs. The **Withdrawal** stage is a transitional stage where both conflicting cultures are rejected without any commitment to any specific set of cultural values. The **Biculturalism** stage is characterized by full involvement with two cultures where effective cultural and linguistic code-switching is accomplished, permitting individuals to function effectively with members of both the mainstream and the home cultures. The **Constructive Marginality** stage involves a position of tentative acceptance of two conflicting cultural value systems in which the individual maintains a conscious distance from both cultural systems. This position is characterized by selective choice or code-switching of one or another value system as required by the circumstances. This permits the marginal person maintenance of personal equilibrium through moderate participation in both cultures. In the final stage, **Compensatory Adaption,** individuals become thoroughly mainstreamed or assimilated and may reject, or at least avoid, any identification with, or display of, their native culture.

The varying degrees of acculturation have led to the formation of bipolar ethnic communities in which Asian and Pacific Island populations are composed of two extremes (Takaki, 1989). One extreme consists of unskilled and uneducated workers, who are generally welfare cases with poor English proficiency and high rates of poverty. The other extreme comprises the educated, successful professionals with high levels of English proficiency and the entrepreneurial upper and middle classes. In general, the upper and middle classes emigrated to pursue a higher education, to seek a better quality of life and to escape political unrest from their countries of origin. The lower socioeconomic status groups left their homeland to seek job opportunities mostly as laborers and unskilled workers in farming and construction industries (Cheng, 1991).

## Factors Influencing Acculturation

Asian students may adopt a variety of adaptation strategies as they experience higher education. Some may cope very well, while others may need to seek counseling in order to maintain personal equilibrium. Educators need to be keenly aware of the differences in their coping strategies in order to work effectively with them. The acculturation pattern of Asian and Pacific Islanders is highly complex and influenced by a host of factors including the preimmigration and migration experience, time of arrival in the United States, educational background, socioeconomic status, personal life history, and the unique history and conditions in the country of origin. For example, prior to 1975 there were few Southeast Asians in the United States. At the end of the Vietnamese War however, there was a marked influx of Southeast Asian refugees (Gordon, 1987). Prior to this, there had been migration of Samoans following World War II. The Samoans brought with them a unique culture and religion which greatly colored their ability to adapt to the American lifestyle (Leung, 1988).

Language proficiency is an additional variable. Immigrants come with a wide range of skills in producing and understanding the English language. For example, many Southeast Asians come to the United States with limited or no English language proficiency. Some of these may even be illiterate in their own native language (Walker, 1985). In contrast, others may be prepared in the English language, and require minimal assistance in communication acquisition. Those groups with high English language proficiency and more education tend to adapt more readily than those who feel alienated and isolated because they are unable to communicate in English (Cheng, 1991). Many refugees and immigrants who live in their own ethnic enclaves (e.g., Flushing, San Francisco, Fountain Valley), seldom come in contact with the mainstream U.S. population and thus do not use English in their daily contacts.

The variable of socioeconomic status is an important underlying factor in why the refugee and immigration populations greatly vary. For example, many recent Hong Kong immigrants came with great financial support, and are in the United States because they feared the takeover of Hong Kong by the People's Republic of China in 1997. On the other hand, refugees from Laos and Cambodia continue to flee their countries with literally no money or resources (U.S. Bureau of Census, 1988a). Socioeconomic status additionally impacts both educational experience and the import placed on it. Some immigrants quickly learn the important aspects of American schooling, and engage their children in activities similar to those of the mainstream American children while others are unaware and unable to provide the essential foundation to their childrens' later academic success (Cheng, Trueba & Ima, 1992).

Other factors such as age and gender may also impact on adaptation process. These complex factors in adaptation, combined with the influences of traditional values on the degree of acculturation, affect how Asian and Pacific Island students view the educational process and conduct themselves in the classroom environment.

## LANGUAGE AND LINGUISTIC ORIGINS

Asian and Pacific Island students come from diverse language backgrounds, many of which contrast with the English language. Languages that are easiest to acquire and pronounce are those that are closest to one's native language. Asian languages are quite dissimilar in phonology, morphology, and syntax from Western languages. Cheng (1991) discusses that Mandarin, Cantonese, Vietnamese, Korean, Tagalog, Khmer, Lao, and Hmong are among the most widely spoken Asian languages in the United States. Hundreds of distinct languages and dialects are spoken in East Asia, Southeast Asia, and the Pacific Islands. The Asian languages that are spoken can be classified into five major families (Cheng, 1991):

1. Malaya-Polynesian or Austronesian family: Chamorro, Illocano, Tagalog, Bahasa Indonesia, Bahasa Malaysia, Javanese;
2. Sino-Tibetan family: Thai, Yao, Mandarin, Cantonese;
3. Austro-Asiatic family: Khmer, Vietnamese, Hmong;
4. Papuan family: New Guinean.
5. Altaic: Japanese, Korean.

Over 1,200 indigenous languages are spoken among the 5 million inhabitants of the Pacific Islands. These include Chamorro, Marshallese, Trukese Carolinian, Papa New Guinea, Korean Yapese, Palauan, Pompean, Samoan, Hawaiian, Fijian, and Tahitian. The five lingua francas used by the Pacific Islanders are French, English, Pidgin, Spanish and Bahasa Indonesian. Familiarity with the names, origins and descriptions of the languages will assist faculty in understanding more about the students they teach. Further understanding the major differences between Asian, Pacific Island and English language systems illustrates the relative difficulty that many Asian and Pacific Island students have learning English. Table 6-1 provides a list of the major native languages spoken by Asian and Pacific Island students.

Students whose native language is tonal may have initial difficulty with the complex multisyllabic and morphological structure of English. This can be explained in part by a review of tonal structure. With tonal languages, each character is phonetically represented by a single syllable (Ruhlen, 1976). Each syllable has a distinct pitch or tone. Tones convey different meanings for the syllables to which they are assigned. For example, when a language has only one tone, there is only one meaning for the word. However, in languages that have several tones, the same word conveys different meanings depending on the pitch variation employed (Grosjean, 1982). As illustrated above, Chinese, Hmong, Lao and Vietnamese are tonal languages. Different from the English language, these latter languages are uninflected and as such use no morphological

**Table 6-1.**
**Asian and Pacific Island Languages**

| Language | Country of Origin and Description |
|---|---|
| Chamorro: | Language spoken in Guam, Saipan and some Micronesian islands; nontonal; inflected system; and contains polysyllabic words. |
| Chinese: | One of a group of languages and dialects spoken in China, including Mandarin, Cantonese, Amoy, Fukien and Shanghai; tonal; uninflected system and monosyllabic words. |
| Hmong: | Language spoken by the Hmong people from the mountain area of Laos; tonal uninflected system and monosyllabic words. |
| Ilokano: | Language spoken in the Philippines; nontonal; inflected system and polysyllabic words. |
| Japanese: | Language spoken in Japan; agglutinatonal; nontonal and polysyllabic words. |
| Khmer: | Official language spoken in the Cambodia nontonal; uninflected system and monosyllabic or disyllabic words. |
| Korean: | Language spoken in Korea; officially unclassified but contains many words of Chinese origin; nontonal inflected system and polysyllabic words. |
| Lao: | Official national language of Laos; a Tai language of Buddhist people living in the area of the Mekong River in Laos and Thailand; tonal; uninflected system and monosyllabic words. |
| Vietnamese: | National language of Vietnam; tonal; monosyllabic noninflectional system. |
| Malay: | Language spoken in Malaysia and other parts of Indonesia; nontonal; inflected and system polysyllabic words. |
| Filipino: | National language of the Philippines; nontonal; inflected system and polysyllabic words. |
| Tagalog: | Native but not official language of the Philippines. |

markers to grammatically mark for pluralization, possession, or past tense.

For Asian students whose own languages are essentially monosyllabic words, the rules for syllabification and syllable stress in English may present difficulty (Walker, 1985). For instance, a Chinese student may misplace English word stress because of the differences in word stress and intonation patterns (e.g., refrige'rator or u'niversity). Because intonation patterns convey different meanings (e.g., statements from questions, demands from requests, excitement from sarcasm, enthusiasm from indifference), it is crucial for both the faculty and students to understand these distinctions to avoid misinterpretation of the actual intent of a message.

Many university students will be fluent English speakers. Others will have difficulties being understood. Students learning a new language frequently are able to comprehend, read and write the language, but may have difficulty with oral expression in regard to the phonological and/or syntactic aspects of the language. Accent is related to how an individual pronounces words. For example, because the phoneme /f/ does not appear in Taiwanese, the word **fix** may be pronounced **hix**. This single sound substitution renders the word unintelligible. When a sentence contains many words with the /f/ sound, the entire communicative attempt may be incomprehensible. Vietnamese-influenced English, Mandarin-influenced English, Singapore-influenced English, Bengali-influenced English will contribute to the speech intelligibility of an Asian speaker's English. Educators may be better able to understand a student's Asian influenced English if they base intelligibility on how close the speech pattern approximates that of standard English. When speech intelligibility is compromised, API students should be encouraged to enhance their English communication skills by improving their articulation, and intonation patterns.

## PREREQUISITE KNOWLEDGE: RELIGION, EDUCATION, LEARNING, COMMUNICATION AND HEALTH

It is critical for faculty to obtain prerequisite knowledge about the diversity, philosophical foundations, cultural beliefs and native and personal histories of API students in order to provide them with a more meaningful education. Philosophical and religious beliefs permeate their cultural values and practices including language of origin, thought patterns, communication and learning styles and even how these cultures view the educational process and conduct educational practices.

Background information including: immigration and migration history to United States; prior education and exposure to English; the home environment, roles, and expectations of family members and the societal support system are critical in understanding API students (Bouvier & Agresta, 1987; Cheng, 1991). It is also important for faculty to keep in mind that extreme heterogeneity exists across and within API populations. Despite the fact that Asians and Pacific Islanders are celebrated as American's "model minority," they are the most poorly understood of all minority groups in the United States (Crystal, 1989; Suzuki, 1989). Despite extreme diversity, API immigrants and refugees have been confronted with stereotyped undifferentiated and often hostile perceptions by mainstream American society. These perceptions ignore distinct lifestyles, customs, traditions, world views, ethnic and social norms, values and folk beliefs with ancient religious and philosophical origins (Asians in America, 1991).

## Foundations for Cultural Beliefs and Practices: Religious and Philosophical Systems

Religious and philosophical beliefs which are an integral part of Asian and Pacific Island cultures, will invariably affect the way these individuals view education and conduct themselves in the educational setting. In order to better understand the learning approaches of their students, faculty would benefit from knowing about how learning and educational views are shaped by the various religious systems. For example, the predominant belief in Buddhism is reincarnation and the acceptance of fate. People are taught to be passive and to accept what has come to them (Ashby, 1983). Following these principles, the preferred style of interaction is a nonassertive or nonaggressive one. Such cultural values reflect and shape the students' educational values, practices, communication and learning styles, and in turn their behavior in the academic setting.

Religious beliefs and philosophical systems dictate sociocultural orientation, values, and customs which also permeate family, communication styles, and health beliefs and practices. It is important to understand this in regard to the Asian and Pacific Island students since their orientation differs markedly from a Eurocentric orientation in a number of significant ways. For example, while the mainstream American culture practices monotheism or the belief in one god, most Asians and Pacific Islanders practice polytheism or the worship of plurality of gods with the coexistence of all supernatural beings. Together with ancestor worship, shamanism, including animism and spirit worship, and Christianity, the three teachings of Confucianism, Taoism, and Buddhism, have evolved into a syncretistic or complementary system of blended beliefs which differ greatly from Western practices.

In addition, these three teachings or doctrines have further shaped a traditional collectivistic orientation for many Asians and Pacific Islanders (Triandis, Brislin & Hui, 1988). In contrast, the mainstream American culture is reflective of an individualistic orientation where the individual is viewed as autonomous, self-reliant, independent, living for the future, striving for personal achievement and self happiness, and where social familial roles and expectations are loosely structured (Chan, 1986).

In a collectivistic society, human relationships are inclusive rather than exclusive (Liu and Yu, 1975). Family is the basic unit of society, and the central focus of an individual's life. Individuals strive for group welfare, loyalty, cooperation, mutual interdependence among group members, and reverence for elders, ancestors, and the past.

According to collectivistic orientation, successful academic achievement is the greatest attribute one can bestow on parents and the family. The key to existence is harmony; harmony with self, others, and nature by observing the rules of propriety and respect for others. This principle of preserving harmony or humanism, translates into observed social behavior of conduct and communication styles that are markedly different from a Eurocentric **mind** or **materialistic** orientation (PAPEP, 1982). A later description in the chapter of these social interactive practices will illustrate how these behaviors do in fact create communication barriers between mainstream American faculty and API students, and between culturally diverse student groups.

Specific examples of the impact of religious beliefs on the behavior of Asian students follows. Students from China, Korea, Vietnam, and Japan will generally follow Confucianism (MacMahon, 1977). This philosophy of behavioral codes dictates relationships between family members and filial piety. Chinese students may also practice Taoism, which is derived from the doctrines of Lao Tzu who preached total acceptance of the determined course of nature or "**the way**" (Porter, 1983; Tom, 1989). Ancestral worship is also practiced in China, Japan, Korea, and Vietnam (Cheng, 1989). Japanese students will generally follow Shintoism which emphasizes the worship of nature, ancestors, and ancient heroes, and reverence for the spirits of natural forces and emperors.

Students from Southeast Asia are predominantly Buddhist. Buddhism which is an offshoot of Hinduism, emphasizes kindness and nonviolence. Brahmanism or Hinduism with its associated Indian philosophy, deities, and traditional worship of Brahma, the Supreme Being, the Creator, the Preserver, and the Destroyer, is practiced by mainly Indian students and some Malaysian, Indonesian, and Filipino students (Chhim, 1989).

Students from the Pacific Islands (e.g., Hawaii, American Samoa) and Philippines, and some from Korea and Vietnam practice Christianity. This is combined with practicing a mixture of spirit worship and folk beliefs about the supernatural world such as Taotaomuna (Chamorro), or Menehune spirits (Hawaiian) (Ashby, 1983). Animism which is practiced by many Southeast Asians and Koreans, is the basic principal of shamanism that holds all forms of life and things in the universe as maintaining their existence by virtue of the soul or anima (Mun, 1979). Moslem is practiced by students from Pakistan but also by some students from Malaysia, Indonesia, and parts of the Philippines.

While these religious and philosophic systems are the foundation for most Asian cultural beliefs and practice, the Filipino culture is set distinctly apart from other Asian cultures (Ashby, 1983; Winter, 1988). The Filipino culture is a mosaic with input from the Spanish, American, Chinese, Malay, Indian, and other cultures. It differs from other Asian cultures because it is essentially monotheistic, and has a bilateral kinship system where one is obligated to both sides of the family. Roles between men and women are more egalitarian. While similar to the Chinese culture where child obedience is highly valued, familial relations are based more on mutual respect. Parents persuade and model concepts of conduct and compromise rather than demand obedience or absolute submission to authority (Enriquez, 1987).

During this century, Americans have had a major influence on the pedagogy of the Filipino education (Okamura and Abgayani, 1991). American curriculum and teaching methodologies have been imported on large scale dimensions. The Filipine culture has remained unique (Carino, 1987), although influenced by Hispanic Catholics and Euro-christian ethnics, combined with the Philippines' indigenous Malay roots and a history of Hindu, Confucianism, and Islamic teachings. There is, however, a sense of identity and values which reflect the Asian culture.

## Educational Beliefs and Learning Practices

Most Asian and Pacific Island parents secure a good education for their children and in return their children, particularly the males, strive toward academic and occupational excellence and high socioeconomic status (Leung, 1988). Most Asian cultures which follow the teachings of Confucius maintain a life-long respect of education (e.g., knowledge, wisdom, intellect, and love of learning). The oldest educated child provides educational support for the next oldest child in the family and so on.

Wong-Filmore (1985) indicates that differences in styles of classroom conduct and interaction exist among Asian and Pacific Island students, and American mainstream students and educators. From an early age,

Asian and Pacific Island students are taught a strict formal code of ethics for classroom conduct and obedience (Cheng, 1991). Traditional cultural values convey respect for authority so obedience and status are conferred on teachers by use of honorific terms to address teachers. There is a definite social and psychological distance between the teacher and students. API students may be perceived as being shy or uncomfortable when they talk to their American professors. In most Asian schools, students are taught to be quiet and remain in their assigned seats during class. In general, when the teacher enters or leaves the classroom, Asian and Pacific Island students must stand up and bow to the teacher as an indication of respect and reverence. The teacher's instructions are to be obeyed and not challenged. These written and culturally defined rules are to be strictly adhered to and without question.

Cheng (1991) reports that Asian parents revere educators and expect them to assign their children a great deal of homework. They additionally expect classrooms to be disciplined, and thus may not approve of the American mainstream educational system which allows students a great deal of freedom in the classroom. Incongruencies may arise between parents' perceptions of the teacher's role and the mainstream teacher's perception of their own role as an educator. Consequently, students may be unsure regarding behavioral expectations and how to conduct themselves in the American educational setting.

In American classrooms, Asian and Pacific Island students often become confused by the spontaneous and outspoken verbal behaviors of their mainstream peers since they have been taught that such behaviors show disrespect for authority. Active classroom participation and discussion may be foreign concepts to Asian and Pacific Island students, who may consider volunteering answers, commenting, interrupting, criticizing, asking questions, or seeking clarification, as bold and immodest practices. Asian and Pacific Island students may seem at a loss when they are asked by their professors to participate in the decision making process regarding course content (Tran, 1991).

Because of cultural and family teachings, API students usually avert direct eye contact and tend to bow their heads when communicating with a teacher. While mainstream American teachers consider direct eye contact as a sign of attention and respect, Asian children are taught early on that it is disrespectful to look someone of authority directly in the eyes. Understanding these nonverbal cues and the passive verbal behaviors described above will insure that non-Asian educators will interpret signs of respect that are generated by their API students.

It is imperative that educators understand the major cultural differences in learning styles, teaching styles and the interactive participant styles between students and professors in the classroom. Most Asian and Pacific Island students behave in a formal manner in the educational setting. In order for Asian and Pacific Island students to more easily adjust to the cultural social rules of mainstream American education setting, they must be acquainted and comfortable with the relative informality and freedom of expression within American classrooms (Jackson, 1986).

### Variations in Learning

Cheng (1991) reports that in most Asian and Pacific Island countries the learning style is passive in which students learn by listening, reading, observing, and imitating, rather than by discovery learning or engaging in critical thinking. Students are not encouraged to ask questions during class or to seek answers. Professors lecture during the entire class and students take and memorize copious notes. Examinations usually require the recall of factual information. Study habits of Asian and Pacific Island students differ from those of mainstream American students in that they read word by word, page by page, often failing to integrate, organize, and synthesize information, particularly when it is counterfactual and hypothetical in nature (Bloom, 1981; Cheng, 1991).

In the mainstream American educational setting, faculty encourage creativity, discussion, and debate. Students are expected to volunteer information and to ask questions. The shift from a lecture method of teaching to a cooperative learning environment, from observation and memorization of facts to problem solving, from total dependence on teachers to self-reliance in finding information, may require a period of adjustment for the Asian and Pacific Island students. The differences in learning styles in Asian and Pacific Island students present challenges for mainstream American faculty where flexibility and adaption in the use of learning and instructional strategies is required of their students (Leung, 1988).

A further example of the marked difference between Eastern and Western educational practices is reflected in styles of writing. The linear writing style of mainstream American educational practices demands a syllogistic, logically patterned sequence of thought where one idea is introduced, supported with arguments and reiterated. On the other hand, the circular writing style of Asian and Pacific Island educational practices focuses on the simultaneous development of many parallel points which all lend explanation to the topic (Cheng, 1991). Circular writing style may be construed by faculty as reflective, incomplete, or disorganized thoughts. As one might imagine, an Asian or Pacific Island student who has received formal training in the circular mode of writing

1. Compared to some other Chinese dialects, tone sandhi phenomena in Mandarin are so straightforward that they have rarely been discussed in detail, thus many problems have been left uninvestigated. This paper is an attempt to explore some of those problems.

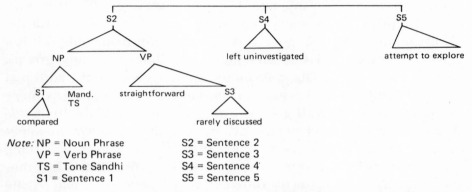

*Note:* NP = Noun Phrase     S2 = Sentence 2
VP = Verb Phrase     S3 = Sentence 3
TS = Tone Sandhi     S4 = Sentence 4
S1 = Sentence 1     S5 = Sentence 5

2. This paper is an attempt to explore some of the neglected problems concerning Mandarin tone sandhi phenomena, which have been rarely discussed in detail because they appear to be straightforward in comparison to other dialects.

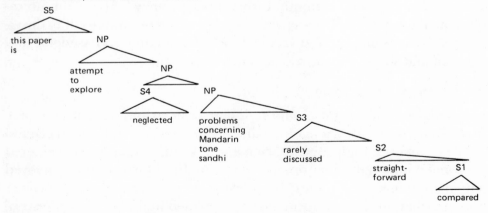

Figure 6-1. Sample of nonlinear versus linear written expression. (From Chen, M.: Three Representations of Two Semantically Equivalent Paragraphs. In Cheng, L.: *Assessing Asian Language Performance.* Courtesy of M. Cheng and Academic Communication Association, 1991.)

may have considerable difficulty not only switching to a linear writing style, but also in the very way they absorb, understand and cognitively process written information in the linear writing style. Figure 6-1 illustrates two semantically equivalent sentences that are grouped by their differences in linear and non linear circular styles of writing (Chen, M., 1985).

## Communication Patterns and Styles

Cultural differences in communication styles may affect social, academic, and professional success. Many students who have good English language skills may not be competent social communicators. Students may lack communication competency because they are unfamiliar with the social pragmatic rules that govern American mainstream interactions. Effective communication is defined differently by different cultural groups. Many Asian and Pacific Island communication styles reflect traditional beliefs and values where the goal of communication is to promote unity and harmony among social groups. An example of how different cultural codes may be contradictory is a Chinese student who remains silent rather than voicing disagreement or anger.

Subtle aspects of API communication styles that are not readily meaningful to speakers of distinctly different Eurocentric style may create barriers between students and faculty. In addition, a verbal **yes** or an affirmative head nod may be used when an API student really means **no.** Mismatches in social communicative practices may cause communication breakdown and misunderstanding, and perhaps even result in development of resentment and hostility between faculty and student, and student and student interactions in the classroom.

### High Context Orientation

Communication patterns and styles are basic to and serve to reinforce traditional cultural orientations and values. Asian and Pacific Island cultures reflect a high context orientation. In this situationally-centered or context bound orientation, most meaningful information is conveyed either in the physical context or internalized in the person who receives the information. Little information is contained in the verbally transmitted part of the message (Hall, 1976). Effective communication is dependent upon the receiver's ability to correctly interpret the speaker's intent without direct reference to what he/she means. For example, an Asian may critique a classroom presentation by providing a lengthy acknowledgement of the honor of hearing the information and never directly critique what was said. This style contrasts with that of low context Eurocentric cultures where information is conveyed mainly through a precise, explicit, and straightforward verbal message.

**Formal Honorific Systems**

Communication patterns of high context Asian cultures are discussed by Cheng (1991). She describes a collectivistic orientation where the goal is to promote harmony, unity, and preserve face. This goal is facilitated by communication styles that employ formality and an honorific language system. Respect for authority, status, and possession is conveyed by special terms of address. The formal roles of propriety that convey respect for authority dictate what is communicated, how communicated and to whom. For example, in Japanese the way one says **you** depends largely on whether **you** are a man or woman, a young or an older person, or a person with high or low societal status. From an early age, children quickly learn to figure out the contextual cues for relating respect and reverence to the various people in their lives. Faculty who possess a low context orientation, may perceive such a formal orientation as excessive and unnecessary.

**Indirect and Nonverbal Styles of Communication**

As mentioned earlier, Asian and Pacific Islanders have been taught an indirect style of communication which may be viewed by faculty as evasive, devious, lacking knowledge or understanding. Along with this, they show respect for the professor's authority by purposefully not volunteering information or engaging in challenging educational debate. The student may be behaving in a culturally taught manner which may preclude providing a truthful answer that they feel might offend the professor. This mismatch of the pragmatic rules of the language of Asian students and Western professors contribute to the interpretation of the Asian student's behaviors as being passive, uncooperative, nonparticipatory or unenthusiastic (Cheng, 1991).

The following nonverbal behaviors may serve as a guide in understanding and promoting effective communication exchanges among faculty and students. For most Asian and Pacific Island cultures, nonverbal communication or so-called **Reading the Eyes** takes precedence over verbal communication (Wieman, Chen & Giles, 1986). Gestures, facial expressions, silences, body movements and spatial arrangements are used to convey the meaning and intent of pragmatic rules. Leubitz (1973) identified four functions of nonverbal communication: to relay messages, to augment verbal communication, to contradict verbal communication and to replace verbal communication. As opposed to an Eurocentric orientation, Knapp (1972) suggested that 35 percent of social meaning is actually transmitted by words, whereas 65 percent of social meaning is conveyed through nonverbal channels in Asian cultures.

**Silence.** Silence is highly valued in most Asian and Pacific Island cultures. The Asian proverb, "He who knows, he who talks, knows not," appropriately summarizes Asians' use of silence a central strategy during conversation (Weinman, Chen and Giles, 1986). Depending on the situation, silence conveys different connotations. For example, maintenance of silence during conversation serves as an expression of respect and intent. Silence following another speaker's verbal response serves to indicate disagreement or even anger as stated in the expression **silent treatment** (Wiemann, Chen & Giles, 1986).

**Eye Contact and Facial Expression.** As previously stated, where direct eye contact is viewed as a sign of hostility, impoliteness, disrespect, or shamefulness in most Asian and Pacific Island cultures, it is considered a polite, attentive and even a trusting behavior in Eurocentric cultures. Faculty may interpret the lack of facial expression by Asian and Pacific Island students as flat, stoic, unmotivated, and disinterested.

From an early age, many Asian and Pacific Island children are taught to overtly control their behavioral expression of emotions. However, in other instances smiling, laughing, or giggling, for example, can serve various functions in Asian and Pacific Islander cultures. Students may smile when embarrassed or to apologize in lieu of a verbal statement (e.g., "I'm sorry"); as an acknowledgment that an error has been committed; in response to a compliment; to mask other emotions (e.g., pain) or to avoid conflict. In Eurocentric cultures, smiling generally conveys happiness and acceptance. Also, in Filipino cultures, persons may laugh at a critical point during a discussion to indicate the importance of what is being said at that moment (Roces and Roces, 1985).

**Gestures and Body Language.** Gestures are not cross-cultural. A given movement gesture will have a different meaning for API communicators then for mainstream Americans. The American gesture for waving **good-bye** for example, is equivalent in meaning to **come here** in most API cultures. On the other hand, the American hand gesture for **to come here**

is viewed by most Asian cultures as a hostile, aggressive gesture, or even a way of beckoning a less inferior person or an animal (e.g., a dog) (Devine & Braganti, 1986). Most Asian and Pacific Islanders avoid touching and making body contact with the opposite sex. However, public hand holding by members of the same sex is acceptable. Further, Asians in general, and Cambodians, Laotians, and Hawaiians consider head touching as inappropriate because the head is the most sacred part of the body. Most Asian and Pacific Island cultures will maintain a greater social and physical distance from the speaker according to the age, social or marital status of the speaker than Anglo Americans. In mainstream American culture, the distance is usually an arms length or 12 inches away from their communication partner (Devine & Braganti, 1986).

## Variations in Health Beliefs and Practices

### Health Beliefs

Many Asian and Pacific Island cultures employ a pluralistic system of health care in which a Western medical practitioner is consulted at the same time indigenous medicines are used. Individuals may seek artificial insemination, while drinking herb tea for infertility problems. Also they may simultaneously use acupuncture treatment, medication and physical therapy. These practices are in part a factor of how recent, and at what age the individual's family migrated to the United States. The differences in health beliefs and practices including how disability is viewed, may impact on how students view and successfully adjust to the clinical training process (Cheng, 1990). Faculty will need to provide a clear understanding of how the API students' own health beliefs differ from those of American mainstream practices. Students may even have difficulty grasping and absorbing specific health related course materials in the allied health disciplines. From a practical viewpoint, what an Asian or Pacific Island student considers as an acceptable or justifiable medical absence from attending a class (or from taking an exam), may be very different from the viewpoint of the educational institution.

Traditional Chinese medicine practices a balanced harmony between the opposing faces of Yin (i.e., a passive, negative energy force) and Yang (i.e., an active, positive energy force) and a belief in the power of nature and the fundamental forces (Tom, 1989). Diseases and their treatment are classified by **hot** and **cold** conditions or forces. When an imbalance of opposing forces results in a medical illness, an individual's diet may be adjusted where **hot** or **cold** foods and medicines are prescribed to restore the proper balance in the body (Randall-David, 1989). For example, **hot** foods (e.g., pigs feet, chicken soup) may be used to cure a common cold. **Cold** foods (e.g., cucumber, melon) may be used to cure a fever. Further, body parts are subdivided as Yang-surface organs or Yin-internal organs. Different from a Western orientation, the Yang and Yin orientation fails to separate mental from physical illnesses. Rather illness is viewed as an affliction of the whole person's forces of the body, mind, and emotions (Cheng, 1990). API students may require greater assistance in differentiating traditional cultural health teaching from Western health practices in allied health disciplines.

Many Asian and Pacific Island students may continue their cultural health practice by consulting folk healers who rid illness attributed to supernatural causes (McKenzie & Crisman, 1977). Priests, shamans, surhanos, folk medicine men, spirit masters, sorcerers, or witch doctors all practice healing. The methods include: chanting sacred prayers, providing herbal medicines (e.g., snake, rhinoceros), performing exorcism or moxibustion (i.e., burning magwort leaves on skin at site of acupuncture hole), dermabrasion (e.g., abrading the skin to treat fever, sore throat, head ache) or coin rubbing (Lew, 1989; Meyerson, 1990). Acupuncture and acupressure also serve as alternative methods of healing.

### Views on Disability

Most Asian and Pacific Island cultures view disability as a stigma whether it be an emotional, developmental, or physical disability. Disability is seen as being caused by natural, metaphysical forces. For example, many believe that disability is caused by: wrong doing of one's ancestors or the individual him/herself; an imbalance in the body because of too strongly felt emotions or improper diet, or spiritual attributions such as an evil spirit or a demon. More specifically, Pacific Islanders may believe that a disability such as a cleft palate is caused by evil spirits, a supernatural power (e.g., exposure to an eclipse during pregnancy) or may be the result of a **susto** or a frightful situation (Cheng, 1990; Cheng-Hammer, 1992).

API cultures that view the cause of a disability as spiritual in nature may believe that nothing can be done for an individual with a disability except to nurture and support them. Other API cultures may believe that a disability does not exist unless it can be physically seen, and thereby deny the presence of a disability such as retardation (Matsuda, 1989). Still other cultures (e.g., the Chamorro) view a handicap as a gift from God, and hence the individual belongs to everyone for shelter and protection. And still other cultures, like the Chinese and the Filipino, view a physical deformity as a curse, and may ostracize the individual from society (Lew, 1989). Because of the different cultural views of disability, Asian and Pacific Island students who engage in their initial stages of clinical training, need guidance in differentiating between their traditional health beliefs and mainstream American clinical intervention that will be beneficial for an individual with a disability. Because students may fail to culturally separate a physical from a mental disability, they will need to learn what type of professional to whom they should refer the client or patient, such as a physical therapist or a psychologist, a neurologist or a psychiatrist.

## CONCLUSION

The information presented in this chapter is intended to help facilitate the recruitment and retention of API students in the professional programs of allied health by providing a means for better understanding and addressing the impact of traditional cultures on the educational styles of Asian and Pacific Islander students. Due to the steady increase of students from diverse API countries in U.S. institutions of higher education, it is crucial that faculty examine the cultural and religious beliefs and customs, including communicative, linguistic, and learning styles, as well as the degrees of acculturation of their API students. The challenge to effectively educate all students calls for nothing less than a drastic revision of our educational practices and perceptions of API students, a challenge that demands an increased sensitivity and awareness to the many cultural and linguistic factors discussed in this chapter, a challenge that will lay the foundation for a more diverse, pluralistic American classroom.

## REFERENCES

Ashby, G.: *Micronesian Customs and Beliefs.* Eugene, Rainy Day Press, 1983.
Bloom, A.H.: *The Linguistic Shaping of Thought: A Study on the Impact of Language on Thinking China and the West.* Hillsdale, Lawrence Erbaum Associates, 1981.

Bouvier, L.F. & Agresta, A.J.: The fastest growing minority. *American Demographics,* 7 (46): 31–36, 1987.

Carino, B.V.: The Philippines and Southeast Asia: Historical roots and contemporary linkages. In Fawcett, J.T. & Carino, B.V. (Eds.): *Pacific Bridges: The New Immigration from Asia and the Pacific Islands.* New York, Center for Migration Studies, 1987, pp. 305–325.

Chan, S.: Parents of exceptional Asian children. In Kitano, M.K. & Chinn, P.C. (Eds.): *Exceptional Asian Children and Youth.* Reston, Council for Exceptional Children, 1986, pp. 35–53.

Chen, M.: Three Representatives of Two Semantically Equivalent Paragraphs. Presentation given at San Diego State University, San Diego, 1985.

Cheng, L.: Ethnic, cultural, linguistic diversity: Challenges and opportunities for faculty, students and curriculum. In Ripich, D. (Ed.): *The Graduate Council in Communication Sciences and Disorders 1989 Annual Conference Proceedings.* Tampa, Author, 1989.

Cheng, L.: Asian American cultural perspectives on birth-defects: Focus on cleft palate. *Cleft Palate Journal, 27* (3): 294–300, 1990.

Cheng, L.: *Assessing Asian Language Performance.* Oceanside, Academic Communication Associates, 1991.

Cheng, L. & Hammer, C.S.: *Cultural Perceptions on Disability.* San Diego, Los Amigos Research Associates, 1992.

Cheng, L., Trueba, H.T. & Ima, K.: *Myth or Reality: Adaptive Strategies of Asian Newcomers in California.* London, Falmer Press, 1992.

Chhim, S.H.: *Introduction to Cambodian Culture.* San Diego. San Diego State University's, Multifunctional Resource Center, 1989.

Crystal, D.: Asian Americans and the myth of the model minority. *Social Casework,* 405–413, September, 1986.

Devine, E. & Braganti, N.L.: *The Traveler's Guide to Asian Customs and Manners.* New York, St. Martin's Press, 1986.

Enriquez, V.G.: Filipino values: Toward a new interpretation, *Tagsibol,* 29–34, November, 1987.

Gardner, R.W., Robey, B. & Smith, P.C.: Asian Americans: Growth, change and diversity. *Population Bulletin, 40:* 1–44, 1985.

Gordon, L.W.: Southeast Asian refugee migration to the United States. In Fawcett, J.T. & Carino, B.V. (Eds.): *Pacific Bridges: The New Immigration from Asia and the Pacific Islands.* New York, Center for Migration Studies, 1987, pp. 243–173.

Grosjean, F.: *Life With Two Languages: An Introduction To Bilingualism.* Cambridge, Harvard University Press, 1982.

Hall, E.: *Beyond Culture.* Garden City, Anchor, 1976.

Jackson, P.: *Life in Classrooms.* New York, Holt, Rinehart and Winston, Inc., 1986.

Knapp, L.: *Nonverbal Communication in Interaction.* New York, Holt, Rinehart and Wilson, 1972.

Leubitz, L.: *Nonverbal Communication: A Guide for Teachers.* Skokie, National Textbook, 1973.

Leung, E.K.: Cultural and acculturational commonalities and diversities among

Asian Americans: Identification and programming considerations. In Ortiz, A.A. & Ramirez, B.A. (Eds.): *Schools and the Culturally Diverse Exceptional Student: Promising Practices and Future Directions.* Reston, Council for Exceptional Children, 1988, pp. 86–95.

Lew, L.S.: Understanding the Southeast Asian Health Care Consumer: Bridges and Barriers. Paper presented at the National Symposium on Genetic Services for the Medically Underserved. Washington, May 1989.

Liu, W.T. & Yu, E.S.H.: Asian-American youth. In Havinghurst, R.J., Dreyer, P.H. & Rehage, K.V. (Eds.): *Youth,* Chicago, National Society for the Study of Education, 1975, pp. 367–389.

MacMahon, H.: *Confucianism: The Korean Way.* Seoul: Samsumg, 1977.

Matsuda, M.: Working with Asian parents: Some communication strategies. *Topics in Language Disorder, 9* (3): 45–53, 1989.

McKenna, B.: Good news and bad on the diversity front. *On Campus, 11* (5): 3, 1992.

McKenzie, J.L. & Crisman, N.J.: Healing, herbs, gods and magic: Folk health beliefs among Filipino Americans. *Nursing Outlook, 25:* 326–329, 1977.

Meyerson, M.D.: Cultural considerations in the treatment of Latinos with craniofacial malformations. *The Cleft Palate Journal, 27:* 279–288, 1990.

Mun, S.H.: Shamanism in Korea. In Shin, Y.C. (Ed): *Korean Thoughts.* Seoul, International Cultural Foundation, 1979, pp. 17–36.

Okamura, J.Y. & Agbayani, A.: Filipino Americans. In Mokuau, N. (Ed.): *Handbook of Social Services for Asians and Pacific Islanders.* Westport, Greenwood, 1991, pp. 97–115.

Pan Asian Parent Education Project.: *Pan Asian Child Rearing Practices: Filipino, Japanese, Korean, Samoan, Vietnamese.* San Diego, Union of Pan Asian Communities, 1982.

Porter, J.: *All Under Heaven: The Chinese World.* New York, Pantheon, 1983.

Randall, D.E.: *Strategies for Working with Culturally Diverse Communities and Clients.* Washington, Association for Care of Children's Health, 1989.

Roces, A. & Roces, G.: *Culture Shock! Philippines.* Singapore, Time Books International, 1985.

Ruhlen, M.: *A Guide to the Language of the World.* Palo Alto, Stanford University, 1976.

Spindler, G.: *Educational and Cultural Process: Anthropological Approach,* 2nd ed. Prospect Heights, Waveland Press, 1987.

Spindler, G., Spindler, L., Trueba, H. & Williams, M.: *The American Cultural Dialogue and its Transmission.* Philadelphia, Falmer Press, 1990.

Suzuki, B.H.: Asian Americans as the model minority: Outdoing Whites or media hype? *Change,* 13–19, November/December, 1989.

Takaki, R.: *Strangers From a Different Shore: A History of Asian Americans.* Boston, Little Brown, 1989.

Tom, K.S.: *Echoes from Old China.* Honolulu, University of Hawaii, 1989.

Tran, M.: *Hidden Curriculum: An Asian Perspective.* Unpublished manuscript. San Diego, San Diego State University, 1991.

Triandis, H.C., Brislin, R. & Hui, C.H.: Cross-cultural training across the individualism-collectivism divide. *Internal Journal of Intercultural Relations, 12:* 269–289, 1988.

U.S. Bureau of Census: *Asian and Pacific Island Population in the United States Washington.* U.S. Government Printing Office, 1988a.

U.S. Bureau of the Census: *We, the Asian and Pacific Island Americans.* Washington, U.S. Government Printing Office, 1988b.

U.S. General Accounting Office: *Asian Americans: A Status Report.* Washington, Human Resources Division, 1991.

Walker, C.L.: Learning English: The Southeast Asian refugee experience. *Topics in Language Disorders, 5* (3): 53–65, 1985.

Wiemann, J., Chen, V. & Giles, H.: Beliefs About Talk and Silence In a Cultural Context. Paper presented at the Speech Communication Association Convention. Chicago, November, 1986.

Winter, F.H.: *The Filipinos in America.* Minneapolis, Lerner, 1988.

Wong-Filmore, L.: Learning a second Language: Chinese children in the American classroom. In Alatis, J.E. & Staczek, J.J. (Eds.): *Perspective on Bilingualism and Bilingual Education.* Washington, Georgetown University Press, 1985, pp. 436–452.

# Chapter 7

# PROFILE OF NATIVE AMERICAN STUDENTS

Marilyn A Pipes, Carol E. Westby and Ella Inglebret

## INTRODUCTION

The Native American population presents unique challenges for educators. Unlike other minority groups, Native Americans assume a special status within the United States. The various tribal and native groups exist as sovereign nations and maintain government-to-government relationships with the United States. Over the years, through treaties and other federal acts, Native Americans have exchanged land for services, particularly education, from the United States Government. Because of this, the United States assumes a special responsibility for the education of Native American youth. Another unique characteristic, lack of visibility, is a result of the small size of the Native American population. As a minority among the minorities, they comprise only slightly less than 1 percent of the total United States population. As a result, when the status of the minorities in the United States is examined, the unique characteristics of the Native American population are often not specified.

This chapter will consider factors which impact upon the academic success of Native American students in higher education. The heterogeneity of the population will be emphasized, and cautions will be reiterated to avoid generalizing and stereotyping. A brief review of the history of education for Native Americans will be presented. Limited information is available on Native Americans at postsecondary levels. Consequently, this chapter will review data on preschool and school age Native American children and tie this information to higher education through reference to personal experiences with Native American college students at our respective settings. Our three graduate programs, the University of Arizona, the University of New Mexico, and Washington State University, sponsor federally funded projects to recruit and retain Native American students.

# HISTORY OF EDUCATION FOR NATIVE AMERICANS

## Traversing Two Worlds

Perhaps more than any member of a minority group in the United States today, Native Americans traverse two worlds; one being the community of their tribal members, the other being the mainstream society. McDonald (1989b) attributed the following statement to Johnathan Buffalo, a teacher on the Mesquaki Indian settlement in Iowa, "Indians are like people split in two. Economically, they have to get along with the outside world. Spiritually and culturally, they have to get along with themselves" (p. 12). Many Native Americans report a sensation of being in limbo, trying to participate in the American mainstream without losing their unique cultural identity, this state one tribe refers to as "stuck in the horizon—part of neither the earth nor the sky" (Staff, "Stuck in the Horizon", 1989, p. 1).

Participation in these two worlds is validated by the concept of dual citizenship. A Native American person may be considered a citizen of his or her tribal nation, as well as a citizen of the United States. As independent nations, tribal communities can offer their members broad societal support. Participation with the mainstream society may not be as crucial for Native Americans as for other minorities who lack this strong community and governmental support. Although many proponents of self-determination for Native Americans consider a "White man's education" critical to self-sufficiency in the mainstream world, such an education may not be essential for self-sufficiency within the tribe. Dr. Joseph Suina, a Cochiti Pueblo Indian and faculty member at the University of New Mexico (in personal communication), has commented that a college education is not necessary for a position of leadership and respect within the tribe. Positions such as storyteller, medicine person, council person, or governor/chief are valued, and allow individuals to contribute positively to their tribal community. No other minority group in the United States has this same option. An ethnographic study of students from nondominant cultures in an academic setting (Ford & Westby, 1992) provides one student's assessment of this unique position:

> At the university I feel like I'm just one of the people walking around going to school. I don't feel like I'm somebody here, and I don't feel I'm a nobody here. I'm just an anybody. I feel good about myself at home because I'm a mother and I'm somebody that people in the pueblo will talk to, and they'll tell me

what's going on with them. I can be an authority figure there, or I can be an informative person there . . . I'm a person someone can come and talk to, and I can take care of them (p. 3).

## Educational Demographics

Few would argue that mainstream educational institutions have difficulty bridging the gap between the culture of the school and the cultural values retained by Native American students. Indeed, Henry and Pepper (1990) describe the school experience as a culturally incongruent situation for many Indian students, resulting in a feeling of culture shock. Wright and Tierney (1991) quote a Native American high school senior, who elucidated this conflict:

> When I was a child I was taught certain things, don't stand up to your elders, don't question authority, life is precious, the earth is precious, take it slowly, enjoy it. And then you go to college and you learn all these other things, and it never fits (p. 18).

The cultural dissonance experienced by many Native Americans has contributed to a disastrous outcome. Among all racial minorities, Native Americans have achieved the lowest educational levels (Lin, LaCounte & Eder, 1988). As compared to all racial and ethnic groups, a 1985 report from the Arizona State Department of Education indicated that Indian students achieved the poorest scores on reading, language, and mathematics tests across grades 1 through 12 (Red Horse, 1986). Additionally, dropout rates for Native American high school students are alarmingly high, ranging from 45 to 85 percent (Red Horse, 1986). Statistics for higher education are similarly depressing. The U.S. Department of Education (1987, as cited in Green, 1989) indicated that only 10.8 percent of 1980 Native American high school seniors had attained a baccalaureate degree and .0 percent had attained a master's degree by 1986.

## Attitudes Toward Education for Native Americans

Advocates of Indian education believe that a long-standing history of racist attitudes continues to pose significant obstacles to equal educational opportunities for Native American students. Initially, the racism took overt forms, expressed through physical and psychological abuse. When Europeans first arrived on North American shores, they regarded the indigenous people as subhuman and denied them basic civil rights.

The educational, social, religious, and governmental structures of Indian societies were viciously attacked (Duchene, 1988).

Assimilationist educational policies were in full force from the late 1800s through the early 1900s with the goals being to **civilize** Native Americans by eradicating their language and culture, and incorporating them into the mainstream of American life. Education emphasized agricultural, industrial, and domestic arts, rather than higher academic study (Wright & Tierney, 1991). Many Native American children were **legally** kidnapped and shuttled to boarding schools, far removed from their family and community networks. Laws prohibited Indian children from speaking their native languages in school (Duchene, 1988). Some institutions boarded students year round, fearing that pupils would lapse into traditional ways if allowed to go home for the summer (McDonald, 1988a & b).

As assimilationist educational policies failed, the mid 1900s brought the termination and relocation era. Selected Indian reservations and their educational programs were terminated, and individuals were relocated away from reservations into urban areas. Those individuals that were relocated to urban areas were generally met with poorly funded vocational training programs, no assistance in learning English, and only short-term employment. Most Native Americans had difficulty adjusting to the urban conditions and eventually returned to their reservations (Eder & Reyhner, 1988; McDonald, 1989). Although these urban relocation policies were relatively short-lived, the end result was "extreme poverty and disease on reservations and the creation of Indian ghettos in the cities" (Fixico, 1989, p. 59). Further, Native Americans were left with an "almost ineradicable suspicion of the government's motives for every policy, program, or action concerning Indians" (McDonald, 1989a, p. 6).

The generations of subjugation and overt racism have contributed to a sense of cultural isolation, a loss of identity and a sense of inferiority felt by some Native Americans today. Many are neither comfortable in the mainstream culture nor in their native culture. While recognizing that a good education is crucial to self-determination, they are understandably reluctant to pay the cost of cultural genocide. Wolcott (1987) suggested that Native American students may perceive the teacher as the enemy, where teachers are not assigned to teach students about their own way of life, but to teach them about the mainstream way of life. Consequently, teachers are viewed as captors charged with instructing the prisoners (students) in the ways of mainstream life with the underlying purposes encouraging students to defect from their home culture, and to give them skills for successful defection.

Cummins (1988) maintained that Native American students continue to fail in school because educators inadvertently reinforce this **bicultural ambivalence.** He asserted that the historical pattern of overt racism currently persists through more covert, subtle means. Interviews with Native American students in our programs have revealed that a number of them were discouraged by guidance counselors, teachers, and college professors from continuing their education. In high school, they were told that they would not need certain skills because "Indians don't go to college." In college they were dissuaded from entering particular areas of study because "Indians don't do well in that program."

Subtle racism takes on many forms in contemporary educational institutions. In most United States schools today, an Anglo-conformity orientation prevails. Educators are often unaware of and even insensitive to cultural and linguistic differences, and curricula reflect the views of the dominant society. Very few public or Bureau of Indian Affairs' schools demonstrate respect for Native American customs and beliefs (Locust, 1988). Although research indicates considerable differences in learning styles among culturally diverse groups, educators continue to view these as deficiencies, rather than difference (Red Horse, 1986). Teaching style may conflict with traditional cultural patterns emphasized at home. Swisher & Deyhle (1989) observed that in many classrooms, teachers generally provide instruction and introduce new concepts through verbal rather than visual channels. This puts an Indian student, who comes from an environment where visual strengths are stressed, at a definite disadvantage. Culturally-biased methods of educational instruction persist, and minority students may become victims of professional **credibility** when teachers lack training and expertise in alternative styles of teaching (Cummins, 1988).

As we move toward the twenty-first century, there are some bright spots in Indian education. The more recent policy of Indian self-determination has fostered increased Indian control over education for their youth. As the colleges are held accountable to the local Indian leadership, opportunities for postsecondary education in native communities have increased, reflecting greater cultural relevance and sensitivity (Bill, 1987). Tribal colleges, along with other two-year institutions, are the higher education entry point for over one-half of Native American students (Wright & Tierney, 1991). Today, twenty-two tribally controlled community colleges are operated on reservations in the Western and Midwestern states of Arizona, California, Kansas, Michigan, Montana, Nebraska, North Dakota, South Dakota, Washington, and Wisconsin. From 1987 to 1991, enrollment in these colleges increased dramatically from 5,000 to 7,050 students (BIA, 1987; BIA, 1991).

## HETEROGENEITY WITHIN THE NATIVE AMERICAN POPULATION

### Cautions in Making Cultural Assumptions

"One of the major problems of American Indians at present is the fact that they are seen as 'one people with one need,'" (Reeves, 1989, p. 4). This is one of many fallacies that White people assume of Native Americans. They are **not** a monolithic, generic group, and do not appreciate being perceived as such. The population is comprised of distinct tribal and native groups, with vast observable differences in governance, customs, language, wealth, and religion. This diversity contributes to different world views and varied approaches to problem solving. Thus, "Indian people do not speak with one voice any more than America does" (Tijerina & Biemer, 1987–1988, p. 89).

As opposed to the stereotype of the Indian as the **vanishing American,** the contemporary Native American population is a young and rapidly growing group. According to the 1990 U.S. Census, 1,959,234 persons (or 0.8% of the total U.S. population) identified themselves as American Indians, Eskimos, or Aleuts. This figure represents an increase of 37.9 percent over the 1980 population total (Bureau of the Census, 1991). A large proportion of the population is of childbearing age, which contributes to a birth rate that is 78 percent greater than for the general U.S. population (Indian Health Service, 1991).

Demographic population counts, such as those conducted by the U.S. Census Bureau, raise the question, "Who is an Indian?" This is a difficult question to answer since no single federal or tribal definition is used to determine membership in this population. For the purpose of the census and many other demographic surveys, anyone who declares him or herself an Indian is considered one. To qualify for tribal or native association membership, only a minimum amount of Indian blood, varying from one-half to a trace, is necessary. In addition, an individual may be adopted by a tribal group (Bureau of Indian Affairs, 1991). This lack of consistency leads to variation in the basic definition of Indian.

There is a need to examine how members of the dominant culture have formed impressions of what it means to be **Indian.** In the popular media, Native Americans are generally depicted as relics of the past. Deloria (cited in Elliott, 1991) stated that "the tragedy of America's Indians—that is, the Indians that America loves, and loves to read about—is that they no longer exist, except in the pages of books" (p. 10). Very little information is readily available that accurately portray modern day Native Americans. As with any group of people, Native Americans have adapted and changed over time. To recognize the contributions of Indians in today's world, stereotypes associated with Native Americans of the past must be overcome (Heinrich, 1991).

No consensus exists with regard to the appropriate terminology to use in reference to members of this group: **Indians, American Indians, Native Americans.** When the clinical staff of our educational programs ask students what term they prefer, various responses are given, and no term is uniformly given. Thus, in this publication, the terms **Native American** and **Indian** are used interchangeably.

It should be remembered that there were no **Indians** prior to the arrival of Europeans in America. Those so-called **Indians** identified themselves using terms specific to their native groups, such as Nee-me-poo (Nez Perce) or Dineh (Navajo). Native Americans of one nations were, and are, as different from Native Americans of another nation or tribe, as the English are from the Spanish or the Swedes are from the Italians (Heinrich, 1991). The difficulty in collectively referring to all native groups become apparent when one considers that there are over 500 federally recognized tribes and native groups in the United States (BIA, 1991).

As seen in Figure 7-1, Native Americans reside in every region of the United States in vastly different environments and geographic locations. The majority reside in the southern and western portions of the country. While most Native Americans reside off their reservations, about 48 percent live on or adjacent to Indian reservations (Bureau of Indian Affairs, 1991). Reservations vary in size from 16 million acres of land on the Navajo Reservation to less than 100 acres on smaller reservations. Some reservations are occupied primarily by tribal members, while others are inhabited by high percentages of non-Indian land owners (BIA, 1991). In recent years with many Native Americans shifting resi-

# FEDERALLY RECOGNIZED INDIAN TRIBES

Prepared by the U. S. Geological Survey

in cooperation with the Bureau of Indian Affairs

October 1991

dency from reservation to urban locations, direct exposure to the dominant American culture has resulted. Thus, levels of acculturation widely vary among Native Americans.

## Levels of Acculturation

To understand the cultural diversity of Native American individuals, an examination of the concept of acculturation is imperative. Acculturation refers to learning the rules of another, nonnative culture. It differs from assimilation in that it is an additive, rather than subtractive process, and has positive rather than negative psychosocial ramifications. For Native Americans, the level of acculturation typically relates to the quality and quantity of cultural contact with the U.S. mainstream or White, middle class culture. It is useful to consider acculturation to the mainstream culture on a spectrum (Red Horse, 1988), while acknowledging that each Native American possesses some degree of acculturation. Red Horse proposed a spectrum of acculturation for Native Americans ranging from traditional to panrenaissance with reference to language, kin structure, religion, views of land, and health at various points of the acculturation process. (See Appendix 7-A). For example, a Native American who demonstrates relatively less contact with mainstream culture might show the following behaviors characteristics:

| | |
|---|---|
| **Language:** | Generally prefers use of native language in most settings. |
| **Kin Structure:** | Maintains social relations with extended kin system. |
| **Religion:** | Practices native religion with retention of clans and ritual means. |
| **Land:** | Retains sacred view of land and links to land through rituals. |
| **Health:** | Retains traditional beliefs regarding etiology and healing. |

By contrast, a Native American who has become fully acculturated into the mainstream culture may show the following behavioral characteristics:

| | |
|---|---|
| **Language:** | Maintains English as the language of home and community with total loss of native language. |
| **Kin Structure:** | Maintains nuclear household arrangements with primarily non-Indian social relations and a minimal kin system. |

**Religion:**        Converts to nonnative religion with loss of historic religious practices.

**Land:**            Unconcerned with traditional sacredness of land, except perhaps in terms of conservation.

**Health:**          Accepts mainstream cultural explanations for illness and uses American institutional health services.

In recent years, a panrenaissance is occurring among highly acculturated Native Americans where there is an effort to renew their native language uses, reorganize extended kin systems, revitalize aspects of historic customs, and pursue traditional Native American health care practices.

It is important to realize that any one individual might show differing degrees of acculturation across different behaviors. That is, a person may retain traditional views about health and religion, yet speak English without having knowledge of his or her native language. The individual experience of acculturation will determine how each Native American fits in to both native and nonnative mainstream cultures. Thus, it is incorrect to assume that all Indian students will have difficulty achieving and **fitting into** a predominately White, middle class, academic institution, as it is equally erroneous to assume that all Native American students will be knowledgeable about the origin story of their people or traditional tribal beliefs. Each Native American will have differing values, beliefs, and world views depending on degree of acculturation.

## Linguistic Heterogeneity

While it is true that the majority of Native Americans speak a variety of English dialects (Payne, 1986), over one-fourth solely speak their native language at home (McArthur, 1984). These latter speakers use one of the approximately 250 Native American languages spoken in the U.S. today (BIA, 1991). Some of these languages are spoken by only a few individuals, others, such as Cherokee, Navajo, and Teton Sioux, are spoken by thousands (BIA, 1987). This wide variation in native language use reflects varying levels of language acculturation.

Maintenance or loss of Native American languages has a profound effect on the acculturation process. Geographically and socially isolated Native communities have tended to successfully maintain their traditional languages (Saville-Troike, 1989). For example, Zepeda (1988) attributed the fact that approximately 70 to 75 percent of the Tohono O'odham tribal members still speak the Papago language fluently because many Tohono O'odham villages are isolated and **uncontaminated** by outside influences. In other less isolated native communities, traditional languages have been completely lost or on the verge of being lost with the passage of elders. Ahenkaw (1986) discussed that the loss of language is viewed by many Native Americans as one of the most critical dilemmas facing them today, since it leads to communication breakdown between generations, and to their children being "cut off from their past and their heritage" (p. 1).

With some native groups, characteristics of the native language have been transferred to spoken English (Wolfram, 1991). As a consequence, distinctly indigenous ways of speaking English have been maintained. Phonological, semantic, syntactic, and pragmatic characteristics of some **Indian English** dialects have been described by Bayles & Harris (1982), Fletcher (1983), Weeks (1975), and Wolfram (1984). Bayles and Harris (1982) noted linguistic variations in the English spoken by Papago (Tohono O'odham) children involving verbs, auxiliary verbs, adjectives, prepositions, and personal pronouns. These variations appeared to correspond with grammatical rules of the Papago language. For example, in Papago, tense is not marked by verbs but may be expressed by adverbs of time. Thus, a Papago child speaking English might say, "His shirt got unzipper" (p. 17).

An example of both linguistic and dialectal variation among one Native American group is provided by Grobsmith (1979). She reported that the Rosebud Sioux demonstrate five varieties of speaking: two are forms of Lakota, and the other three are nonstandard English varieties. The two forms of Lakota represent formal and informal speech styles. The formal Lakota which is context specific, is reserved for traditional healing rituals and is restricted to individuals considered to be **good speakers** (e.g., medicine men, public orators, and elders). The informal Lakota form is the common, everyday speech spoken by persons on the reservation. Level of acculturation determines who speaks the other three nonstandard English dialects. The first is a form generally spoken by elderly full-blood Sioux, the second is used by native speakers who have encountered off-reservation experiences with regular exposure to English, and the third is spoken by younger Indians and non-Indians living in the reservation area.

U.S. governmental policy toward native language use has radically changed over time. Previous assimilation and termination policies played a major role in the decrease of native language use. However, the recent shift to Native American self-determination has resulted in native language revival efforts (Reyhner, 1988). The Native American Languages Act of 1990 recognized the important of traditional native languages to the survival of Native American cultural identity, and ensures that the U.S. government acts together with Native Americans in preserving and promoting the use of native languages.

## FACTORS IMPACTING ON ACADEMIC SUCCESS

Living in two worlds requires the development of bicultural knowledge and skills. Both students and faculty must have knowledge of both the Native American and mainstream culture if Native American students are to be successful in the university environment. They must understand how students' culture affects their language preferences, social interactions, and communication styles. Faculty can facilitate students' effective coping and learning abilities by functioning as cultural brokers who provide students with the necessary skills to function in the mainstream world without devaluing the students' own culture.

### Cultural Dimensions

Mainstream educational philosophy assumes a particular value system regarding the focus of human behavior and how people relate to one another. In addition, formal education requires the ability to use a literate communicative style with specific types of narrative and expository genres. These value systems and genres of mainstream schools frequently differ from value systems and language genres of culturally nondominate students. Several frameworks have been suggested to understand these cultural variations in beliefs and communication patterns. The broadest and most encompassing dimensions of cultural variability that have been isolated are individualism and collectivism views, and low and high context communication. Where mainstream culture tends to be individualistic, Native American cultures tend to be collectivistic. Individualistic cultures emphasize the individual's goals, while collectivistic cultures stress that group goals have precedence over the individual's goals. In individualistic cultures, people solely look after themselves and their immediate family, while in collectivistic cultures, people who belong to ingroups or collectives look after each other in exchange for loyalty (Hofstede & Bond, 1984). The **I** identity in individualistic cultures has precedence over the **we** identity in collectivistic cultures. Individualistic cultures emphasize the individuals' initiative and achievements. Collectivistic cultures emphasize the goals, needs, and views of the group over those of the individual; the social norms of the group rather than individual pleasure; the shared group beliefs rather than unique individual beliefs; and place a value on cooperation with group members rather than maximizing individual outcomes.

Hall (1959; 1976; 1983) differentiated cultures on the basis of the communication style that predominates in the culture. A high context communication or message is one in which "most of the information is either in the physical context or internalized in the person, while very little is in the coded, explicit, transmitted part of the message" (1976, p. 79). In contrast, a low context communication or message is one in which "the mass of the information is vested in the explicit code" (Hall, 1976, p. 79). While no culture exists at either end of the low or high context continuum, the communication style of the mainstream United States culture falls toward the lower end, slightly above those of German, Scandinavian, and Swiss cultures. Communication styles of most Asian and Native American cultures fall toward the high context end of the continuum. The level of context affects the functions of communication (why people talk), the topics of communication (what people talk about), and the structure of communication (how people organize what they talk about). Gundykunst and Ting-Toomey (1989) view the dimensions of low and high context communication, and individualism versus collectivism as isomorphic because cultures that Hall labels as low context are all individualistic while those labeled as high context are all collectivistic. It, therefore, appears that low and high context communication are the predominant forms of communication in individualistic and collectivistic cultures, respectively.

Kluckhohn and Strodtbeck's (1961) value orientation taxonomy provides an additional perspective on cultural variation. They proposed five problems all cultures must deal with. These issues give rise to five corresponding value orientations. The issues and value orientations include:

1. **How do humans relate to one another? Relational orientation,** or the individualistic versus collectivistic construct discussed earlier.

2. **What is the character of innate human nature? Human nature orientation** where human beings are innately good, evil, or neutral with a combination of good and evil.

3. **What is the temporal focus of human life? Time orientation** where life is concerned with the past, present, or future. Cultural systems, such as many Native American cultures, highly value traditions or **past** orientations. Systems with **present** orientations pay relatively little attention to traditions or what might happen in the future. For example, some Hispanic cultures believe that humans are victims of natural forces. In **future** oriented cultures, change is highly valued such as with mainstream U.S. culture.

4. **What is the focus of human activity? Activity orientation** emphasizes self-expression on being, being-in-becoming, or doing in activities. In the **being** orientation, the kinds of activities that are performed are "spontaneous expressions of what are conceived to be given in the human personality" (p. 16). Some traditional Hispanic value this **being** orientation. They believe that humans are born with innate worth and importance. They cannot be held accountable for their lot in life. Status is possessed by existing, and everyone is entitled to **respecto.** The being-in-becoming orientation, which is characteristic of many Native Americans, is concerned with who we are, not what we can or have accomplished. The focus in human activity is on striving for an integrated whole in the development of self. Mainstream U.S. culture epitomizes the **doing** orientation, in which there is "a demand for the kind of activity that results in accomplishments that are measurable by standards conceived to be external to the acting individual" (p. 17).

5. **What is the relation of man to nature? The human environment orientation** can be categorized into mastery over nature, harmony with the nature or subjusation to nature orientations. **Mastery over nature** involves the perspective that all natural forces can and should be overcome and/or put to use by humans (e.g., mainstream U.S. culture). The **harmony with nature** orientation makes no distinction between or among human life, nature, and the supernatural (e.g., traditional Chinese and Native American cultures). **Subjugation to nature** involves the belief that nothing can be done to control nature, and thus individuals must accept their fate (e.g., traditional Spanish-American cultures).

These three frameworks for describing cultures (collectivistic versus individualistic, high versus low context, and values orientations) can aid faculty in understanding the types of conflicts Native American students experience in the university environment.

## Communication Variable

There are communication variables that may potentially impact upon a Native American student's performance in higher education. These variables, however, will not apply to all Native American students, so care must be taken to achieve a balance between being sensitive to cultural characteristics and stereotyping (Cole, 1989). This can be accomplished through examination of attributes specific to each Native American student's cultural background.

### Verbal Communication Styles

**Narratives.** Narrative genres which exist in all cultures are particularly susceptible to the influence of culture. Cross-cultural variations are evident in terms of functions and genres of narratives, content and thematic emphasis, structural organization and style, who is allowed to produce narratives, and how children are socialized into understanding and producing narratives (Westby, 1992).

Native Americans maintain rich oral traditions that are the central means of communication among their societies. Oral traditions serve many purposes, including defining cultural values and traditions, teaching and maintaining native languages, entertaining, communication between past and present generations, and teaching social and cultural skills. The coyote stories of the North American Indians for example, have been likened to Aesop's fables and exemplify indirect means of teaching socially appropriate behavior. Many varieties of oral traditions exist, including stories, prayers, songs, chants, and genealogical accounts (Benally, 1990).

University programs in health and education often require that students use narratives to relate their own experiences, and to record the case histories of clients they serve. Narratives of U.S. mainstream cultures are organized linearly. They begin with some disruptive initiating event to which persons must respond with goal-directed actions that lead to an outcome. Effective narratives of mainstream culture should have a theme or plot. Native American narratives do not generally follow the mainstream story structure format. Native American narratives portray a different view of space, time, and motion than do narratives produced by persons from Western cultures (Highwater, 1981). In most Navajo stories, plots are de-emphasized, and a good deal of attention is given to describing events such as walking and the landscape (Westby, 1992). The emphasis in the storytelling process is on detail, rather than temporal sequence or major points (Rhodes, 1988). There may be an attempt towards sequencing events in time, however, if details are remembered out of sequence, they are likely to be inserted as they are recalled. When discussing texts produced by Native American students, Benally (cited in Westby, in press) observed, "Navajo thought is like Indian fry bread. An idea bubbles up here, then another idea over there, and another idea there." The whole picture, including the details, the context, and the feelings, is as important as the main points (Rhodes, 1988). Part of the reason for the apparent lack of plot or goal-directed behavior in the Navajo stories may be related to the Indian value of living in harmony with nature. Such a world view does not require that persons try to change their world, but rather that they learn to live in and with their world.

To persons from the mainstream U.S. society, Native American stories may not seem like stories (Westby, 1992). Indeed, oral narratives of Native Americans are often described by Anglo Americans as **unorganized** and **rambling** (Cooley & Lujan, 1982). However, close analysis of speeches made by Native American students and elders reveal an organization that reflects cultural integrity. Cooley and Lujan (1982) reported that Native American students model the structure of their speeches after exemplars from elders, that speeches tend to be organized according to implicit and not explicit relationships between topics; and that lack of across-topic cohesion exists. These features are in accordance with a culture that fosters respect for elders and a preference for ambiguity. From a Native American perspective, there is no need for cohesive ties across topic changes since an implicit commonality exists across subjects that binds them together. The differences in discourse organization, however, can result in Native American students seeming deficient in language skills in the university environment because their narratives do not have an explicit point or theme, and their expository texts do not have explicit topic sentences and supporting statements.

**Social Communicative Interactions**

Not only are the functions, structures, and styles of discourse different across cultures, but also the rules about who talks to whom, about what, and when. Philips (1983) elucidates the cultural conflict Indian children experience between their community socialization experiences and their classroom socialization. In her ethnographic study of Native American elementary school children on the Warm Springs Indian Reservation in Oregon, Philips asserted that the children's preschool and community socialization prepared them to communicate nonverbally and verbally in ways that are in conflict with typical mainstream classroom communication patterns. She additionally noted differences in verbal communication patterns, in comparison to Anglo age-matched peers. Indian children tended to participate less as speakers, respond less often when specifically requested to speak, use interruption less frequently as a device for **getting the floor,** and less often behaved in ways that indicate to the teacher that they wished to speak. Scollon and Scollon (1981) noted that Athabaskan Indians avoid direct questions, have long pauses between conversational turns, and avoid explicit direct comments about others.

Cultural preferences for indirectness and ambiguity that are characteristics of high context communication are common among some Indian people (Zepeda, 1990). Often, Native American cultures stress the use of indirect forms in making requests. For instance, at an early age, Navajo children learn to ask for information indirectly, using forms to express that they **wish** something were true rather than using more direct forms to indicate their wants and needs (Saville-Troike, 1989). As a result, metaphors and proverbs, which provide a means of depersonalizing and allowing for more indirectness, are commonly used by Indian elders in teaching their youth.

Both the high context nature of Native American communication, and the collectivistic orientation of Native American culture account for many aspects of social communication interaction. While Saville-Troike (1989) has cautioned against ethnocentric interpretations, teachers in mainstream academic settings sometimes report that Native American students appear verbally reticent and unresponsive in the classroom, noting that they do not ask questions or volunteer answers to questions (Dilworth, Pipes & Weeks, 1991). Students may not volunteer answers to questions because in a collectivistic culture, it is important not to draw attention to oneself. Rather, one should be humble, and not seek attention or praise. Culture dictates the asking of questions. Some Native American university students in our settings report that they did not feel comfortable asking questions to persons of authority (e.g., professors, clinical supervisors) since they are taught at a young age that this is impolite behavior.

Collectivistic cultures discourage competition and individual recognition but encourage group cohesion and consensus. Rather, many Native American tribal groups maintain values such as generosity and sharing, cooperation and group harmony. Indian persons who are held in the highest esteem are those who have achieved success helping others, rather than helping oneself (Mankiller, 1991). Wealth is not likely defined as an abundance of material acquisitions. Rather, wealth may relate to the size of one's family. Native American students express conflict in mainstream educational settings that emphasize individual achievement and competition (Dilworth et al., 1991). Deeply rooted cultural teaching are in opposition with an environment in which they are asked to excel and compete with their peers. At home, they are taught to avoid drawing attention to oneself, or to act as if they are better than another person (Philips, 1983).

In educational settings, Native American students have been observed to engage in a high frequency of cross-talk (i.e., peer verbal exchange during a **lecture** situation) (Dilworth et al., 1991; Philip, 1983). Although peer interaction and cooperative effort are highly valued in many Indian cultures, demonstrating such behavior puts Indian students at risk in the educational environment. Mainstream teachers tend to view these behaviors as inattentive, rude, and even as disrespectful. Similar behaviors have been observed among Native American adults. For example, while giving an inservice to Native American staff and parents at an Indian Head Start, an Anglo presenter experienced cultural conflict when the behaviors of the audience differed from her expectations. Additionally, rather than listening to her presentation, the audience talked among themselves. Instead of remaining in their seats during the talk, the audience meandered in and out of the room. The audience failed to look at the presenter as she spoke and seemed to be ignoring her. Initially, the presenter assumed her presentation was a failure, and that the audience was disinterested in her content. However, following a long pause at the end of the presenter's talk, audience members initiated comments that demonstrated that they had, indeed, been listening and were interested.

## Nonverbal Communication Style

Just as culture influences verbal communicative behavior, it also impacts on nonverbal communication. In high context cultures, much information is conveyed nonverbally than verbally.

**Eye Contact.** Faculty often cite a lack of eye contact as one of the most notable nonverbal communication differences between Native American and White students. Some Native Americans consider it rude and disrespectful to make direct eye contact with authority figures. A bowed head is a sign of respect (Harris, 1982). It is important to note that Native Americans do not demonstrate an absence of eye contact. Rather, their culture may reinforce a different schedule and patterning of eye contact.

**Use of Silence.** Faculty often describe Native American students as quieter than White students in the classroom (Philips, 1983; Dilworth et al., 1991; Greenbaum, 1985; Saville-Troike, 1989). As previously mentioned, they may be less likely to initiate a verbal exchange or volunteer a verbal response. This verbal reticence in the classroom may reflect a cultural reinforcement of learning through silent listening and watching (Harris, 1985), as well as respect for rank and authority (Dilworth et al., 1991). Also, response time differs where Native Americans may pause for up to several minutes before responding to a question or taking a turn in conversation (Saville-Troike, 1989). Faster-paced mainstream professors and students might respond to these delays with impatience or find them embarrassing, because they are unaccustomed to silent pauses during conversation. In observing groups of Anglo and Native American students, the Native American students appeared to have difficulty entering into conversations, and when they did, they were frequently interrupted by the Anglo students. Informing the members of the student group about pause time differences facilitated student interactions, but did not totally resolve the tendency for Anglo students to take charge of the conversation.

As Basso (1970) noted, Native Americans are reputed to have a preference for remaining silent, and to speak only when absolutely necessary. An ethnocentric interpretation of this behavior might lead to the conclusion that Native Americans are either language impaired or are antisocial. In other instances, cultural interpretations for silent behavior among Native Americans are numerous (Basso, 1970). For example, Basso further reported that among certain situations in Apache tribal cultures, silence is expected, particularly when meeting strangers, interacting during initial periods of courtship, during reunions of parents and children following a child's long absence, being **cussed out,** and being with people who are sad. The similarity among these situations is that the participants perceive their relationship with the other person as ambiguous. While they are silent, Native Americans are reducing the ambiguous relationship by getting to know the person through watching and listening (Basso, 1970). Perhaps, then, the relative silence of some Native American students in the classroom is a reflection of a feeling of ambiguity about their relationships with the professor and other students, and their role in a culturally alien setting.

**Listening Behavior.** Listening behavior varies cross-culturally. It is important for faculty to realize this fact to avoid misinterpretation of the behavior. Mainstream educational settings reinforce domination and control of talk by a single individual, the professor. Typically, it is the professor who determines who talks and when. Many Indian cultures are group rather than individual oriented. Thus, Native American students may be less likely than Anglo students to perceive a sharp distinction between the audience and the speaker, and might distribute their attention over the entire group rather than solely on the professor. Philips (1983) differentiated the listening behavior of Native American and Anglo elementary age children, specifically stating that Indian children provide less feedback (e.g., head nods) to show speakers that they are attending, interject fewer comments when the teacher is talking to indicate that they have heard what was said, and gaze less often at the teacher and more often at their peers. Sometimes faculty may wrongly interpret the lack of directed gaze as an indication of the student's inattentiveness or ill preparedness.

## Cognitive and Learning Styles

It is well known that different individuals favor different learning styles. The approach that an individual takes to learning and the demonstration of learning is, however, culturally determined. Additionally, early socialization experiences influence the ways in which children learn prior to their entering school (Philips, 1983; Swisher & Deyhle, 1989). It is our observation that many Native American students' early socialization practices continue to exert considerable influence on their learning behavior into adulthood. Suggesting that a specific **Indian** learning style predominates can perpetuate negative stereotyping. There is no absolute Indian learning style that exists (Henry & Pepper, 1990).

However, Native Americans collectively demonstrate some particular learning style tendencies that warrant consideration.

Many Native American cultures stress listening and watching as the preferred means of learning skills (Harris, 1982; Harris, 1985; Henry & Pepper, 1990; Dilworth et al., 1991; Swisher & Deyhle, 1989). Much of the formal learning that occurs in Indian communities is nonverbal in nature (Harris, 1985; Locust, 1988; Henry & Pepper, 1990). Verbal interaction between the child and caregiver is minimal when Indian children learn the skills and customs important to their cultures (e.g., weaving, singing, dancing, and basketry). It is not unusual for Native American children to sit passively and observe for long periods of time, participating only as a spectator. Verbal instruction is viewed as unnecessary and redundant, since the child shares close proximity to the observable action (Henry & Pepper, 1990). Demonstration of skill is accomplished through physical evidence (e.g., a well performed dance) or material evidence (e.g., a woven rug), rather than verbal performance (Harris, 1985). This preference for visual learning continues into college. When Native American students were questioned regarding which classes they found learning to be the easiest, they tended to report preferences for anatomy classes because there were so many pictures in the book, the instructors used three dimensional models and the laboratory classes allowed a watching and hands-on learning experience.

For many Native American students, competence precedes performance in the demonstration of new skills. Trial and error learning, and close approximations are not reinforced in many Native American cultures (Swisher & Deyhle, 1989; Dilworth et al., 1991). Swisher & Deyhle ( 1989) provide numerous, cross-tribal examples which suggest that many Native American students are uncomfortable performing new skills unless allowed ample time to practice and perfect them in private. For instance, Navajo children favor observing an activity many times before attempting public performance of the activity. Oglala Sioux children prefer initial observation, then self-testing in private, followed by demonstration of a task as sequential steps in learning. And Yaqui children avoid unfamiliar ground where trial and error learning is required (Swisher & Deyhle, 1989). **Child talk** or **baby talk** is not often encouraged for children speaking a tribal language (Harris, 1985). Rather, the children are discouraged from publically using the language until they have mastered it. Often, beginning clinical training experiences as part of an allied health program, can be difficult for Native American college students. This is because they are immediately expected to translate theoretical information into practical activities for clients, while having had little or no opportunity to observe how this is done.

Native American thought processes have been described as being circular and holistic, with the whole being more important than the parts. In contrast to the U.S. model of formal education, which is linear in nature, traditional Indian education is circular in nature. Thus, there is evidence to suggest that Indian youth appear to learn best when information is presented to them in this latter way (Emerson, cited in Locust, 1988). Locust (1988) vividly described this learning model:

> Indian children learn by watching their elders, by having the grandparents identify for them the whole of the task, the complete circle, the perfection of completion. The whole is then marked into meaningful parts, just as the wheel is divided into the four sacred points of life itself. From these reference points on the circle, the elder begins to teach, always relating the parts to the whole, not treating them in isolation—for a part must remain in the whole or the circle is broken—but in reference to the whole, so there is comprehension of the entire task, not just completion of the work (p. 115).

So, parts can be studied, but only in relationship to the whole (Rhodes, 1988). Collectively, Native American students do better on global processing tasks (i.e., those that emphasize the whole and the relationships between parts) than on analytic processing tasks (i.e., those that process individual parts sequentially) (More, 1987). Indeed, the first author experienced this situation in tutoring undergraduate and graduate Native American students. Students initially expressed discomfort discussing the speech mechanism in terms of the respiratory, laryngeal, articulatory, and resonatory subsystems and in dividing language into the components of form, content, and use.

More (1987) summarized research findings pertinent to Native American learning styles. He noted that relative strengths included processing visual spatial information, using imagery for coding and understanding, simultaneous processing (i.e., tasks that require synthesis of separate elements into a group), and global processing on both verbal and nonverbal tasks. Relative weaknesses were observed with sequential processing, verbal coding, and verbal understanding. Again, More reported a **watch-then-do** rather than trial and error preference to learning. Yet most university programs rely on a verbal, sequential learning process.

## Attitudes and Beliefs Regarding Health and Illness

Communication and social interaction patterns and learning styles have a major impact on Native American students' university performance. Attitudes about health and illness, however, impact on students' behaviors in academic and clinical settings. For most Native Americans, spirituality is an integral part of life. Locust (1986) summarized Native American spiritual beliefs that are common to the majority of tribes. Most Native Americans believe that all creation has a spiritual basis, where plants, animals, and inanimate objects in nature (e.g., lightening, stones, soil) all are viewed as possessing spirits, and where the spirit world communicates with the physical world (Locust, 1986). Spirits exist both prior to entering a physical body and after that body dies. Health, or wellness, is defined as harmony in body, mind, and spirit (Locust, 1986). Thus, wellness depends not only on a healthy physical state, but a healthy spiritual state. Harmony does not equal utopia or perfection, but, rather, is described as an attitude toward life that creates peace (Locust, 1986). Illness, or unwellness, is defined as disharmony in body, mind, or spirit. If one of the three parts is out of harmony, it will adversely affect the others. Many Native Americans believe illness has two possible causes: natural illness caused by violation of a tribal taboo, and unnatural illness caused by witchcraft (Locust, 1986).

Most Indian cultures do not differentiate between beliefs about religion and beliefs about health. Worship and healing are not separated. Thus, no differences exist between religion and medicine, or between a church and a hospital (Locust, 1986). When a Native American person is out of harmony, all three components of being must be treated: the mind, the spirit, and the body. For a Native American, what constitutes a cure from a medical doctor may only reflect treatment of the symptoms (Locust, 1986). Depending on the degree of acculturation a particular Native American experiences, treatment of illnesses may consist of a combination of modern Western medical practice and traditional Indian medicine. The medical doctor treats the physical ailments, and a medicine person helps the individual heal himself/herself by restoring harmony among mind, body, and spirit (Locust, 1986). Even a highly acculturated Native American student may return to traditional healing during times of stress. For example, one of our students was experiencing a reportedly intense academic semester. She became ill with a cold and the flu. Several visits to the local public health clinic did not alleviate her symptoms. Although she has not used traditional medicine for many years, she called her mother to arrange for her to see the medicine man. She then made an eight hour trip home to see her medicine man.

Native Americans are described as possessing a **beautiful blindness** toward disabilities. Persons who are labelled as disabled by non-Indians may not be considered as such by Indians. For example, if mentally retarded Indian persons serve as functional, contributing members within their community, they are not viewed as handicapped. Many traditional Indian languages have no words for **handicapped, disabled, retarded.** Rather, they provide descriptive terms that create a visual image of the disability, such as **One-Arm, One-Who-Walks-with-a-Limp.** Locust (1988) reported that an Indian who limped badly as a result of a congenital hip dislocation was not considered handicapped. However, after undergoing surgery to correct the hip deformity, the Indian was considered handicapped, because he could no longer straddle and ride a horse.

It is imperative that educators understand Native American beliefs regarding health and illness. They are the core beliefs of tribal cultures, and are fundamental to the health and spirituality of Indian students (Locust, 1988). Cultural beliefs regarding health and sickness may put Native American students at risk for culture conflict in mainstream educational settings. For instance, the educational institution's definition of sickness and the Indian student's concept of illness may vary considerably. As Western medicine is based on treating physical symptoms, school personnel are quick to recognize and excuse students from classes for symptoms such as fever, vomiting, or physical pain. In contrast, it is unlikely that an educational institution will recognize spiritual sickness, such as **ghost sickness,** which produces lethargy and a nonspecific feeling of unwellness, and is caused by spirits of dead relatives calling the student to join them (Locust, 1988). Thus, a student may face ridicule and punishment on his/her return to the educational institution, since the institution does not consider **ghost sickness** as one of its allowable absences. Also, the student's return to the educational institution may be delayed for a several days because possibly the healing ceremonies that the student underwent utilized pungent herbs, and, thus, bathing was contraindicated for a few days (Locust, 1988).

Many Native Americans believe that it is wrong to mutilate an animal's body, and that retribution will be served for doing so. Biology classes that require dissection of animals present a dissonant situation for Indian students. Most will elect to not dissect. As a result, they may risk failing the class to avoid the disastrous consequences for themselves or their families that breaking of the taboo might bring (Locust, 1988).

## STRATEGIES FOR ACADEMIC ACHIEVEMENT AND ADJUSTMENT

In our work with Native American university students, strategies are implemented to enhance cultural relevance in the curriculum, and to facilitate recruitment and retention of Indian students. Strategies for academic achievement are not necessary to implement with all Native American students. The degree of acculturation, and the individual student's level of comfort in the mainstream institutional setting, will determine the amount and type of strategies required. Students in our programs have identified faculty support and a mentoring relationship as crucial to their academic success and adjustment to the university setting.

### Faculty Role as a Cultural Broker

As mentors, faculty can model the role of cultural broker for students. In this capacity, faculty helps bridge cultural gaps by negotiating between the student's culture and the institution's culture. The role of a cultural broker is multifaceted and involves much more than simply "showing students the ropes." It often involves teaching specific cross-cultural survival strategies. We advocate role playing, as a means of teaching Native American students the different patterns of social interactions they may need to effectively participate in mainstream society. Role playing can demonstrate different ways of behaving as a cultural choice.

### Oral Interactive Strategies

In this chapter, we have discussed a number of differences in the verbal and nonverbal communication styles between Native American and mainstream students, and have illustrated how these may create cultural conflict for Indian students in the educational setting. Less acculturated Native American students can, however, be taught specific oral interactive strategies that parallel mainstream communicative interactions. For instance, we have role played such situations as the formal admission interview situation with our students. Students are taught the expectations of the situation, are given suggestions for specific forms of interaction, and then given opportunities to rehearse these interaction. We discuss the fact that the interviewer will expect the interviewee to ask questions, make comments, and discuss his/her qualifications and accomplishments.

Clinical supervisors in our speech-language pathology and audiology training programs have noted differences between Native American students and Anglo students during supervisor and supervisee interactions. They found that, as a group, Native American students tend not to initiate, ask questions, or **take charge** of management issues. Additionally, supervisors have observed special tendencies about Native American clinicians during therapy sessions: not verbally reinforcing the client enough or enthusiastically, letting the client take control of the session, not providing clients with enough modelling, and allowing for too much silence to persist during therapy sessions. However, these patterns of clinical interactions appear to mirror family childrearing practices and, therefore, should be addressed as differences and not as deficiencies.

Traditional Native American childrearing practices have been described as permissive in comparison to mainstream societal practices (Henry & Pepper, 1990; Dilworth et al., 1991). This misconception likely arises from the observation that Indian childrearing practices stress self-exploration and limit restriction. During the preschool years, Indian children are trained to be self-reliant and independent by having the freedom to make many of their own choices. Many Indian parents view childhood as a time to discover the world, and nurture curiosity through experimenting and testing. Individual autonomy is respected. Noninterference is stressed, where Indian children are taught not to interfere in others' affairs (Henry & Pepper, 1990). Indian parents are unlikely, even at the preschool level, to interfere with their children's choices (Dilworth et al., 1991). While Anglo mothers interpret active speech and physical behavior in a positive regard, Navajo mothers interpret the same behaviors as rude, restless, self-centered, and undisciplined. Additionally, where Anglo mothers use a verbal means to obtain their infant's attention, Navajo mothers remain silent and use their eyes (Harris, 1985).

To resolve conflict between the supervisor and student in the clinical training setting, supportive faculty can intercede as cultural brokers. The clinical supervisors should be inserviced as to cultural differences in communicative styles that Native American students may demonstrate.

Expectations of both parties can be clearly defined. Role-plays of supervisory conferences and therapy sessions can be enacted, thus, allowing students the opportunity to practice newly learned skills in a non-threatening environment.

## Enhancing the Curriculum Content

To enhance cultural relevance, the academic curriculum should include Native American cultural issues and concepts, particularly those pertinent to the specific native or tribal background of the enrolled students. Native American university students indicate that inclusion of native cultural characteristics and viewpoints in the standard coursework, as well as opportunities to observe and gain practicum experiences with Native Americans, is a key element to their academic and clinical success (Inglebret, 1991). Indian Nations At Risk Task Force Study (1990) supports the inclusion of Native American issues in all areas of academic study so as to "build pride, confidence, and understanding" (p. 97) for students of Native American heritage.

Inclusion of Native American issues in the standard coursework may be accomplished through use of the pyramid, unit, infusion, and course approaches described by Battle in Chapter 10. The unit approach can be effectively implemented through guest lectures by Native Americans and others knowledgeable in Native American issues. Guest lectures may be supplemented with commercial and originally made videotape presentations, reading assignments, and student projects. Assigning novels written by Native American authors may be a means of both facilitating knowledge of the culture and Indian issues, as well as, providing role models. Implementation of the infusion approach may involve presentation of content relevant to Native American cultures throughout an entire course. It can also be a by-product of the unit approach, as the course instructor becomes exposed to pertinent cross-cultural information. The course approach may involve offering an indepth single course of Native American issues as they relate to an allied health field. An important benefit of these cross-cultural educational approaches is that nonnative students in the professional education programs, potentially gain a better prospective of Native Americans. Therefore, these approaches can provide a more supportive classroom atmosphere for Native American students, as well as, provide a cultural knowledge base for students when interacting with Native American clients and families.

## Teaching Strategies

### Compatible Learning Styles

Academic success for Native American students can be facilitated through matching faculty teaching styles to student learning styles. It has been observed that Native American students often learn more when concrete or practical information is initially presented, and then is followed by presentation of abstract or more theoretical information. Additionally, it has been observed that by presenting the overall purpose and structure of a topic prior to the more typical analytic sequence of teaching, effectiveness of the learning process is achieved for Native American students (More, 1989).

Use of visual aids to accompany classroom lectures may facilitate the visual learning strengths displayed by many Native American students. Developing students' knowledge of the organization of different types of oral and written discourse and text patterns (including their own oral and written patterns). Further, by depicting these organizational patterns using diagrams, flow charts, or use of symbols may enhance the learning process for some Native American students. Some students also benefit from the use of mental imagery in understanding and recalling concepts (More, 1989).

Native American students react favorably to the use of cooperative learning strategies. A small group format can bridge inconsistencies between home and school communication and learning patterns by allowing students to incorporate their own background and language into the learning situation (Beaumont, 1992). Cummins (1988) indicated that experiential and interactive instruction empowers minority students. This is in direct contrast to an instructional approach that emphasizing transmission of information from the teacher to the students where opportunities for the student to actively integrate the new information with his or her current knowledge base, are reduced.

New information is effectively taught through an individual's preferred learning style. However, presentation of information through other learning modes is recommended. Use of a variety of learning approaches will allow students to strengthen alternative styles of learning that they might not otherwise exercise. Encouraging flexibility in the learning process can prepare students to handle variations in multicultural world (Henry & Pepper, 1990).

## Planning and Organizing

A major source of difficulty for a number of Native American students is the mainstream orientation to time, planning ahead, and organizing. Scollon and Scollon (1981) reported that Athabaskan Indians believe that it is inappropriate to speak of one's plans or to anticipate the future. Navajos believe that one should live a long life, and not limit one's potential with a specific plan or time line. In other words, if one sets a specific plan for future actions, one may limit all other possibilities for living a long life (Mike, Bidtah, & Thomas, 1989). Native American students have frequently grown up in environments where planning ahead was not done and where time was not rigidly scheduled. Thus, they may not be consciously aware of the reasons why they tend not to plan ahead.

Time is viewed differently by many Native American cultures. Activities are done "when the time is right." Although one may be told that a ceremonial dance or a chapter house meeting may begin at a particular time, this may only mean that the event will occur in the near future. The actual event may not begin for several hours. The idea of what constitutes **being late** then differs in mainstream and Indian cultures.

In our training programs, faculty complained about several students arriving late for morning classes. When project staff questioned the students, the students denied that they had been late for class. While they admitted that they arrived after all the other students, the fact that they had arrived absolved their concerns of tardiness. Project staff needed to make explicit to the student that faculty viewed any arrival after the start of class as late. One student reported that she could not arrive on time because her baby often did not waken early enough, and it was considered inappropriate for her to awaken the baby. Program staff talked with her about possible options, such as having a sister, mother, or aunt come to the house to look after the baby. They also role played with the student how she could talk with her family about the importance of her getting to class on time, and the need to wake the baby and take him to her sister's home.

Many of our students have had difficulty in meeting deadlines. They would fail to check their course syllabi to note upcoming assignments and exams, or they would not allow sufficient time to complete assignments or study for exams. To assist the students in managing their time, staff required that students purchase daily calendar books. At the beginning of the semester, staff reviewed each course syllabi with the students. Students then had to enter dates in their calendars for exams, and for the completion of projects and papers. They discussed the necessary steps for completing each assignment, and assisted students in backtracking from these dates by marking their calendars with the subcomponents of projects they would complete by specific dates. For new students in the program, staff regularly checked that the students were maintaining their time schedules. As students continued in the program, they were given increasing responsibility for developing their own plan books and determining time schedules.

## SUMMARY

A diverse student body is an asset to any educational institution. Diversity enriches the learning experience for students and faculty by providing broader perspectives and promoting flexibility in thinking. Native American students offer unique contributions to the educational setting. These contributions should be sought after and valued. One of the many strengths of Native American students is their tenacity. They are **survivors,** having fought against the odds for decades. As Philips (1983) comments:

> Even where teachers are well-intentioned, the results are similar, because the minority students' efforts to communicate are often incomprehensible to the teacher and cannot be assimilated into the framework within which the teacher operates. The teacher, then, must be seen as uncomprehending, just as the students are. And it is primarily by virtue of the teacher's position and authority that the students and not the teacher come to be defined as the ones who do not understand (p. 129).

Traditionally, teachers have blamed students for their academic difficulties. Native American students, as well as other minority students, have been expected to accommodate, adapt, and integrate into the culture of the mainstream American university. Poor performance of Native American students has been attributed to individual characteristics such as poor motivation, lack of skills, or an inability to "deal with a difficult situation." While it may be true that Native American students confront a difficult situation on a predominately White campus, as Lin et al., (1988) remind us, the question to ask is, "Who created the difficult situation?". Perhaps it is time for educational institutions to share the onus for accommodation and create a more **user-friendly** environment for students from culturally diverse backgrounds. To continue blaming the victim is nothing short of institutionalized racism. Indeed, students must acquire mainstream knowledge and ways of communicating. Faculty, however, hold the power to allow Native American students access to the behaviors and knowledge necessary in the mainstream world or to deny them such access. Often, access has been denied, because faculty have made erroneous assumptions about students' abilities based upon their culturally determined ways of talking, thinking, and writing. The staff of our student training projects have sought to identify Native American students' issues not as the students' problems, but as issues that collectively belong to all students, clinical supervisory staff, and faculty. With this in mind, it is hoped that as educators, we can begin to clear a path that leads to success in the academic setting for all students, regardless of their cultural backgrounds.

## REFERENCES

Abenally, A.: Oral Traditions, Key to Creative Learning. Paper presented at the American Indian Languages Development Institute, The University of Arizona, Tucson, 1990.

Ahenakew, F.: Text based grammars in Cree language education. In Weryackwe, S. (Ed.): *Proceedings: Selected Papers and Biographics.* Choctaw, Sixth Annual International Native American Language Issues Institute, 1986, pp. 1–4.

Basso, K.H.: "To give up on the words": Silence in western Apache culture. *Southwestern Journal of Anthropology, 26* (3): 213–230, 1970.

Bayles, K.A. & Harris, G.: Evaluating speech-language skills in Papago Indian children. *Journal of American Indian Education, 21:* 11–21, 1982.

Beaumont, C.: Language intervention strategies for Hispanic language-learning disabled students. In Langdon, H.W. & Cheng, L.L. (Eds.): *Hispanic Children and Adults with Communication Disorders.* Gaithersburg, Aspen, 1992, pp. 272–342.

Bill, W.: *From Boarding Schools to Self Determination.* Olympia, Superintendent of Public Instruction, 1987.

Bureau of the Census. 1990 census profile. Race and Hispanic origin: *U.S. Census.* U.S. Department of Commerce, Washington, 1991.

Bureau of Indian Affairs: *American Indians Today.* Washington, Department of the Interior, 1987.

Bureau of Indian Affairs: *American Indians Today: Answers to Your Questions.* Washington, Department of the Interior, 1991.

Cole, L.: E pluribus pluribus: Multicultural imperatives for the 1990's and beyond. *ASHA, 31* (8): 65–70, 1989.

Cooley, D. & Lujan, P.: A structural analysis of speeches by Native Americans. In Barken, F., Brandt, E. & Ornstein-Garcia, J. (Eds.): *Bilingualism and Language*

*Contact: Spanish, English and Native American Languages.* New York, Teachers College Press, 1982, pp. 80–92.

Cummins, J.: Empowering Indian students: What teachers can do. In Reyher, J. (Ed.): *Teaching the Indian Child: A Bilingual/Multicultural Approach.* Billings, Eastern Montana College, 1988, pp. 301–317.

Dilworth, R.P., Pipes, M.A. & Weeks, L.E.: A cross-cultural perspective of academic and clinical preparation. *National Student Speech Language Hearing Association Journal, 18:* 56–65, 1991.

Duchene, M.: Giant law, giant education, and ant: A story about racism and Native Americans. *Harvard Educational Review, 58* (3): 354–362, 1988.

Eder, J. & Reyhner, J.: The historical background of Indian education. In Reyhner, J. (Ed.): *Teaching the Indian Child: A Bilingual/Multicultural Approach.* Billings, Eastern Montana Press, 1988, pp. 29–54.

Elliot, J.: America to the Indians: Stay in the 19th century. In *Rethinking Columbus.* Milwaukee, Rethinking Schools, 1991, p. 10.

Fixico, M.: The road to middle class Indian America. In Trafzer, C.E. (Ed.): *American Indian Identity: Today's Changing Perspectives.* Sacramento, Sierra Oaks, 1989, pp. 55–75.

Fletcher, J.: What problems do American Indians have with English? *Journal of American Indian Education, 23* (1): 1–13, 1983.

Ford, V. & Westby, C.E.: Successes and struggles of students from nondominant cultural backgrounds in an academic setting: An ethnographic study. Albuquerque, University of New Mexico, unpublished manuscript, 1992.

Green, M.F.: *Minorities on Campus: A handbook for Enhancing Diversity.* Washington, American Council on Education, 1989.

Greenbaum, P.E.: Nonverbal differences in communication styles between American Indian and Anglo elementary classrooms. *American Educational Research Journal, 22* (1): 101–115, 1985.

Grobsmith, E.S.: Styles of speaking: An analysis of Lakota communication alternatives. *Anthropological Linguistics, 21* (7): 355–361, 1979.

Gundykunst, W. & Ting-Toomey, S.: *Culture and Interpersonal Communication.* Newbury Park, Sage, 1988.

Hall, E.T.: *The Silent Language.* New York, Doubleday, 1959.

Hall, E.T.: *Beyond Culture.* New York, Doubleday, 1976.

Hall, E.T.: *The Dance of Life.* New York, Doubleday, 1983.

Harris, G.A.: ASHA interviews Gail Harris, Indian advocate. *ASHA,* June, 388–392, 1982.

Harris, G.A.: Consideration in assessing English language performance of Native American children. *Topics in Language Disorders, 5* (4): 42–52, 1985.

Heinrich, J.S.: Native Americans: What not to teach. In *Rethinking Columbus.* Milwaukee, Rethinking Schools, 1991, p. 15.

Henry, S.L. & Pepper, F.C.: Cognitive, social, and cultural effects on Indian learning style: Classroom implications. *Educational Issues of Language Minority Students, 7:* 85–97, 1990.

Highwater, J.: *The Primal Mind: Vision and Reality in Indian American.* New York, Harper & Row, 1981.

Hofstede, G. & Bond, M.: Hofstede's cultural dimensions: An independent validation using Rokeach's value survey. *Journal of Cross-Cultural Psychology, 15:* 417–433, 1984.

Indian Nations At Risk Task Force Study: Part VI—Indian nations at risk task force study. In *Toward the Year 2000: Listening to the Voice of Native America.* Washington, National Advisory Council on Indian Education, 1990, pp. 89–111.

Indian Health Service: *Trends in Indian Health 1991.* Rockville, U.S. Department of Health and Human Services, Public Health Service, 1991.

Inglebret, E.: *Retention of Native Americans in a Communication Disorders Training Program.* Paper presented at the Annual Convention of the American Speech, Language and Hearing Association, Atlanta, 1991.

Kluckhorn, F. & Strodtbeck, F.: *Variations in Value Orientation.* New York, Row, Pederson, 1961.

Lin, R., LaCounte, D. & Eder, J.: A study of Native American students in a predominantly White college. *Journal of American Indian Education, 27* (3): 8–15, 1988.

Locust, C.: *American Indian Beliefs Concerning Health and Unwellness.* Monograph, Native American Research and Training Center, College of Medicine, University of Arizona, Tucson, 1986.

Locust, C.: Wounding the spirit: Discrimination and traditional American Indian belief systems. *Harvard Educational Review, 58* (3): 315–330, 1988.

Mankiller, W.: Entering the twenty-first century on our own terms. *National Forum: The Phi Kappa Phi Journal, 71* (2): 5–6, 1991.

McArthur, E.: What language do you speak? *American Demographics, 6* (10): 32–33, 1984.

McDonald, D.: Education: The first condition. *Education Week,* 5–7, August 2, 1989.

McDonald, D.: The quest for cultural identity: 'Indian people just want to be themselves'. *Education Week,* 12–16, August 2, 1989.

Mike, E.H., Bidtah, L. & Thomas, V.: *Cultural Conflict.* Central Consolidated Schools, District 22, Title VII, Bilingual Education Program, 1989.

More, A.J.: Native Indian learning styles: A review for researchers and teachers. *Journal of American Indian Education, 27* (1): 17–29, 1987.

More, A.J.: Native Indian learning styles: A review for researchers and teachers. *Journal of American Indian Education, Special Issues:* 15–28, August, 1989.

Payne, K.T.: Cultural and linguistic groups in the United States. In Taylor, O. (Ed.): *Nature of Communication Disorders in Culturally and Linguistically Diverse Populations.* San Diego, College-Hill Press, 1986, pp. 19–46.

Philips, S.U.: *The Invisible Culture: Communication in Classroom and Community on the Warm Springs Indian Reservation.* New York, Longman, 1983.

Reeves, M.S.: The High Cost of Endurance. *Education Week,* 2–4, August 2, 1989.

Red Horse, J.: Education reform. *Journal of American Indian Education, 25* (3): 40–44, 1986.

Red Horse, J.: Spectrum of Indian family systems with illustrative modal behaviors.

In Jacobs, C. & Bowles, D. (Eds.): *Ethnicity and Race: Critical Concepts in Social Work.* Washington, National Association of Social Workers, 1988, pp. 93–95.

Reyhner, J.: Bilingual education: Teaching the native language. In Reyhner, J. (Ed.): *Teaching the Indian Child, A Bilingual/Multicultural Approach.* Billings, Eastern Montana College, 1988, pp. 10–28.

Rhodes, R.W.: Holistic teaching/learning for Native American students. *Journal of American Indian Education, 27* (2): 21–29, 1988.

Saville-Troike, M.: *The Ethnography of Communication.* New York, Basil Blackwell, 1989.

Scollon, R. & Scollon, S.B.K.: *Narrative, Literacy, and Face in Interethnic Communication.* Norwood, Ablex, 1981.

Staff.: Stuck in the horizon. *Education Week, Special Issue:* 1, August, 1989.

Swisher, K. & Deyhle, D.: The styles of learning are different, but the teaching is just the same: Suggestions for teachers of American Indian youth. *Journal of American Indian Education, Special Issue:* 1–14, August, 1989.

Tijerina, K.H. & Biemer, P.P.: The dance of Indian higher education: One step forward, two steps back. *Educational Record, 68* (4): 86–93, 1987–1988.

Weeks, T.: The Speech of Indian Children: Paralinguistic and Registral Aspects of the Yakima Dialect. Paper presented at the Annual Meeting of the National Council of Teachers of English, San Diego, 1975.

Westby, C.E.: The effects of culture on genre, structure, and style or oral and written texts. In Wallach, G.P. and Butler, K.G. (Eds.): *Language Learning Disabilities in School-Age Children and Adolescents: Some Underlying Principles and Applications.* Columbus, Charles Merrill, 1992.

Wolcott, H.F.: The teacher as an enemy. In Spindler, G. (Ed.): *Education and Cultural Processes.* Prospect Heights, Waveland Press, 1987, pp. 136–150.

Wolfram, W.: Unmarked tense in American Indian English. *American Speech, 59* (1): 31–50, 1984.

Wolfram, W.: *Dialects and American English.* Englewood Cliffs, Prentice Hall, 1991.

Wright, B. & Tierney, W.G.: American Indian in higher education: A history of cultural conflict. *Change, 23* (2): 11–18, 1991.

Zepeda, O.: *A Papago Grammar.* Tucson, University of Arizona Press, 1988.

Zepeda, O.: Personal Communication, 1990.

**APPENDIX 7-A: SPECTRUM OF INDIAN FAMILY SYSTEMS WITH ILLUSTRATIVE MODAL BEHAVIORS**

| | *MODAL BEHAVIORS* | | | | |
| --- | --- | --- | --- | --- | --- |
| *FAMILY TYPE* | *LANGUAGE* | *KIN STRUCTURE* | *RELIGION* | *LAND* | *HEALTH BEHAVIOR* |
| Transitional | Prefers native language in the home and intimate social relations, but not in community use and other external relations. Language homogeneity across generations declines. | Extended kin system is fractured, but modified system will be available if a colony is organized. Fractured, isolated groups form nuclear households. System opens to outsiders, particularly among children. | Retains beliefs associated with historic custom, but struggles to act it out on a daily basis because of absence of natural system. Travels frequently to homeland to reinforce religion through ritual ceremonies. | Retains sacred view of land and acts this out when visiting homeland. However, begins to acquire utilitarian view of residence and often other land in general. | Retains traditional sense of the etiology of disease and makes frequent trips to homeland for health care. Daily ritual behavior in health matters begins to deteriorate, and American institutional services begin to dominate. |
| Bicultural | English is preferred language in the home and community. Parents may know native language, but homogeneity across generations declines rapidly. | Nuclear household arrangements predominate, but a strong sense of American Indian identity leads to fictive extended kin structures. Prefers social relations with other American Indians and system is open to them. | Retains a symbolic sense of native religion, but does not practice it on a daily basis. Adopts new religion, but does not adapt it to traditional beliefs; hence, ritual customs are absent. | Aware of the symbolic meaning of the sacredness of land, but adopts utilitarian behaviors with respect to land in general. | Uses American institutional services, but prefers services that involve other American Indians. Has developed extensive parallel network of all-Indian services that mirror systems common to the general population. Prefers non-Indian view on etiology of disease. |

| FAMILY TYPE | MODAL BEHAVIORS | | | | |
| --- | --- | --- | --- | --- | --- |
| | LANGUAGE | KIN STRUCTURE | RELIGION | LAND | HEALTH BEHAVIOR |
| Acculturated | English is preferred language in the home and community. Exhibits total loss of native language. | Nuclear households outside of general parameters of an identifiable American Indian community. Primary social relations are with non-Indians and no fictive system develops. System is open. | Converts to nonnative religion and loses ties to historic religious customs and practices. | Not generally concerned with sacredness of land. Except in narrow terms of secular views on conversation, land view is utilitarian. | Prefers American institutional care without need for all-Indian parallel systems. Adopts non-Indian view on the etiology of disease. |
| Panrenaissance | English generally is the primary language in the home and community. Language renewal is emphasized, but homogeneity across generations is low. | Nuclear household arrangements predominate, but a strong effort to reorganize natural extended kin systems prevails. Fictive kin arrangements are common and system is open. | Attempts to revitalize aspects of historic ritual custom. Generally organizes hybrid forms to replicate traditional religious beliefs. | Revitalizes the sacred view of land, but retains utilitarian views with respect to residence and other property in general. | Is extremely critical of American institutional system. Actively pursues expansion of all-Indian parallel networks of care. Attempts to revitalize historic beliefs around the etiology of disease. |

From Red Horse, J.: Spectrum of Indian family systems with illustrative modal behavior. In Jacobs, C. & Bowles, D. (Eds.): *Ethnicity and Race: Critical Concepts in Social Work*. Courtesy of National Association of Social Workers, 1988, pp. 93–94.

# Chapter 8

# FACULTY CHALLENGES IN THE EDUCATION OF FOREIGN-BORN STUDENTS

Li-Rong Lilly Cheng

## INTRODUCTION

Foreign-born students who come to the United States to study comprise 8 percent of the student population in American institutions of higher education (Cheng, 1990). A majority of these students come from Taiwan, China, Japan, India, Latin America, Korea, and Arab countries. These foreign-born students represent a heterogeneous group in terms of their native language, socioeconomic and occupational status, as well as their cultural and religious beliefs and values. These factors permeate their individual views of education and health, and their unique styles of communication and learning. A common element shared by this diverse group of students, however, is English as a Second Language (ESL). Additionally, those adults who newly immigrate to the United States and immediately begin pursuing academic studies in higher education, experience similar educational obstacles to those of the non-immigrant foreign-born ESL students (Green, 1989).

Most foreign students pursue degrees in science, mathematics, engineering, and business administration (Green, 1989). It is vital, however, that more of these students be recruited and retained in the professional educational programs of allied health. There are increasingly important professional health care and educational roles that these foreign students can assume upon returning to their countries of origin (Cole, 1989). Foreign-born students who receive American educational degrees can help to fill both the shortages that exist in healthcare and higher education in their country of origin. Additionally, where students' country of

The information presented in this chapter is abstracted from previous works by the author including Cheng, L.: Ethnic, cultural, linguistic diversity: Challenges and opportunities for faculty, students and curriculum. In Ripich, D. (Ed.): *The Graduate Council of Communication Sciences and Disorders 1989 Annual Conference Proceedings.* Tampa, 1990, pp. 37–61.

origin fails to offer professional degrees in certain of the allied health disciplines, students should be encouraged to pursue both U.S. masters' and doctoral degrees before returning to their home country. These students will then be prepared to develop professional allied health programs at universities in their own countries.

Foreign students, as well as American faculty, bring to the educational setting a set of internalized cultural values and beliefs that are second nature to them, but which affect both students' and faculty's communicative and social interactive competencies, as well as students' learning competencies and faculty's teaching effectiveness. Some foreign students may feel socially isolated, frustrated and self-conscious because of the difficulty they experience in communicating effectively. They may additionally feel discouraged by the negative feedback they receive from American faculty regarding their general lack of English communication skills. These skills go beyond speech intelligibility. Communication facility involves factors such as understanding the nuances of idiomatic language, correctly reading nonverbal language, as well as demonstrating appropriate pragmatic usage of the language. These aspects are, for the most part culturally determined. Because of this, it is important for American faculty and foreign students to work together to achieve cultural literacy. Just as foreign students should be encouraged to study the culture of the American institutions of higher education, faculty should become knowledgeable about the native cultures, and the learning and communication styles of their foreign students. In regard to these issues, this chapter will emphasize the educational obstacles that foreign non-American and recent adult immigrant ESL students commonly encounter when they begin their educational studies. Suggestions for faculty in assisting foreign students to adapt to the mainstream American educational environment will be outlined.

## PROBLEMS IN RECRUITING FOREIGN STUDENTS

As mentioned, it is essential that faculty in the allied health professional programs encourage foreign students to enter their programs. Some of the reasons why foreign-born and nonnative students generally have not chosen professional programs in allied health, such as audiology or speech-language pathology include the following areas (Cheng, 1991). Knowledge of these reasons may assist faculty in developing nontraditional or alternative recruitment procedures for foreign students. The three primary reasons include: stringent admission requirements, high level of academic written language competency, and verbal proficiency.

Many institutions' admission policies require foreign students to obtain high test scores in the Test of English as Foreign Language (TOEFL) and/or the Graduate Record Examination (GRE). And in some instances, students may also have to pass English written competency examinations as an admission requirement.

Often, allied health programs require students to demonstrate proficiency of written expression in both academic and clinical assignments. These tasks include critiquing research articles, conducting research, applying scientific knowledge to clinical practice, and writing clinical reports. Furthermore, foreign students may feel that they do not and never will possess the native-like spoken English language proficiency required to competently complete their clinical training.

## EDUCATIONAL OBSTACLES OF FOREIGN STUDENTS

Inaccurate perceptions and lack of familiarity with the culture, history, and contemporary experiences of different foreign student groups can lead American faculty to develop generalizations about the educational potential of foreign-born ESL students (Ramirez, 1988). As mentioned earlier, foreign student populations are heterogeneous in terms of their native language, cultural beliefs and practices, and socioeconomic status. They do, however, share some of the following problems when they enter mainstream American institutions of higher education (Cheng, 1990).

### Insufficient English Communication Competency

While some foreign students may have received English reading instruction through exposure to English textbooks, they may have had limited exposure to other types of English reading materials. Their previous experiences with written English may have been restricted to school grammar exercises, homework, and examinations. Because of this, they may experience difficulty comprehending a variety of course reading assignments. These limitations may additionally interfere with their training and practice in the linear analytical style of writing required by American mainstream educational institutions (Kaplan, 1966). Those students who have had limited exposure to spoken English may experience comprehending difficulty when listening to a faculty lecture.

Other more subtle aspects of the English language may further compound and limit foreign students' communicative competency. Such factors may include: accent, nonliteral language, pragmatic variability and nonverbal language, in addition to cultural literacy. Personal experience and prior world knowledge impact on the ability to successfully interact. The following elaborations describe these subtle components.

### Accent

Accent serves to immediately identify a person as a nonmember of the particular linguistic community (Ainsfeld, Bogo & Lambert, 1962). Accents are not characteristic of only foreign born individuals. As is apparent, everyone speaks with an accent, ranging from a Bostonian or Southern American accent to that of a Cantonese Chinese accent. An accent is determined by how an individual pronounces words. First or native language influences how an individual will produce the sounds of the English language. For example, the phoneme /f/ does not appear in Taiwanese and, therefore, the word *food* may be pronounced as /*hood*/. In some Indian dialects, voiceless plosive stops result, for example, in the word **cat** sound like **gad**. Negative attitudes toward different accents and the subtle social meanings behind these attitudes need to be examined for successful intercultural communication (Gallois & Callan, 1981; Ryan, Carranza & Molfie, 1977). The primary factor is not whether a foreign student's speech is characterized by an accent, but whether the student's speech is intelligible (Giles, 1973).

Although many foreign, nonnative speaking students communicate adequately in English they may become withdrawn and reluctant to participate in the classroom and clinical environments because of the stigma attached to speaking with an "accent." Additionally, they have already experienced communication breakdowns because of problems in making themselves understood by their faculty, peers, and clients.

### Nonliteral Language

Understanding language involves more than recognizing the surface structure. Language also involves being able to read "between the lines," and interpreting inflectional patterns as in a questioning or sarcastic tone. Nonnative speaking students may lack the linguistic awareness needed to ascertain the subtle communication intent. They may not be able to decipher the implied meaning from the literally expressed words. The nonliteral, idiomatic aspects of language are problematic for new speakers of a language. For example, a very bright Turkish student working in the school cafeteria was left confused when customers complained that his soda was **flat.** Many English words have frequently unfamiliar and contextually unobvious multiple meanings, e.g., **cool** or **bad.** Further, the same words or phrases used in one language may mean something quite different in another language. For example, the literal translation of "Turn off the light" in English is "Close the light" in Chinese. In the Vietnamese language the word **hair** may also refer to **hair, fur** and **feather.** Also, idiomatic and colloquial expressions such as "Too many cooks spoiled the broth," "Give me a break," "Break a leg," "Knock them dead," or "That's a piece of cake" are difficult for foreign speakers to grasp.

## Pragmatic Variations

The pragmatic aspects of any language refers to how the forms of the language are used to perform particular communication functions in various social settings, i.e., Who may say what to whom. Foreign and nonnative English speaking students require direction and instruction in order to follow the pragmatic rules of the English language that govern a variety of social contexts such as the classroom. Given the variety of factors that a native speaker of English must consider prior to choosing a strategy for performing a speech act, it is not surprising that the appropriate choice of a strategy is doubly challenging for foreign ESL students. For example, deciding whether a particular communication intent would best be phrased as a protest or a request. For a communication interaction to be successful, knowledge of the speech form for a particular social context must be learned by the participants (Prutting, 1982). Pragmatic variables come into play when a person, for example, walks into a kitchen and asks if there is any water. The intent is a request for a glass of water, however, the words and structure appear to reflect an inquiry.

## Nonverbal Communication

Foreign and nonnative English-speaking students may encounter additional obstacles when interpreting the nonverbal communication intentions of mainstream American instructors. Nonverbal communication (e.g., eye gaze, gestures, body movement, facial expressions), as well as pauses, silence periods, intonation patterns, and spatial arrangements are used to convey meaning and intent. These aspects of language serve to: relay messages, augment or contradict verbal communication or replace verbal communication (Leubitz, 1973). In fact, in some Asian cultures for example, social meaning is actually transmitted more through nonverbal channels than by words (Knapp, 1972). Because communication styles tend to be culturally-based, foreign students' nonverbal communication patterns may be different from those of American mainstream students and faculty. Overt effort must be exerted to assure that there has not been an intercultural mismatch of nonverbal language interpretation resulting in failed communications.

## Restricted Social, Cultural and World Knowledge

Foreign students represent a wide variety of countries and unique heritages. They bring to the academic and clinical environments, varying degrees of experience and world knowledge. They, additionally, come from different educational backgrounds with the focus on the history and cultures of their people, and may have little knowledge of U.S. society, history, and culture. Generally they have not been exposed to the same social and educational experiences as their native-born peers. Because of this lack of exposure to communicating in American social contexts, they may experience difficulty adapting to American mainstream educational settings.

Social context and the social relationships of the participants are crucial to the conversational format of all languages. Conversation involves selecting a topic of conversation, initiating a conversation, taking turns talking, maintaining a topic, and closing a conversation (Wolfram, 1992). Being in the process of acquiring and perfecting English communicative skills puts foreign and nonnative English speaking students at a loss when engaged in social discourse. Nonnative speakers have difficulty identifying communicative effectiveness from the American perspective, because this requires an understanding of the American mainstream cultural values and beliefs that significantly affect communication behaviors.

Calling someone on the telephone, for example, requires the use of certain ritualized phrases, such as "How are you?", "I have to go now," and "May I leave a message?". Vocabulary selection and syntactical form alone will not insure a socially successful communicative interchange. It is through practice and experience that foreign students become more competent. Each culture has a different set of rules that determines what behavior is considered appropriate.

Other cultural factors influence communication behavior as well. The American Eurocentric orientation produces a direct, assertive, analytical, and linear communication style. Americans are additionally characterized as being time and results-oriented. This results in the expectation of quick and direct responses. They find silence periods intolerable and have little patience for "beating around the bush." They may also view the more reflective or circular communicators who possess a collectivistic orientation as slow, even evasive and ineffective communicators (Hale-Benson, 1982). These American expectations may cause problems for foreign ESL students in classroom and clinical training environments. In the classroom, breakdowns in faculty and student interactions may result. Foreign students may have difficulty completing written course projects on time, as well as taking exams when scheduled. This may be a factor of their viewpoint or a collectivistic viewpoint, which does not reflect on present and future times.

Cummins (1981) stated that education is viewed as a formal process by most collectivistic cultures. In these cultures, reading of actual information is considered of valuable study. Many foreign students learn by observation, memorization, and patterned practice, with rote learning preferred over learning critical analysis and self-discovery. Cheng (1991) reports that collectivistic cultures view teachers as carriers of knowledge and transmitters of information. The American educational system, on the other hand, stresses critical thinking and discovery learning in a less formal and more open atmosphere. Incongruities in educational practices between Eastern and Western cultures may result in confusion, communication breakdowns, and failure to achieve on the part of many foreign students.

In the clinical setting, foreign students demonstrate difficulty interacting appropriately with clients. It is important for foreign students to gain clinical experience as an essential component of their training program in learning to apply academic course content. Cultural differences and adaption must not stand in the way of this. Cultural differences should be addressed as though the students were, for example, applying to ASHA for their Certificate of Clinical Competency, and not returning to their native countries.

Cheng (1989) provides the following example to illustrate how foreign students may become lost in classroom discussions due to their lack of familiarity with the American culture.

> Although I had heard the names Dick and Jane many times before, I must confess that I had no idea who they were. My immediate reaction was, "Were they a couple?" (like Ronald and Nancy), "Were they singing partners?" (like Simon and Garfunkel), or "Were they the names of a store?" (like Lord and Taylor). Were they cartoon characters (like Mickey and Minnie Mouse)? Were they characters from a movie (like Bonnie and Clyde)? Were they historical figures (like Franklin and Eleanor)? Were they pets (like Flipper and Lassie)?
>
> Then more thoughts came to my mind. Were they young? Were they old? Have they done something bad or good? Were they rich and famous? They were probably not designers since most designers use their full names or their last names. I was pretty sure that Dick was the name of a boy or man, and Jane was the name of a girl or woman, although I had some slight doubt, since I knew there was a song that talked about a boy named Sue. In any event, my thoughts lingered on and my desire to find out who they were increased (p. 4).

Cheng (1989) elaborated that if one is not familiar with the old elementary school-book characters of Dick and Jane, then modern-day references, such as the movie "Fun With Dick and Jane" (with George Segal and Jane Fonda) or the popular T-shirts imprinted with stick figures of Dick, will have no meaning. The primary issue here is that a lack of cultural familiarity can become an obstacle to learning. A nonnative speaker of English, for example, might be confused by a reference to Tricky Dick, even though he/she might be aware that Richard M. Nixon was a U.S. President. Although most native English speakers in the United States would automatically translate the name Tricky Dick to mean Richard Nixon, many foreign students are at risk of becoming lost in discussions that require this type of culturally-bound translation. By the same token, a reference to Watergate during a discussion may require a brief explanation in order for foreign students to understand the significance of Watergate. By being sensitive to the existence of culturally bound meanings in English, faculty may prevent misunderstandings and greatly increase the effectiveness of their communications with foreign students.

## WHAT FACULTY CAN DO
## TO EMPOWER FOREIGN STUDENTS

There is a significant need for faculty in the allied health programs to examine their methods of teaching and to endorse the resultant paradigm shifts to embrace diversity (also refer to Chapter 1). As with all students, curricular and clinical training materials must be adapted to students' cultural bases. It is most important for educators to infuse multicultural and pluralistic perspectives into their course content, approach, style of instruction and evaluation processes. It is important to consider that when students perceive a respect from others for their primary language and culture, a positive self-image and esteem is fostered for healthier educational and social development (Trueba, 1989).

Faculty can empower foreign students, and thus improve the quality of their life on campus and in the classroom and clinical environments. This can be accomplished by preparing foreign students for anticipated problem areas in a course, and by becoming proactive in helping the students adapt to the academic setting. Faculty can encourage foreign students to practice mainstream social conduct within the safety of the classroom by having them ask questions, participate in projects, seek advice, and to express their concerns. Faculty can direct foreign students to the diversity of learning resources on their campuses such as language tapes, books on American culture, writing skills classes, term paper clinics, library search services, academic skills classes, counseling and career guidance centers. Students can also be referred to accent or communication enhancement programs, when their English speech intelligibility is compromised. Faculty need to understand that students may require time to shift their styles of learning, and that students should not be expected to make great gains in a short period of time.

Programs that deal with multicultural issues and content must be sure to consider the affective domain of foreign students and the need for foreign students to maintain their own cultural identity. To improve the communicative competence of foreign students in American mainstream educational settings, bicultural identity needs to be nurtured. Improving language skills means infusing cultural literacy information into the curriculum, and providing awareness of the phonological, morphological, pragmatic, and semantic aspects of the English language, as well as the ritualized discourse patterns practiced in the classroom. Students need to be provided with opportunities for experiencing a variety of narrative styles and an explanation of the written and unwritten rules that govern these styles. They also need to know about the different occupational environments, such as schools, hospitals, health care, social and governmental systems. Students need experience in working with a wide variety of clients of different age groups and disorders. Similarities and differences in writing style, as well as models of what is appropriate, need to be explicitly discussed in detail with the students.

It is important for faculty and foreign students to work together to achieve cultural literacy (Gollnick & Chinn, 1990). While foreign students should be encouraged to study the American culture, faculty need to learn of the native cultures of their students. The following suggestions by Cheng (1989) may be helpful for faculty:

- Read about foreign countries and cities including geography, languages spoken, native foods, and the people's names and origins.
- Visit the ethnic communities in ones own city or town (e.g., Little Saigon, Little Tokyo, Little Havana, German town, Italian town) and attend their cultural exhibits and events, such as art shows and theatrical performances.
- Read well-known, classic foreign stories, and folktales.
- Conduct interviews with foreign adults and children to learn about their life histories.

Also refer to those chapters in the text that specifically describe the different cultural backgrounds of students.

The following suggestions can be made to foreign students who are trying to familiarize themselves with the American culture (Cheng, 1989, p. 5):

- Read American literature (Bettleheim, B., 1977; Von Dongen, R. & Westby, C. 1986) about famous people, both living and dead (e.g., Jesse Jackson, Robert E. Lee, John F. Kennedy, Patrick Henry).
- Read magazines, newspapers, poetry and comic books.
- Do crossword puzzles and other English word games.
- Learn words that have special multiple meanings (e.g., **petite** is not used to describe a man, and **sheepish** has negative connotations).
- Directly ask people to explain why a particular joke is funny.
- Understand social and cultural calendars (e.g., proms, the Super Bowl, the World Series, Monday night football).
- Learn about events that are culturally bound, such as Halloween, Valentine's Day, and St. Patrick's Day.
- Attend a variety of celebrations (e.g., showers, graduations, weddings).
- Eat at a variety of restaurants and study what is on the menu.
- Attend movies, theater shows, lectures, art exhibits, fashion shows, and musical performances.

- Watch and listen to the television news and listen to the radio.
- Listen to oral presentations (e.g., sports interviews, newscasts, talk shows, speeches).
- Study maps to learn the names of cities, historical and geographic landmarks (e.g., Mississippi River, Smithsonian Institute, Hearst Castle, Radio City, Lincoln Center, Arlington Memorial, the White House).
- Be an ethnographer by observing interactions and taking notes (Spindler, Spindler, Trueba & William, 1990).
- Study magazine and newspaper advertisements to learn about unfamiliar, culturally loaded items (i.e., items in which the use and meaning are culture-bound), such as kitchen items (e.g., food processor, microwave), clothing (e.g., clam diggers, Bermuda shorts), brand names (e.g., Kleenex®, Xerox®), and furniture (e.g., loveseat, waterbed).

## CONCLUSION

Foreign students provide faculty with a wide array of challenges. In order to facilitate their learning, faculty will need to examine the intricate relationship between communication and culture so as to enhance their own cross-cultural sensitivities to effectively teach foreign students. This chapter has focused on specific issues that are problematic to foreign and nonnative, English-speaking students: educational obstacles, insufficient English communicative competency, limited social, cultural and world knowledge, and improving students' cultural literacy and cross-cultural communicative competency as a means of enhancing academic success. In order to achieve cross-cultural communicative competency, both students and faculty must recognize the differences and similarities between their cultures, appreciate diversity and understand that while misunderstandings may arise, they should strive for better communication.

## REFERENCES

Ainsfeld, M., Bogo, N. & Lambert, W.: Evaluational reactions to accented English speech. *Journal of Abnormal and Social Psychology, 65:* 223–231, 1962.

Bettleheim, B.: *The Uses of Enchantment.* New York, Vintage Books, 1977.

Cheng, L.: Dick and Jane: A journey to cultural literacy. *Clinical Connections, 3* (3): 4–5, 1989.

Cheng, L.: Ethnic, cultural, linguistic diversity: Challenges and opportunities for faculty, students and curriculum: In Ripich, D. (Ed.): *The Graduate Council of Communication Sciences and Disorders 1989 Annual Conference Proceedings.* Tampa, 1990, pp. 37–61.

Cheng, L.: Recognizing diversity. *American Behavioral Scientists, 34* (2): 263–278, 1990.

Cheng, L.: *Assessing Language Performance.* Oceanside, Academic Communication Associates, 1991.

Cole, L.: Multicultural Imperatives of the 1990's. Lecture presented at the Patricia Roberts Harris Lecture Series, San Diego State University, San Diego, April 1989.

Cummins, J.: The role of primary language development in promoting educational success for language minority students. In California State Department of Education, Office of Bilingual, Bicultural Education (Ed.): *Schooling and Language Minority Students: A Theoretical Framework.* Los Angeles, Evaluation, Dissemination and Assessment Center of California State University, 1981.

Gallois, C. & Callan, G.: Personality impressions elicited by accented English. *Journal of Cross-Cultural Psychology, 12:* 347–359, 1981.

Giles, H.: Communicative effectiveness as a function of accented speech. *Speech Monographs, 40:* 330–331, 1973.

Green, M.F. (Ed.): *Minorities on Campus: A Handbook for Enhancing Diversity.* Washington, American Council on Education, 1989.

Gollnick, D., M. & Chinn, P.C.: *Multicultural Education in a Pluralistic Society.* Columbus, Merrill, 1990.

Hale-Benson, J.E.: *Black Children: Their Roots, Culture, and Learning Styles.* Baltimore, John Hopkins University, 1982.

Kaplan, R.: Cultural thought patterns in intercultural education. *Language Learning, 16:* 1–20, 1966.

Knapp, L.: *Nonverbal Communication in Human Interaction.* New York, Holt, Rinehart & Winston, 1972.

Leubitz, L.: *Nonverbal Communication: A Guide for Teachers.* Skokie, National Textbook, 1973.

Prutting, C.A.: Pragmatics as social competence. *Journal of Speech and Hearing Disorders, 47:* 123–133, 1982.

Ramirez, B.A.: Culturally and linguistically diverse children. *Teaching Exceptional Children,* Summer 1988.

Ryan, E.B., Carranza, M.A. & Moffie, R.W.: Reactions toward varying degrees of accentedness in the speech of Spanish-English bilinguals. *Language and Speech, 20:* 268–273, 1977.

Spindler, G., Spindler, L., Trueba, H. & Williams, M.: *The American Cultural Dialogue and its Transmission.* Philadelphia, Falmer, 1989.

Trueba, H.T.: *Raising Silent Voices: Educating the Linguistic Minorities for the 21st Century.* Cambridge, Newburg House, 1989.

Von Dongen, R. & Westby, C.: Building the narrative mode of thought through children's literature. *Topics in Language Disorder, 7* (1): 70–83, 1986.

Wolfram, W.: Grammatical, phonological and language use differences across cultures. In Cole, L. & Deal, V. (Eds.): *Communicative Disorders in Multicultural Populations.* Rockville, American Speech, Language and Hearing Association, 1992.

# PART THREE
# SUCCESSFUL LEARNING STRATEGIES
# AND CURRICULUM APPROACHES

## Chapter 9

# FACILITATING TEXT COMPREHENSION IN COLLEGE STUDENTS: THE PROFESSOR'S ROLE

CAROL E. WESTBY AND GERALDINE RODRIGUEZ ROUSE

## INTRODUCTION

"I read it, but I don't understand it," is a statement commonly heard from students. University faculty across the nation are increasingly expressing concern that large numbers of students do not possess the basic skills essential for college-level work. Books such as Allan Bloom's *The Closing of the American Mind* (1987) and E.D. Hirsch's *Cultural Literacy* (1989) have popularized the concern. Actual test data documents that the problem indeed exists. The New Jersey Basic Skills Council (1985) reported that only 26 percent of students entering universities in the state were sufficiently proficient in verbal skills to succeed in university curricula. Students from nondominant cultures, with the exception of Asian Americans, are disproportionately under represented at all professional degree levels (United States Bureau of Census, 1991). While statistics on entry, retention, and drop-out rates at institutions of higher learning are not easily available or are inconsistent across schools, the available data does indicate that it is difficult for large numbers of individuals, including minorities, to either enter college or to remain after acceptance.

Students from all ethnic, racial, and socioeconomic backgrounds are entering universities underprepared (Alpert, Gorth, & Allen, 1989; Carpenter & Johnson, 1991; Pugh & Pawan, 1991). There are a number of factors that contribute to students' poor academic performance. Some factors, such as family and job demands, inadequate finances, and/or discomfort in the university environment, are indirectly related to classroom achievement. Other factors, however, are more directly related to academic performance. Two factors within this latter category are: (1) underpreparation for university work, and (2) cultural patterns of

189

interacting, communicating, and learning that may affect the ways in which students approach academic learning. Faculty frequently attribute students' poor performance to lack of ability. Before such judgements are made, however, other possibilities need to be considered. This chapter will discuss the ways in which cultural learning and communication styles may affect minority students' academic performance, the nature of academic texts, and strategies for facilitating students' comprehension of texts and learning.

## FACTORS IN ACADEMIC PERFORMANCE OF MINORITY STUDENTS

### Underpreparedness

Students from nondominant cultures and low socioeconomic backgrounds, are especially likely to be underprepared for college, particularly if they come from inner city or rural high schools. The underpreparedness may be related to three factors: (1) some public schools may not have the resources to prepare students well for the university environment, (2) faculty of these schools may be unfamiliar with the types of skills the students will need, or (3) minority students may specifically be discouraged from taking college preparatory classes. Ethnographic data from students in the Multicultural Education Program (MEP) in Communicative Disorders at the University of New Mexico provide support for these factors. For example, MEP students have reported that high school guidance counselors failed to encouraged them to consider college. A Native American student who asked about college preparatory classes was told, "Indians don't go to college," and an Hispanic student reported that when she asked the guidance counselor about taking a college entrance examination, she was told "Oh, no, no, no dearie. You are not college material. What you need to do is go to the vocational school and take secretarial courses."

### Learning and Communication Styles

Other major factors contributing to minority students' academic difficulty may be their cultural communication and learning styles. Many nondominant students come from cultures that rely heavily on oral rather than written communication. In such cultures, learning is based on watching and listening rather then being formally taught. Such cultures can rely on shared information in their communications, and consequently, their spoken language need not be explicit. The communication may, as a result, be ambiguous to the listener who is not part of the group. In most traditional, or non-Western cultures (that is, cultures other than Euro-Americans and individuals with a high degree of acculturation to Euro-American culture) learning styles are field-dependent and holistic, rather than field-independent and analytic. Witkin (1967) described field-dependent learners as highly sensitive to the social environment. They approach learning in a gestalt manner and rely heavily on nonverbal cues to interpret events and expectations. They are, additionally, likely to prefer a group-oriented approach to learning and to memorize rather than analyze information to be learned. Field-independent learners, on the other hand, attend to discrete aspects of the environment or task, focus on verbal information (sometimes to the exclusion of contradictory nonverbal information), and prefer both independent study and the provision of their own organization to tasks. Because American university environments require a field-independent approach to learning, many minority students who are field-dependent learners are placed at risk for academic success.

Students from literate non-Northern European cultures may also experience difficulty in American universities related to the ways in which they organize or structure their communication. The study of contractive linguistics in second language learning has described differences in text structures across languages and cultures (Connor & Kaplan, 1987; Purvis, 1988). Kaplan (1966) who explored the writing styles of foreign students in writing English, noted that although these students had mastered the vocabulary and grammar of English, their writing appeared disorganized and not to the point. Kaplan hypothesized that different cultures had developed different logical systems and, consequently, different organizational formats for texts. Figure 9-1 presents his diagrams for text organization in several cultures. He later clarified his ideas (Kaplan, 1987), stating that although one might find all examples within each culture, one type of text structure predominates within each culture.

Kaplan proposed that English texts are direct and straightforward, with one point following logically from the preceding, and with minimal digressions. Semitic texts (e.g., Arabic and Hebrew) are based on a series of parallel constructions. This construction is particularly obvious in the

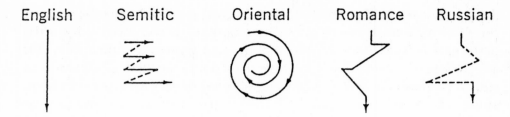

Figure 9-1. Patterns of discourse organization. (From Kaplan, R.: Cultural thought patterns in intercultural education. Courtesy of *Language Learning, 16* (1 & 2: 15, 1966).

King James version of the Bible. Semitic texts tend to rely on coordinate constructions (e.g., use of *and, therefore, but*), whereas maturity in English texts is measured by increasing subordination (e.g., use of *when, that, because, if*). This lack of subordination in Semitic texts makes it difficult for English speakers to realize the interrelationships among the elements of the text. Kaplan described Asian texts as indirect compositions that develop in a widening gyre. The circles or gyres turn around the topic and show it from a variety of tangential views. Because of this style, the topic is not explicitly addressed. Ideas are developed in terms of what they are not, rather than in terms of what they are. To comprehend Asian texts, one must have additional shared knowledge with the speaker/writer. In the romance languages, (e.g., French and Spanish), it is permissible to introduce what appears to be extraneous or superfluous material. For listeners/readers unfamiliar with this style, the digressions lead them away from the main point of the story and, consequently, result in difficulty following the story line. To the writer or speaker, however, these apparent digressions are a means to elaborate on aspects of the text and to provide greater contextualization for the reader/listener. Russian texts appear to operate on a dialectic model of thesis and antithesis. Speakers begin presenting information to substantiate their point, but then give information contradictory to the point, in effect, giving both sides of the argument. If one is unfamiliar with this type of text, however, it is difficult to determine whether the speaker is supporting or opposing a particular position.

A number of studies have reported that many African American students use an anecdotal or topic-associating style of communication rather than the linear topic-centering strategies used in mainstream schools (Gee, 1989; Michaels, 1981; Michaels & Collins, 1984). Speakers present a number of anecdotes that are related to a central theme, but they do not make the theme explicit in words, nor do they explain the relationship among the anecdotes. Variations in stress and intonation patterns are used to link anecdotes and emphasize points. Teachers who are generally unfamiliar with African Americans' integrative use of stress and intonation, find it difficult to recognize the point of such texts, and think students have gotten off the topic. Native Americans may also use a discourse style that is unfamiliar and confusing to faculty. When discussing this matter with a Native American faculty member, I was told, "Navajo thought is like Indian fry bread. An idea bubbles up here, then another idea over there, and another idea there" (Benally, 1989). In Navajo thought there is no need to indicate the relationships among the ideas. It should be recognized that these text organizations are proposed from a mainstream American point of view. Text structures vary, but the nature of the variation is in the eyes of the beholder. The text organization pattern a particular cultural group uses is the most logical and straightforward to them. A Korean woman attending a workshop I taught commented, "I thought he (Kaplan) wasn't Korean. I always thought it was we Koreans who talked in a straightforward manner and it was you Americans who talked in circles."

Universities have provided academic support services for underprepared students for many years. The effectiveness of these programs has been somewhat equivocal. Most of these programs have been generic, teaching the theory of learning or study strategies with material unrelated to the specific coursework the students are taking (Anderson, 1988). In academic settings, language and literacy are used in the service of thought. Clifford (1984) reported that academic institutions define literate individuals as those who are able to synthesize, organize, and interpret ideas, as well as apply information learned from reading to new situations. To foster such development, curricula designed to develop learning strategies and thinking skills are proliferating in junior and senior high schools as well as universities (Beyer, 1988; Clarke, 1990; Deshler & Schumaker, 1986; Nickerson, Perkins, & Smith, 1985; Pressley & Associates, 1990). Such curricula assume a proficiency in a formal style of language use that can be brought to the learning strategies and thinking skills curricula. Furthermore, many of the learning strategies and thinking curricula are generic. Instructors assume that thinking is thinking, and consequently, that once thinking strategies are taught they can be applied equally across the curriculum. This is not, however, truly the case. Clarke (1990) suggested that different courses, and their underlying

disciplines (e.g., math, science, literature, social studies), require different types of thought. Individuals within a discipline think like others
within that discipline. Therefore, sociologists think like sociologists,
linguists think like linguists, historians think like historians, speech-
language pathologists think like speech-language pathologists. Because
different learning strategies are shaped by the thinking patterns typical
of the various disciplines, they require different approaches to the development of instructional support activities (Clarke, 1990). Students must
not only learn the content of their chosen discipline, but they must also
learn to think in the ways required by their chosen discipline.

Students must be able to engage in both inductive and deductive
thought. Inductive thinking is the process of constructing ideas from
experience. For example, students must be able to observe the behaviors
of a client and arrive at conclusions about possible conditions and
causes. Deductive thought is the process of applying ideas or concepts to
specific problems in experience. In a reverse process, students must be
able to take the theoretical information learned in classes and generate
appropriate intervention plans for clients. Learning proceeds in a widening
spiral with new experiences supporting the development of new ideas
(inductive thinking) and those ideas being further developed and tested
in new experiences (deductive thinking). Clarke (1990) proposed six
aspects to thinking. Beginning with the data of experience, the individual thinks inductively by (1) scanning the experience searching for
meaningful information (e.g., noting a client's articulation errors), then
(2) grouping together aspects of the experience into classes or categories
(e.g., identifying phonological processes), which are then used for (3)
creating abstract ideas or propositions from the facts (e.g., client may
have velopharyngeal incompetence). Once the abstract idea or proposition is formed, the individual thinks deductively by (4) hypothesizing
other possible relationships between concepts and events (e.g., velopharyngeal incompetence is primarily observable when the physical
system is stressed), (5) using the hypothesis to predict future events (e.g.,
predicting phoneme combinations which would be most affected by the
condition), and finally (6) designing problem-solving procedures to
develop a specific plan to deal with experience (e.g., planning an appropriate intervention strategy).

## Academic Support Systems

Universities providing academic support through learning strategies classes should enable students to comprehend texts at multiple levels and then use this knowledge in the service of inductive and deductive thought, the type of thought required in Euro-American institutions of higher education. These classes need to be offered in a way that acknowledges the competencies of nondominant culture students. Many students, dominant and nondominant, can benefit from strategies classes designed to facilitate learning in specific disciplines.

At the University of New Mexico, we have offered a 2-semester credit course called Learning Strategies. The course is available for undergraduate or graduate credit to all students in speech-language pathology and audiology. Although the focus of the course is on language-learning strategies for adolescents and adults, the techniques presented are applicable to elementary and mid-school students as well. Students cover the literature on language learning strategies and discuss implications for culturally different and language learning disabled students. With the increasing emphasis on the role of speech-language pathologists as consultants to classroom teachers, this course is of interest to many students. As the various strategies are presented, students practice using the strategies when reading and studying for their own classes. Graduate students are also given the opportunity to obtain clinical hours by working with adolescents or college students who are referred to the clinic because of academic difficulties.

This course approach provides important information to all students regarding language learning issues of adolescents and adults. The inclusion of information on cultural variations in language learning helps diminish the idea that certain cultural groups are "just not as capable." By using the strategies when reading and studying for their own courses, students from both dominant and nondominant cultures are provided with support without any student being singled out as incompetent or as being perceived as receiving special assistance that is not available to other students. Response to the course has been very positive. Review of student transcripts indicates that students' grade point averages have improved. In addition, on course evaluations **A** students who have taken the course report that they've learned how to get **A** grades more easily.

University programs that are unable to provide learning strategies classes can still facilitate the learning of all students. Many faculty may feel that it is not their role to adapt their teaching for underprepared students. Most faculty, however, want their students to master the content of the courses they teach. Incorporation of learning strategies principles into academic teaching will not only enable underprepared and culturally different students to succeed, but will also improve the performance of all students. Although the strategies discussed below were recommended to and implemented by some faculty members in the Communicative Disorders Department at University of New Mexico, they are general enough to be employed in most disciplines.

Voluntary partnerships were established between students. Those students experiencing difficulty in a course and who were amenable to peer tutoring, were matched with students who had previously taken the course or were presently in the course and not experiencing difficulty. In one instance the tutee was taking another class with the tutor in which the tutor was experiencing difficulty. The roles of the tutor and tutee were reversed for that particular class.

Class instructors were encouraged to provide alternatives for required class participation. For example, an instructor who required class participation could define it as: voluntary comments during class discussion; meeting individually with the instructor to discuss class topics; or written dialogues to the instructor about class readings and discussion. The opportunity to engage in group, as well as individual class projects, was also suggested as a way to allow students with different interaction and learning styles to display knowledge.

Different styles of communication and use of space, time, and language were discussed with faculty members. For example, it is important to realize that, although there is variation within every culture, there are also trends within cultures (Hall, 1959; Hall & Hall, 1987, 1990). For example, it is inappropriate for individuals in some cultures to perform and stand out as individuals. Rather than displaying competitiveness, group members are taught how to learn and display knowledge through group interactions. In addition, it is important for faculty to realize that in some cultures it is taboo for women to obtain something (e.g., education) for themselves. Rather, they can **achieve** only if they are doing it for someone else. If students from those cultures do not complete or volunteer to do an assignment on their own, they may do so if the instructor specifically asks them for an assignment. In this instance, the student may readily do the assignment because they can justify doing the assignment **for the instructor.** Completing the assignment is no longer viewed as a **selfish** act to obtain a high grade, but rather as providing something that someone else wanted. Failure by some faculty and peers to understand this issue leads to the perception that the student is lazy, lacks motivation, or is incompetent.

At the University of New Mexico, faculty members were given ideas for facilitating group discussion, eliciting an awareness of background knowledge necessary for understanding texts, using question taxonomies in class discussions and tests, and analyzing written projects. These and other techniques provided to the faculty are presented under the section of this Chapter entitled: "Facilitating Comprehension and Thinking." One final, but crucial means of assisting all students to function more effectively in school, is to employ faculty members who represent the ethnic make-up of the community. These individuals serve not only as role models, but also will likely have an understanding of interactions and learning styles of particular groups. The recognition of abilities and the increased expectations of nondominant culture students will serve to empower students.

## TEXT DIMENSIONS

To assist students effectively in acquiring learning strategies, faculty need to understand the nature of text content and structure. Thinking in a particular discipline requires the ability to comprehend the texts of that discipline. Comprehension involves more than being able to read the words in a book. A great deal of research has shown that students' knowledge of **content schemas** and **text grammar schemas** is critical for successful text comprehension (Britton & Black, 1985; Muth, 1989). Content schema refers to hierarchical organization of information on a topic; text grammar refers to the overall organization of the text. A number of classification systems have been presented for texts. The simplest is a classification into narrative and expository texts. Within each of these subcategories are additional categories. Narratives can include newspaper articles, novels, personal accounts of experiences, fairy tales, dramas, history, etc. Expository texts can include scientific articles, advertisements, technical descriptions, editorials, operating instructions, etc. The majority of texts that university students are expected to read are expository, yet much of their experience has been with narrative texts.

Cazden and Hymes (1978) documented the ways in which university students' discourse changed during the course of their education, moving from personal experience examples to using impersonal comments and reasoning from the propositions in texts to relate to course material. This movement from narratives of personal experience to reasoning from texts represents an aspect of what Cummins (1984) has termed BICS (basic interpersonal communication skills) and CALP (cognitive-academic language proficiency). BICS is defined as "the manifestation of language proficiency in everyday communicative contexts"; CALP is defined in terms of "the manipulation of language in decontextualized academic situations" (Cummins, 1984, p. 137). A BICS level of language is not sufficient for success in the academic world. To be successful, students must master the CALP language essential for comprehending and discussing expository texts.

Differences between the content and structure of narrative and expository texts are widely accepted (Black, 1985; Grabe, 1987; Graesser & Goodman, 1985; Kieras, 1985). Compared to expository texts, narrative texts are read faster, are easier to comprehend, and are retained better in memory (Freedle & Hale, 1979; Graesser, 1981). Awareness of the characteristics of narrative and expository genres can provide faculty with some insights into the differences between BICS and CALP and reasons why students experience difficulty comprehending expository academic texts. Although there is considerable diversity within narrative and expository genres, some generalizations can be made regarding differences between these two genres.

## Text Functions

Black (1985) claimed that expository texts are the meat and potatoes of the textual world because expository texts are ones that contain new information and explain new topics to people. In contrast, he suggested that narratives are dessert; they describe new variations on well-learned themes and serve to entertain. Narratives are associated with relaxing and having fun, whereas expository texts are associated with learning and working. It is not difficult to motivate persons to eat dessert; similarly, it is generally not too difficult to motivate students to read an interesting story. Eating a healthy meal, or reading expository texts is another matter. Students frequently will procrastinate and seek to do other things, rather than read textbooks.

## Text Content

Narrative and expository texts differ in the familiarity and nature of their content. Although the specific content of each narrative is different, there are a relatively limited number of themes. Many themes involve an aspect of lack or loss of something desired or a villainous or destructive action of one set of individuals against another (Botvin & Sutton-Smith, 1977). In Western cultures the content of many narratives report on a problem that must be solved. The behavior of persons, which forms the content of stories, is familiar to readers. In contrast, the content of each expository text is unique and usually unfamiliar. Anderson (1988) has reported that minority students who are field-dependent find learning easier when the material has a human content (like narratives) than when the content is inanimate and impersonal (like expository texts).

Graesser and Goodman (1985) proposed a representational knowledge system consisting of statement nodes and arc categories to describe the content of texts. **Statement nodes** are idea units that correspond to an event, state, process, action, or fact. **Arc categories** interrelate the statement nodes. Table 9-1 lists, defines, and gives examples for each of the six statement nodes and six arc categories.

The types of knowledge and the relationships among aspects of this knowledge differ in narrative and expository texts. Narratives have more reason arcs, initiate arcs, goal nodes and style nodes. Expository texts have more physical state and physical event nodes and property, consequence, and support arcs (Graesser, 1981). Students daily interact with people and talk about or narrate these interactions. Consequently, they are more familiar with the physical events, internal states, internal events, and goals of persons and the reason and initiate arcs that explain the relationships among these components than they are with the using support and property arcs in expository texts and reasoning from physical states and events that do not involve persons to consequences.

## Text Structure

The majority of narratives have highly similar and predictable structures. All stories are about behaviors of characters, and stories usually focus on the emotions of characters in response to events and their attempts to cope with these events. Consequently, all stories share the same basic structure (see Fig. 9-2). Stories consist of one or more episodes.

**Table 9-1.**
**Node and ARC Categories**

*A. Node Categories:*

| Category | Definition | Examples |
|---|---|---|
| Physical state | Statements that report an ongoing state in the physical or social world. | There is a hole in the ozone layer. The child has a cleft palate. |
| Physical event | Statements that report changes in the the physical or social world. | The sound was amplified. The patient pressed the computer keys. |
| Internal state | Statements that describe an ongoing mental or emotional state of a person. | The parents were relieved when they heard the diagnosis. |
| Internal event | Statements that report a change in the mental or emotional state of a character; statements that refer to metacognitive thought processes. | The client demonstrated frustration when she could not do the assignment. The teacher knew the child should be referred for evaluation. |
| Goal | Statements that refer to persons' attempts to attain future states and events. | The physician identified the need to perform a myringotomy. |
| Style | Statements that modify action or state. | The angry child screamed furiously. |

*B. ARC Categories*

| | | |
|---|---|---|
| Reason | One goal node is a reason for another goal node. | The speech-language pathologist chose to work with the occupational therapist because she wanted to address the child's general difficulties with praxis. |
| Initiate | This links states, actions, and events to goals. | The parent's stated frustration over the child's poor academic performance brought them to the clinic. |
| Consequence | States, events, and actions can lead to other states and events by causally driven mechanisms. | Inability to produce plosive sounds is a consequence of inadequate velopharyngeal closure. |
| Property | Objects and persons have attributes. Property relations are descriptive relations that link statements about how objects look or relate to other objects and characters. | Persons with traumatic brain injury exhibit several problems that affect their ability to hold a job. They have difficulty remembering sequences of instructions and organizing their time. |
| Support | Support relations link general statement ideas that make assertions. | Facilitative communication has been effective for many children with autism. Children who have never spoken, now are able to communicate. |

Courtesy of author.

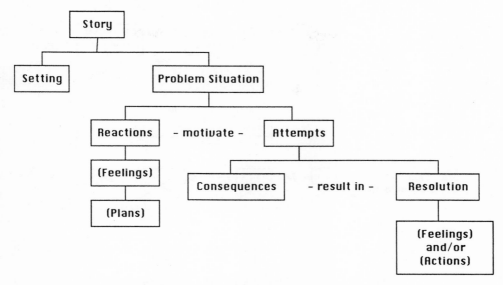

Figure 9-2. Story text structure (Courtesy of author).

Each episode consists of at least a motivation or purpose for the person's behavior (initiating event or internal response), a goal-directed action (attempt), and attainment or nonattainment of the goal (consequence). Narratives increase in structural complexity by adding episodes, either in a linear manner or by embedding one episode within another episode. Each episode has the same structure (Peterson & McCabe, 1983; Stein & Glenn, 1979). All narratives have similar structure because they all have similar content (people and their goals and their actions to attain the goals).

Expository texts have multiple possible structures because they are about a greater variety of ideas than narrative texts, with different structures best fitting each idea (see Fig. 9-3). Not only do different texts have different structures, but also within any given text there may be several different structures. For narrative texts, readers need only acquire a single basic narrative episode structure. To comprehend expository texts, students must recognize a variety of text structures and be able to switch between these structures within a single text. A variety of expository text structures have been proposed (Horowitz, 1985a, 1985b; Richgels, McGee, Lomax, & Sheard, 1987):

1. Descriptive/collection: Tells what something is or gives a list related to a topic.

**DESCRIPTIVE/ELABORATION/COLLECTION**

Level One:     Topic

Level Two:     Attribute/Example     Attribute/Example     Attribute/Example

details     details     details

**SEQUENCE/PROCEDURE**

Level One:     Topic

Level Two:     Action 1 → Action 2 → Action 3 → Action n
(and below)

details details     details details     details details     details details

**COMPARISON/CONTRAST**

Level One:     Topic

Level Two:     Alike     Different
(and below)

details     details     details     details

**CAUSE/EFFECT EXPLANATION**

Level One:     Topic

Level Two:     Antecedent     Consequence
(and below)

ante-cedent → ante-cedent

details     details     details

**PROBLEM/SOLUTION**

Level One:     Topic

Level Two:     Problem → Solution     Solution     Solution
(and below)

details     details     details     details

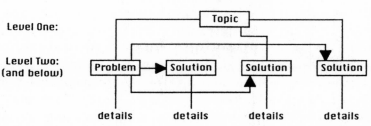

Figure 9-3. Expository text structures (Adapted from Richgels, S.D.J., McGee, L.M., Lomax, R.G. & Sheard, C.: Awareness of four text structures: Effects on recall of expository text. Courtesy of *Reading Research Quarterly, 22:* 183, 1987).

2. Sequence/procedure: Tells what happened or how to do something.

3. Cause/effect explanation: Gives reasons for why something happened.

4. Problem/solution: States a problem and offers solutions to the problem.

5. Comparison-contrast: Shows how two things are the same or different. Awareness of text structure can assist the reader in comprehending the information or the content of the text.

## Content-Structure Links

Three types of information are involved in text comprehension: **text grammars, content schemas,** and **facts** (Kieras, 1985). **Facts** are the propositions conveyed in the prose, either explicitly, or implicitly. A **content schema** represents a superordinate organization of content facts. A **text grammar** is a schema that represents a frequent structure or configuration of textual elements, defined independently of specific content. In narrative texts, the content schema and text grammar are the same because narrative structure is dependent upon the content schemas of persons' goal-directed response to disrupting events or attitudes.

In expository text there is no predictable relationship between content and structure. Nearly any content can be presented in any structure. A unit on neuroanatomy may be presented as a descriptive list of parts of the central and peripheral nervous systems with the functions of each part; or characteristics of the central and peripheral nervous systems can be compared and contrasted (e.g., differences between upper motor and lower motor neuron lesions); or the course may focus on types of central and peripheral nervous system disabilities and interventions (problem-solution type texts). The relative independence of content facts, content schemas, and text grammars marks a major difference between expository and narrative material.

## Time and Order

Narratives take place in a specific time and place (Graesser, 1981). Narratives rely on a sequential temporal order. There may be flashbacks and flashforwards, but within each of these, the information is temporally ordered (with the possible exception of dreams). Time and place in expository texts are usually generic (with the possible exception of history texts). Statements are regarded as universally true at relevant times and locations. Expository texts may report information in temporal order, but they frequently do not. The order of presentation is determined by the point to be made or the function of the text. There are mnemonic advantages of temporal sequences (Gomulicki, 1956). Texts that do not follow temporal order may be harder to process and remember. Spiro and Taylor (1987) suggested that the presentation format of expository texts could present processing problems for readers because the text presentation of the content does not match the underlying representation of the ideas.

## Inferences

Narratives rely on pragmatic inferences, i.e., what makes sense in this particular situation based upon personal experiences. In contrast, expository texts depend on logical inferences from the printed texts. What may be an acceptable pragmatic inference from a narrative text, may not be an acceptable logical inference from an expository text. Relationships affecting important ideas in narratives are often determined on pragmatic grounds, but are determined on logical grounds in expository texts. Nickerson, Perkins, and Smith (1985) report that use of pragmatic inferences rather than logical inferences represent common deductive errors by students in many situations. One example of a substitution of pragmatic inferences for logical inferences is a Native American student's explanation of her choice of a response to a multiple choice examination in stuttering. The student chose the response that she knew to be true for her friend who stuttered, rather than the answer the professor had derived from the text. Matthews (1989) reported a similar example from a Black nursing student. The student was given the following test question:

> Which activity would be appropriate for a patient recovering from kidney surgery within his second postsurgical week?
> A. a game of badminton
> B. a ten-mile drive in the country
> C. a card game with three other friends
> D. none of the above (p. 19).

The correct answer was C. The student answered D (none of the above) because she understood that the principle of a successful recovery requires quiet, sedate activities. She reasoned that badminton requires running and stretching, driving could involve fast turns and sudden stops, and in her family, card games could be pretty wild and exciting.

## Vocabulary, Syntax, and Connective Words

Vocabulary in expository texts lacks the general familiarity of vocabulary in narratives. Much of the vocabulary of narratives has an Anglo-Saxon origin. In contrast, expository texts make greater use of words of Latin and Greek origin, which require knowledge of prefixes and suffixes (Calfee & Drum, 1986). Grabe (1987) noted that narrative and expository texts use differing syntactic and cohesive principles. Narratives generally make more use of active voice and simpler syntactic structure than expository texts which make greater use of passive voice and more subordinate clauses (Spiro & Taylor, 1987). In narratives, transitional phrases and signaling devices play a less critical role than in expository text. Additionally, in narratives, chronology, rather than formal logical relationships is of primary importance. Consequently, vague connectives like "and then" may be sufficient for comprehension. In expository texts transitional words and conjunctions are critical for signaling the structure of the text, relationships among propositions, and relationships between the propositions and macrostructure of the text. Hence, connectives in expository texts are explicit and varied, such as words that signal additive relationships (e.g., in addition, furthermore, moveover), temporal relationships (e.g., then, next, before, after, soon, while), and causal or logical relationships (e.g., therefore, because, consequently), or adversative relations (e.g., but, however, on the other hand). Students must be alert to these signal words and recognize the subtle variations of meaning among the conjunctions.

## Relationship of a Text to Other Texts

With narratives, each text can stand alone. Each story can be understood and enjoyed without drawing information from other stories. Familiarity with other stories on a theme may facilitate story comprehension, but it is not essential for comprehension. For example, students who are familiar with Mr. Spock in Star Trek, may more easily comprehend a Star Trek book or movie, but knowledge of Mr. Spock's behavior is not, however, essential to the comprehension and appreciation of the story.

With expository texts, background knowledge is critical (Lazansky, Spencer, & Johnston, 1987; Spiro & Taylor, 1987; Voss & Bisanz, 1985). A text may be understandable only if one has the necessary background information. In addition, the knowledge gained from expository texts must be integrated with other topically-related knowledge. Information in expository text is used to elaborate or modify content schemas. Stories are complete in themselves; whereas expository texts must be assimilated to other similar texts. When the same instructor teaches a series of courses, students often report that the first course on a topic is the most difficult. Speech-language pathology programs generally offer a sequence of courses: language development, then language disorders, and finally language assessment. Students in our program at the University of New Mexico have generally reported that the language development course is more difficult than the language disorders course, and that the language disorders course is more difficult than the language assessment class.

## Top-Down versus Bottom-Up Processing

Readers can rely heavily on top-down processing in comprehending narratives. Readers familiar with narrative structure match the specific story content to the structure, and in so doing, facilitate their comprehension. Expository texts, on the other hand, require bottom-up processing (Britton, Glynn, & Smith, 1985). Before the initial reading of the text, the reader has no knowledge of the overall text structure, and generally, has limited knowledge of the content to be presented. Consequently, readers must use a bottom-up approach (Britton, Glynn, & Smith, 1985). Black (1985) has suggested that for many unfamiliar expository texts, several readings are required for comprehension. During the first reading, readers do not have a correct or complete schema for either the content or the text structure. Consequently, they must gather general information about the structure and content of the text. On the second reading, readers use awareness of the text structure to relate the individual propositions of the content to the overall structure to gain understanding of the main ideas. On the third reading, readers refine understanding of the content, attaching details to main ideas. This sequential reading process has been of benefit to share with students. Many of the minority students and students at the University of New Mexico who were not **A** students believed that the **A** students got **A**'s simply because they were smart. They were surprised when they learned during a discussion of time management the amount of time **A** students were spending on their studies.

Knowledge of text characteristics can enable faculty to understand what is involved in CALP and provide them with ideas to assist students in comprehending academic texts. Good readers (particularly those with high vocabularies) remember more when texts have clear structures and use explicit words (e.g., connectives) to signal relationships among parts of the text (Meyer, 1984; Meyer, 1987). All students benefit from well-structured texts. Faculty should consider the overall text organization and not just the text content when selecting texts. Reading information presented in different formats can also facilitate learning. For that reason, faculty should consider making available in the library other texts that present the material is a somewhat differ structure.

There is some suggestion that memory for descriptive texts is frequently poorest, perhaps because there is no hierarchical structure to facilitate memory. Memory for cause-effect texts has reportedly been poor in some studies, perhaps because of the conceptual demands required by such texts (Richgels, McGee, Lomax, & Sheard, 1987). Information in texts that place explicit main idea statements at the beginnings of paragraphs is better remembered than information in texts where the main idea is implicit or not placed at the beginning of paragraphs (Hare, Rabinowitz, & Schieble, 1989). Individuals with greater knowledge of a topic remember more after reading a passage on the topic than readers with less knowledge (Voss, Vesonder, & Spilich, 1980). Poor readers and readers with lower vocabulary levels, unlike good readers, perform no differently on texts with clear structure, explicit main ideas, and signal words. They do not appear to recognize and or use this information to facilitate comprehension (Meyer, 1984; 1987). Students in the University of New Mexico program reported particular difficulty with a neuroanatomy course the semester in which the professor selected a detailed book that used primarily an enumerative approach. Such a book had no inherent organization. The book was useful for those who already knew neuroanatomy, but not for those students who required more structure and explicit links between the elements in the text.

## FACILITATING COMPREHENSION AND THINKING

Learning strategies classes at the University of New Mexico have focussed on two major components: time management and learning/study strategies. Some discussion of the time management strategies is presented in the chapter by Pipes, Westby, and Englebret in this book. This section focuses on the learning strategies component of the course. As each strategy was presented, the instructor modeled the use of the strategy while teaching the actual class, after which the students used their textbooks to practice the strategy.

The nature of some of these strategies makes them readily useable only in the strategies class and in independent student study time. Other strategies could be incorporated into the teaching of any class. When using learning strategies, instructors need to explain how to use each of these strategies and to practice them in class. Instructors first introduce each strategy to the students, explaining to them why, when, and where to use them. Second, they provide procedural and mental modeling by thinking aloud while using the strategy and modeling its steps and the reasoning process that regulate its effective use. Third, instructors provide students with guided practice, having students talk through their use of the strategy and offering assistance to those who cannot successfully execute it. Finally, they promote independent practice to ensure that students transfer their use of the strategy to a variety of reading situations.

Strategies to facilitate text comprehension and thinking about topics fall into three areas: (1) preparation for reading, which involves determining and developing students' background knowledge, (2) assistance during reading, which involves activities to develop comprehension, and (3) studying and reflection and thinking after reading (Richardson & Morgan, 1990). Some strategies are used by the instructor in presenting material and other strategies are those that students must employ themselves when reading and studying. Knowing about strategies is not sufficient to ensure their use. Students may know what strategies are available but choose not to use them because they think they will take too much time, or because they do not feel comfortable changing their usual reading and study habits. For this reason, instructors will want to provide opportunities for students to "try out" the strategies, and they will want to monitor students use of the strategies. We have found the use of the Learning and Study Strategies Inventory (LASSI) (Weinstein, Palmer, & Schulte, 1987), helpful in getting students to evaluate their learning and study behavior. Students complete the inventory the first week of class. Results are discussed individually, as well as in class, and then based on their profiles on the LASSI, students generate goals for ways they will change their learning and study behaviors during the year.

The following section describes common learning strategies that are presented in the learning strategies courses at the University of New Mexico.

## Preparation for Reading

Because background knowledge is related to text comprehension, prereading strategies to develop background knowledge are recommended. The strategies detailed below are suggested for the preparation phase.

### Determining Background Knowledge

Students cannot be expected to comprehend material without a certain amount of background knowledge. For instance, the sequence of coursework in speech-language pathology and audiology facilitates students having the necessary background. Students generally do not take a course in language disorders without a prerequisite course in language development, or a course in aphasia without first having a course in neuroanatomy. Even if students have had the prerequisite courses, there is still no guarantee that they will have acquired the necessary background for understanding a particular course content or a particular text. University instructors may find procedures employed in secondary school settings to evaluate whether students' background knowledge is adequate before beginning a new topic, is of value.

1. **Cloze Technique.** Instructors delete words from a text and have students select the words that have been deleted. Discussion of their choices provide instructors with information about students' background knowledge.

2. **PreP (Prereading plan)** (Langer, 1981). PreP has three phases: (a) initial associations in which the instructor introduces the topic and asks students to list everything they think of when they hear this topic; (b) reflections on the initial concepts when students are asked to explain why they thought of a particular response, so as to build an awareness of their prior knowledge and associations; (c) re-formation of knowledge when new ideas that were learned during the first two phases are articulated. Students' responses to these activities give instructors insight into how prepared students are for the material that is to come. If students are able to give precise definitions, analogies, and meaningfully

link the concepts under discussion with other concepts, they should be well prepared for the material. If they are able to give some examples, attributes, and characteristics, they have the basics necessary to comprehend the material. If their responses consist of tangential associations based on personal experiences, they will require considerable assistance in comprehending the material (see Table 9-2).

**Table 9-2.**
**Prep Response Levels to Autism/Autistic**

| Little Knowledge | Some Knowledge | Much Knowledge |
|---|---|---|
| Artistic | Difficulty talking | A type of developmental |
| only interested in | Repeat words and phrases | disability affecting |
| oneself | without meaning | the ability to |
| Dustin Hoffman in | May have severe tantrums | communicate and |
| *Rainman* | Like to rock and spin things | interact normally |
| There's an autistic man | | Manifested within the first |
| in the neighborhood | | two years of life |
| | | Differentiated from |
| | | childhood schizophrenia |
| | | which develops later |
| | | May exhibit marked |
| | | splittering of skills |
| | | (e.g., excellent |
| | | drawing ability and |
| | | limited language skills) |

Courtesy of author.

**Building Background**

The following strategies prepare students for the material that will be presented in the text.

1. **Graphic Organizers.** The instructor identifies the organizing themes or concepts in the material and all the supporting concepts. The instructor then constructs a diagram displaying the interrelationships between the concepts and uses it to introduce the material. Occasionally, chapters in a text begin with an outline or graphic representation of the chapter content. An instructor could provide a graphics organizer in the course syllabus to show students the interrelationships among the sections of the course (see Fig. 9-4).

2. **Anticipation Guides.** Readers are requested to react to a series of statements that are related to the content of the material. In reacting to

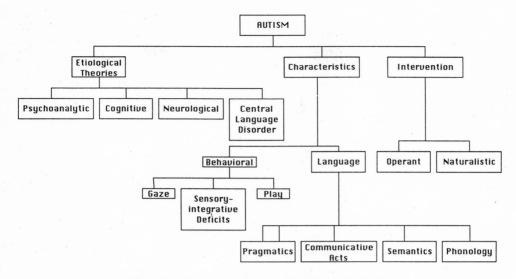

Figure 9-4. Graphic organizer (Courtesy of author).

these statements, students anticipate or predict what the content will be. Anticipation guides enable students to devote attention to the most important information in the text so they can spend time learning it. One problem with anticipation guides is that students sometimes assume that the only information they must know are the answers to the guide questions (see Table 9-3).

3. **Directed Reading-Thinking Activity** (Stauffer, 1969). The Directed Reading-Thinking Activity (DRTA) strategy combines elements of the graphic organizers and anticipation guides. It requires students to attend to both the structural organization of the text and to hypothesize about the content. There are three steps to this activity. (a) Readers preview the title, pictures, subtitles and introduction, discuss what they know about the topic, and predict what the material will be about. Students are required to justify their predictions. (b) Students read the material to verify whether their predictions were correct. (c) Students reflect on their reading, checking and modifying their predictions.

4. **K-W-L.** The initials of K–W–L stand for (a) what I *know,* (b) what I *want* to find out, and (c) what I *learned* (Ogle, 1986). Students are asked to read the title of the passage, and then make a list of everything they know about the topic. Students are encouraged to pool their ideas and classify the items into categories. Next students are asked to write down

**Table 9-3.**
**Anticipation/Prediction Guide**

Put a check by the items you believe to be true before you read the chapter on Neuropathology of Aphasia and after you read the chapter.
Prereading                                                                                          Postreading

_____ 1. Etiologies for aphasia can be divided into acute events and        _____
              insidious processes.

_____ 2. Strokes are most often caused by hemorrhages.                        _____

_____ 3. Ischemic incidents can be thrombotic or embolic.                     _____

_____ 4. Subarachnoid hemorrhages are the most common extra-      _____
              cerebral hemorrhage.

_____ 5. Recovery is similar in ischemic and hemorrhagic strokes.     _____

_____ 6. Insidious processes make their presence known slowly.          _____

_____ 7. Gliomas are the most common intracerebral tumor.                 _____

_____ 8. The brain is readily susceptible to infections.                         _____

Courtesy of author.

what they want or expect to learn from the passage. Finally, after reading the passage, students write down what they learned.

## Assistance During Reading

### Categorizing Comprehension Level

Comprehension occurs at different levels. Students frequently think that if they have memorized material, they have comprehended it. If the instructor asks for other than a regurgitation of the material, however, the student is at a loss. In working with students at University of New Mexico, we have observed that during the first two years of college, course requirements focus primarily on rote memorization of material. Students in their junior and senior years, are expected to do more reading between the lines and integrating information. Graduate school requires them to analyze, synthesize, and evaluate what they have read. A number of taxonomies have been developed to lead students from literal, rote comprehension to critical thinking about a topic (Bloom, 1956; Heber, 1978; Raphael, 1982; 1986). Instructors can use taxonomies to develop questions to be used during the reading process or during class discussions. They can also consider the taxonomy as they develop test questions. Following the test, they should analyze the students' responses to see if there is a pattern to the types of questions that are difficult. The following are three types of taxonomies that can be used to facilitate comprehension:

1. **Three-Level Guides** (Herber, 1978). First students must understand the *facts* in the text; then they must see the **implications** of the topic; and finally they must **apply** what was understood to other topics. Before the reading, instructors prepare study guide questions for the students that include these three levels.

2. **Bloom's Taxonomy** (1956). This is one of the most comprehensive thinking taxonomies. When using this taxonomy with university students, the instructor develops questions on a text and course activities for each level of the taxonomy and alerts students to words that cue them to the types of responses that are required. Table 9-4 (adapted from Tonjes and Zintz, 1987) presents explanations, cue words, and example tasks for the levels of Bloom's taxonomy.

3. **QAR (Question-Answer Relationships)** (Raphael, 1982, 1986). Comprehension requires reading between the lines and bringing to bear all the knowledge one has on a topic. The QAR technique was developed to help students think about the relationship between a text and its questions. It is particularly helpful in fostering an understanding of inferential questions. Students, at times, argue that professors "aren't fair" because the answers to the test questions cannot be found in their notes or texts. Raphael identified the following four types of relationships that students must understand to answer a question, two of which are in the text and two of which require readers to draw from their own knowledge:

*In the book QARs:*

1. *Right there.* The answer is in the text, usually easy to find. The words used to make up the question and words used to answer the question are **Right There** in the same sentence.

2. *Think and search.* Although the answer is in the text, it is not in one specific part of the text. Readers need to put together parts of the text to find it. Words for the questions and words for the answer are not found in the same sentence or even same paragraph. They come from different parts of the text.

*In my head QARs:*

3. *Author and you.* The answer is not in the text. Readers need to think about what they already know, what the author tells them in the text, and how it fits together.

**Table 9-4.**
**Using Bloom's Taxonomy**

| Taxonomy Level | Objective | Cue Words | Example Tasks |
|---|---|---|---|
| Knowledge (facts, rote memory) | show how you know by: | list, tell, identify, label, locate, recognize | List and give the functions of the cranial nerves. |
| Translation and interpretation (put in your own words) | show that you under-stand by: | explain, illustrate, describe, summarize, interpret, expand, convert, measure, translate, restate | Explain how the vocal cords vibrate. |
| Application (use what you know) | show that you can use what is learned by: | demonstrate, apply, use, construct, find solutions, collect information, perform, solve, choose appro-priate procedures | How would you evaluate a 7-year-old child referred for stuttering? |
| Analysis (take apart to solve problem) | show that you can pick out the most important points presented or solve the problem by: | analyze, debate, differentiate, organize, determine, distinguish, take apart, figure out, solve | Analyze this narrative language sample and discuss the student's narrative abilities. |
| Synthesis (put together in a new way) | show that you can combine concepts to create an original idea by: | create, design, develop a plan, produce, synthesize, compile | Based on coursework and the information in the case history and evaluation report, develop an Individual Family Service Plan for this child and family |
| Evaluation (make a value judgement based on criteria) | show that you can judge and evaluate ideas, information, procedures and solu-tions based on your own stated criteria by: | judge, rate, compare, decide, evaluate, conclude, appraise (with reasons given). | Compare the whole language and phonics/basal approaches for teaching reading. |

Adapted from: Tonjes, M.J. & Zintz, M.V.: *Teaching Reading and Thinking Study Skills in Content Classrooms.* Courtesy of Wm. C. Brown, 1987, p. 307.

4. *On my own.* The answer is not in the text. Readers can even answer the question without reading the text. They need to use their own experience. Students may be insecure with questions that require them to pull from their own general knowledge.

## Appreciating Relationships

Text comprehension requires understanding of the concepts and propositions presented in the text and the relationship of the concepts and propositions to the overall theme and structure of the text (Marzano, Brandt, Hughes, Jones, Presseisen, Rankin, & Suhor, 1988; Meyer, 1987). By facilitating students' awareness of text structures and how the text concepts are organized within the text structures, instructors can assist students in comprehending complex texts.

1. *Awareness of text structure.* The instructor explains the structure of various texts, alerts the students to the structure of the text they are about to read, and may even provide them with a study guide diagram of the structure with spaces for them to fill in the main points of the text. Before students read a text, instructors may have them scan the passage, noting headings and subheadings, and ask them to predict the structural organization of the text. This has become an extremely popular strategy in public schools. Directing students' attention to the words that signal the various text structures is useful. Table 9-5 describes each type of text, the words that signal the text structure, and the types of questions that are most likely asked about that particular type of text.

2. *Understanding concept relationships through mind mapping or semantic webbing* (Johnson & Pearson, 1984; Novak & Gowin, 1984). The purpose of mapping is to demonstrate the interrelationship and hierarchies of concepts in a text. The instructor or students identify the topic or main idea of the text. They circle the main idea. Then they identify other ideas or concepts and connect these categories to the main idea with lines. To each of these categories they connect supporting ideas. When the map is complete, they then find linking words to write on the connecting lines that explain the relationships between the concepts.

## Learning Comprehension Monitoring Strategies

An ultimate goal of strategies for developing comprehension is for students to become independent learners, i.e., they must learn to question and monitor their own comprehension. The following comprehension strategies teach students to monitor their own comprehension by asking themselves questions. Instructors must model these strategies.

1. *Think Aloud Strategy.* The think aloud strategy demonstrates to students how good readers read. The instructor selects a passage that contains ambiguities, unknown words, and several other points of difficulty.

**Table 9-5.**
**Guide for Monitoring Expository Texts**

| Text Pattern | Text Function | Key Words | Test Formats |
|---|---|---|---|
| Description | The text tells what something is | is called, can be defined as, is, can be interpreted as, is explained as, refers to, is a procedure for, is someone who, means | Define . . .<br>Describe . . .<br>List the features of . . .<br>What is . . .<br>Who is . . . |
| Collection/ enumeration | The text gives a list of things that are related to the topic | an example is, for instance, another, next, finally, such as, to illustrate | Give examples of . . .<br>What is . . . and give some examples |
| Sequence/ procedure | The text tells what happened or how to do something or make something | first, next, then, second, third, following this step, finally, subsequently, from here . . . to, eventually, before, after | Give the steps in doing . . .<br>When did . . . occur? |
| Comparison/ contrast | The text shows how two things are the same or different | different, same, alike, similar, although, however, on the other hand, contrasted with, compared to, rather than, but, yet, still, instead of | Compare and contrast . . . and . . . /<br>How are . . . and . . . alike and different? |
| Cause/effect explanation | The text gives reasons for why something happened | because, since, reasons, then, therefore, for this reason, results, effects, consequently, so, in order to, thus, depends on, influences, is a function of, produces, leads to, affects, hence | Explain . . .<br>Explain the cause(s) of . . .<br>Explain the effect(s) of . . .<br>Predict what will happen . . .<br>Why did . . . happen?<br>How did . . . happen?<br>What are the causes (reasons for, effects, results, etc.) of . . . ? |
| Problem/solution | The text states a problem and offers solutions to the problem | a problem is, a solution is | Describe the development of the problem and the solutions.<br>What are the solutions to problem . . . ? |

Courtesy of author.

Each student is given a copy of the passage. The instructor reads the passage aloud, verbalizing the thought process he/she is using in trying to make sense of the passage. Davey (1983) suggests that the instructor make predictions about the topic, describe images formed while reading, give analogies to relate the material to personal experience, note confusing points, and demonstrate ways to correct misunderstandings. Imaging and drawing analogies take advantage of field-dependent learners strengths.

2. *ReQuest.* The ReQuest procedure, which also provides a model for self-monitoring, requires students and instructors to alternate asking questions about a text (Manzo, 1969). The instructor and students silently read the first sentence of the text. Then the students ask as many questions as they can think of about the sentence. The instructor answers the questions as completely as possible, verifying his/her responses from the text. If a question cannot be answered, the instructor explains why. The instructor and students read the next sentence, and the instructor takes a turn asking questions about the sentence. The students answer the instructor's questions and verify their answers by showing the answer in the text, or explaining how they arrived at the answer. As the activity progresses, the instructor begins to ask inferential questions as well as factual questions. Once students have grasped the activity at the sentence level, they can move on to reading paragraphs or longer passages before asking and answering questions. Maria (1990) suggested that this technique is useful in situations in which sentence constructions are difficult to understand. She also suggests that this approach assists students in recognizing the relationship of one sentence to another.

3. *Reciprocal Teaching.* Reciprocal teaching has four components: prediction, summarization, questioning, and clarification (Palinscar & Brown (1986). In the initial step, the instructor and students read a paragraph. After reading the paragraph, the instructor summarizes the paragraph and asks several questions about it. The instructor clarifies any misconceptions or difficult concepts. Then, the students predict what will be discussed in the next paragraph. Following that paragraph, student and instructor roles are reversed, and the students summarize the paragraph, ask questions of the instructor (or each other) and clarify any misunderstandings.

These comprehension strategies all require metacognitive processing which require that the students themselves determine if they are comprehending or not comprehending and that they take corrective action when they have failed to comprehend.

## Studying: Reflection and Thinking after Reading

Students must become self learners if they are to succeed in higher education. They must know how to comprehend texts and how to study so that they can remember and apply what they understand.

### Strategy Families

Dana (1989) has proposed a family of strategies for students to use independently: **RAM** to prepare students, **SIP** to help students focus during the reading process, **RIPS** to guide repair in comprehension breakdown, and **EEEZ** to store the information into memory. Students use **RAM** to prepare themselves for the assignment. They are reminded to **Relax** before beginning to read. Many students have reported feeling intimidated with certain course or certain text books and dread even opening the book. Muscle relaxing and imagining techniques can help students relax before reading (Zenker & Frey, 1985). Next students must **Activate** a purpose for reading the material and the knowledge background they have for the material. They must have an idea of what the instructor expects them to be able to do with what they read. They then must **Motivate** themselves for the task. Many students exhibit low motivation because they do not think they can succeed. Students have reported that they thought other students got good grades just because they were smart, and that they did not get good grades because they were not smart. Class discussion has made them aware of how much time the **A** students are spending on schoolwork.

The goal of the **SIP** strategies is to help keep the students on track. **S** reminds the student to **Summarize** the information in each section. **I** refers to **Imagining** or forming an internal visual display of the content encountered while reading. Anderson (1988) suggested that imagining is especially useful for field-dependent students who learn best by having visual and contextual support. **P** is a reminder to **Predict** while reading (i.e., to think about what might be coming next and then to verify one's predictions). The **SIP** strategies, however, are not enough to ensure comprehension. When comprehension breaks down, the student must have some way of dealing with this breakdown. If students are not comprehending, they are told that if one **RIPS** the text apart while reading it will help with comprehension. **R** cues the students to **Read on** and **Reread** the text. If students have not been paying attention, then they should use the **SIP** strategies. If they have been paying attention, then they should read on to the end of the section or at least read the next three paragraphs. If the content is still unclear they should reread the section or the previous three paragraphs. While trying to resolve the problem by reading on or rereading, students should **Image** the content. To check whether comprehension is being repaired, the readers should **Paraphrase** the material, restating the information in their own words. The **S** (**speak up, slow down, seek help**) in the **RIPS** strategy family reminds students to vary their reading rates, and if all else fails, to seek help.

The **EEEZ** strategy family helps the student to hold the information in memory once the reading is completed. Students are told to take it **Easy** and to explain the content of the reading. They might answer questions, generate questions, define a concept, or provide a summary. Two other strategies will enhance their memory. One approach is to **Explore** the same subject matter using other materials and books. Frequently reading a different version of the material helps clarify it. A second approach is to **Expand** the subject matter by reading other sources that go beyond the content covered in the class.

## Cooperative Strategies

Studies have shown that cooperative study techniques facilitate students' understanding and recall of text material and facilitate students' independent study patterns (McDonald, Larson, Dansereau, & Spurlin, 1985). Dansereau (1987) proposed scripts that students could use to guide their study interactions (see Table 9-6). He suggested that without such guidance, study partners would engage in minimal interaction and opportunities to try out new learning strategies. Although the two scripts are quite similar, they lead to different results. The cooperative teaching script leads to better initial learning or recall; whereas the cooperative learning script leads to better transfer to individual studying. In the teaching script, because the partners have not read the same material, they focus on content, rather than the process of learning. As a consequence, teaching partners learn less about the process of understanding the content. With the cooperative script, both the summarizer and the listener have read the same material and thus can concentrate on process. The scripts provide a framework for students to use the monitoring and elaboration strategies that have been presented in class. Students in our program have found these scripts particularly useful.

**Table 9-6.**
**Cooperative Scripts**

| Cooperative **Learning** Script | Cooperative **Teaching** Script |
| --- | --- |
| 1. Both partners read Passage 1. | 1. Partner A reads Passage 1. Partner B reads Passage 2. |
| 2. When both are finished, put the passages out of sight. | 2. When both are finished, put the passages out of sight. |
| 3. Partner A orally summarizes the contents of Passage 1. | 3. Partner A orally summarizes (teaches) the contents of Passage 1. |
| 4. Partner B detects and corrects any errors in Partner A's summary (metacognitive step). | 4. Partner B asks clarifying questions (metacognitive step). |
| 5. Both partners work together to develop analogies, images, etc., to help make the summarized information memorable (elaboration step). | 5. Partners work together to develop analogies, images, etc., to help make Passage 1 information memorable (elaboration step). |
| 6. Both partners read Passage 2. | 6. Repeat steps 3–5 for Passage 2, with partners reversing roles. |
| 7. Repeat steps 3–5 with partners reversing roles. | 7. Both partners read the passage that they did not read originally. |

From Dansereau, D.F.: Transfer from cooperative to individual studying. *Journal of Reading, 30:* 616, 1987. Reprinted with permission of Donald F. Dansereau and the International Reading Association.

## Selecting Strategies

Students must learn what strategies to select for particular purposes, and they must learn which strategies work best for them. Sometimes the goal of reading is to understand, sometimes to remember, and sometimes to apply. Each goal may require different strategies (Levin, 1986). Analyzing context to interpret a word affects understanding, but it may not affect memory for the word. Mnemonic strategies facilitate memory, but do little for understanding and application. For example, saying On Old Olympus Towering Tops A Fin And German Viewed Some Hops, may help students remember the names of cranial nerves, but it will not help them understand the functioning of the cranial nerves or determine what nerves are affected in Bell's palsy. Higher level thinking strategies require a combination of understanding, remembering and applying, and hence require use of multiple strategies.

## CONCLUSION

Students must gain knowledge in the reading process, be able to integrate this knowledge with other information they possess, and use this knowledge in effective problem solving and decision making. Effective problem solving and decision making is dependent upon critical thinking. Critical thinking involves the six components of inductive and deductive thought described by Clarke (1990) at the beginning of this paper. Critical thinking cannot be taught in the abstract or in isolation. It is not a distinct subject, but must be taught as part of the content disciplines. Faculty must not assume that minority students' poor academic performance is due to lack of ability. They should be sensitive to personal factors that may be contributing to poor performance such as family and job responsibilities and to the possibilities that the students have been underprepared or have a learning style that does not match that required by the university setting. Faculty cannot do much about students' personal issues, but they can do something about students' underpreparedness and language and learning style differences. University faculty often maintain that they should not have to deal with underprepared or culturally different students—that is the job of the public schools. Certainly, the public schools need to be addressing these issues. If universities do not also address them, however, a whole generation of minority students who have completed public school will be lost to the professional world.

## REFERENCES

Alpert, R.T., Gorth, W.P., Allan, R.G.: *Assessing Basic Academic Skills in Higher Education.* Hillsdale, Erlbaum, 1989.

Anderson, J.A.: Cognitive styles in multicultural populations. Presented at the ASHA Sea Island Conference, Sea Island, 1988.

Benally, L.: Personal communication, 1989.

Beyer, B.K.: *Developing a Thinking Skills Curriculum.* Boston, Allyn & Bacon, 1988.

Black, J.: An exposition on understanding expository text. In Britton, B. & Black, J. (Eds.): *Understanding Expository Text.* Hillsdale, Erlbaum, pp. 249–267.

Bloom, A.: *The Closing of the American Mind.* New York, Simon & Schuster, 1987.

Bloom, B. (Ed.): *Taxonomy of Educational Objectives: Handbook 1, Cognitive Domain.* New York, Longman, 1956.

Botvin, G.J. & Sutton-Smith, B.: The development of structural complexity in children's fantasy. *Developmental Psychology, 13:* 377–388, 1977.

Britton, B.K. & Black, J.B. (Eds.): *Understanding Expository Text.* Hillsdale, Erlbaum, 1985.

Britton, B.K., Glynn, S.M. & Smith, J.W.: Cognitive demands of processing expository text: A cognitive workbench model. In Britton, B.K. & Black, J.B. (Eds.): *Understanding Expository Text.* Hillsdale, Erlbaum, 1985, pp. 277–248.

Calfee, R. & Drum, P.: Research on teaching reading. In Wittrock, M. (Ed.): *Handbook of Research on Teaching.* 3rd ed., New York, MacMillan, 1986, pp. 804–849.

Carpenter, K. & Johnson, L.L.: Program organization. In Flippo, R.F. & Caverly, D.C. (Eds.): *College Reading & Study Strategy Programs.* Newark, International Reading Association, 1991, pp. 28–69.

Cazden, C. & Hymes, D.: Narrative thinking and story-telling rights: A folklorist's clue to a critique of education. *Keystone Folklore, 22:* 21–35, 1978.

Clarke, J.H.: *Patterns of Thinking.* Boston, Allyn & Bacon, 1990.

Clifford, G.J.: Buch und Lesen: Historical perspectives on literacy and schooling. *Review of Educational Research, 54:* 472–500, 1984.

Connor, U. & Kaplan, R.: *Writing Across Languages: Analysis of L2 Text.* Reading, Addison-Wesley, 1987.

Cummins, J.: *Bilingualism and Special Education: Issues in Assessment and Pedagogy.* San Diego, College-Hill, 1984.

Dana, C.: Strategy families for disabled readers. *Journal of Reading, 33:* 30–35, 1989.

Dansereau, D.F.: Transfer from cooperative to individual studying. *Journal of Reading, 30:* 614–619, 1987.

Davey, B.: Think-aloud — Modeling the cognitive processes of reading comprehension. *Journal of Reading, 27:* 44–47, 1983.

Deshler, D.D. & Schumaker, J.B.: Learning strategies: An instructional alternative for low-achieving adolescents. *Exceptional Children, 52:* 483–590, 1986.

Freedle, R.O. & Hale, G.: Acquisition of new comprehension schemata for expository prose by transfer of a narrative schema. In Freedle, R.O. (Ed.): *New Directions in Discourse Processing,* Vol. II, Ablex, 1979, pp. 121–130.

Gee, J.: Two styles of narrative construction and their linguistic and educational implications. *Discourse Processes, 12:* 287–307, 1989.

Gomulicki, B.R.: Recall as an abstractive process. *Acta Psychologica, 12:* 77–94, 1956.

Grabe, W.: Contractive rhetoric and text-type research. In Conner, U. & Kaplan, R. (Eds.): *Writing Across Languages: Analysis of L2 Text.* Reading, Addison-Wesley, 1987, pp. 115–137.

Graesser, A.C.: *Prose Comprehension Beyond the Word.* New York, Springer-Verlag, 1981.

Graesser, A.C. & Goodman, S.M.: Implicit knowledge, question answering, and the representation of expository text. In Britton, B.K. & Black, J.B. (Eds.): *Understanding Expository Text.* Hillsdale, Erlbaum, 1985, pp. 109–171.

Hall, E.T.: *The Silent Language.* Greenwich, Fawcett, 1959.

Hall, E.T. & Hall, M.R.: *Hidden Differences.* New York, Doubleday, 1987.

Hall, E.T. & Hall, M.R.: *Understanding Cultural Differences.* Yarmouth, Intercultural Press, 1990.

Hare, V.C., Rabinowitz, M. & Schieble, K.: Text effects on main idea comprehension. *Reading Research Quarterly, 24:* 788, 1989.

Herber, H.: *Teaching Reading in the Content Areas.* Englewood Cliffs, Prentice-Hall, 1978.

Hirsch, E.D.: *Cultural Literacy: What Every American Needs to Know.* Boston, Houghton Mifflin, 1987.

Horowitz, R.: Text patterns: Part I. *Journal of Reading, 28:* 448–454, 1985a.

Horowitz, R.: Text patterns: Part II. *Journal of Reading, 28:* 534–541, 1985b.

Johnson, C. & Pearson, P.D.: *Teaching Reading Vocabulary,* 2nd ed., New York, Holt, Rinehart & Winston, 1984.

Kaplan, R.: Cultural thought patterns in intercultural education. *Language Learning, 16:* 1–20, 1966.

Kaplan, R.: Cultural thought patterns revisited. In Connor, U. & Kaplan, R. (Eds.): *Writing Across Languages: Analysis of L2 Texts.* Reading, Addison-Wesley, 1987.

Kieras, D.E.: Thematic processes in the comprehension of expository prose. In Britton, B.K. & Black, J.B. (Eds.): *Understanding Expository Text.* Hillsdale, Erlbaum, 1985, pp. 89–107.

Langer, J.: From theory to practice: A prereading plan. *Journal of Reading, 25:* 152–156, 1981.

LaZansky, J., Spencer, F. & Johnston, M.: Reading to learn: Setting students up. In Tierney, R.J., Anders, P.L. & Mitchell, J.N. (Eds.): *Understanding Readers' Understanding.* Hillsdale, Erlbaum, 1987, pp. 255–281.

Levin, J.R.: Four cognitive principles of learning-strategy instruction. *Educational Psychologist, 2:* 3–17, 1986.

Manzo, A.V.: The request procedure. *Journal of Reading, 11:* 123–126, 1969.

Maria, K.: *Reading Comprehension Instruction: Issue & Strategies.* Parkton, York Press, 1990.

Marzano, R.J., Brandt, R.S., Hughes, C.S., Jones, B.F., Presseisen, B.Z., Rankin, S.C. & Suhor, C.: *Dimensions of Thinking: A Framework for Curriculum and Instruction.* Alexandria, Association for Supervision and Curriculum Development, 1988.

Matthews, J.M.: Preventing text bias in the Texas academic program. In Alpert, R.T., Gorth, W.P. & Allen, R.G. (Eds.): *Assessing Basic Academic Skills in Higher Education.* Hillsdale, Erlbaum, 1989, pp. 19–23.

McDonald, B.A., Larson, C.O., Dansereau & Spurlin, J.E.: Cooperative dyads: Impact on text learning and transfer. *Contemporary Educational Psychology, 10:* 369–377, 1985.

Meyer, B.F.: Text dimensions and cognitive processing. In Mandl, H., Stein, N.L. & Trabasso, T. (Eds.): *Learning and Text Comprehension.* Hillsdale, Erlbaum, 1984, pp. 3–47.

Meyer, B.F.: Following the author's top-level organization: An important skill for reading comprehension. In Tierney, R.J., Anders, O.L. & Mitchell, J.N. (Eds.): *Understanding Readers' Understanding.* Hillsdale, Erlbaum, 1987, pp. 59–76.

Michaels, S.: "Sharing time": Children's narrative styles and differential access to literacy. *Language in Society, 10:* 423–442, 1981.

Michaels, S. & Collins, J.: Oral discourse styles: Classroom interaction and the acquisition of literacy. In Tannen, D. (Ed.): *Coherence in Spoken and Written Discourse.* Norwood, Ablex, 1984, pp. 219–244.

Muth, K.D.: *Children's Comprehension of Text: Research into Practice.* Newark, International Reading Association, 1989.

New Jersey Basic Skills Council: *Effectiveness of Remedial Programs in New Jersey Public Colleges and Universities.* Newark, Department of Education, 1985.

Nickerson, R.S., Perkins, D.N. & Smith, E.E.: *The Teaching of Thinking.* Hillsdale, Erlbaum, 1985.

Novak, J.D. & Gowin, D.B.: *Learning How to Learn.* London: Cambridge University Press, 1984.

Ogle, D.: K–W–L: A teaching model that develops active reading of expository text. *The Reading Teacher, 39:* 564–570, 1986.

Palinscar, A.S. & Brown, A.L.: Interactive teaching to promote independent learning from text. *The Reading Teacher, 39:* 771–777, 1986.

Peterson, C. & McCabe, A.: *Developmental Psycholinguistics: Three Ways of Looking at a Child's Narrative.* New York, Plenum, 1983.

Pressley, M. & Associates: *Cognitive Strategy Instruction that Really Improves Children's Academic Performance.* Cambridge, Brookline Books, 1990.

Pugh, S.L. & Pawan, F.: Reading, writing, and academic literacy. In Flippo, R.F. & Caverly, D.C. (Eds.): *College Reading & Study Strategy Programs.* Newark, International Reading Association, 1991, pp. 1–27.

Purvis, A.C. (Ed.): *Writing Across Languages and Cultures: Issues in Contractive Rhetoric.* Newbury Park, Sage, 1988.

Raphael, T.: Question-answering strategies for children. *The Reading Teacher, 36:* 186–190, 1982.

Raphael, T.: Teaching question-answer relationships, revisited. *The Reading Teacher, 39:* 516–522, 1986.

Richardson, J.S. & Morgan, R.F.: *Reading to Learn in the Content Areas.* Belmont, Wadsworth, 1990.

Richgels, D.J., McGee, L.M., Lomax, R.G. & Sheard, C.: Awareness of four text structures: Effects on recall of expository text. *Reading Research Quarterly, 22:* 177–197, 1987.

Spiro, R.J. & Taylor, B.M.: On investigating children's transition from narrative to expository discourse: The multidimensional nature of psychological text classification. In Tierney, R.J., Anders, P.L. & Mitchell, J.N. (Eds.): *Understanding Readers' Understanding.* Hillsdale, Erlbaum, 1987, pp. 77–93.

Stauffer, R.G. (1969). *Directing Reading Maturity as a Cognitive Process.* New York: Harper & Row.

Stein, N. & Glenn, C.: An analysis of story comprehension in elementary school children. In Freedle, R.O. (Ed.): *New Directions in Discourse Processing.* Norwood, Ablex, 1979, pp. 53–120.

Tonjes, M.J. & Zintz, M.V.: *Teaching Reading and Thinking Study Skills in Content Classrooms.* Dubuque, Wm. C. Brown, 1987.

U.S. Bureau of the Census: *Statistical Abstract of the United States. Washington, DC, 1991.*

Voss, J.F. & Bisanz, G.L.: Knowledge and the processing of narrative and expository texts. In Britton, B.K. & Black, J.B. (Eds.): *Understanding Expository Text.* Hillsdale, Erlbaum, 1985, pp. 173–198.

Voss, J.F., Veosonder, G.T. & Spilich, G.J.: Text generalization and recall by high knowledge and low knowledge individuals. *Journal of Verbal and Verbal Behavior, 19:* 651–667, 1980.

Weinstein, C.E., Palmer, D.R. & Schulte, A.C.: *Learning and Study Strategies Inventory.* Clearwater, H & H Publishing, 1987.

Witkin, H.A.: A cognitive style approach to cross-cultural research. *International Journal of Psychology, 2:* 233–250, 1967.

Zenker, E.R. & Frey, D.Z.: Relaxation helps less capable students. *Journal of Reading, 28:* 342–344, 1985.

# Chapter 10

# CURRICULUM APPROACHES
# FOR TEACHING CULTURAL DIVERSITY
# IN THE PROFESSIONAL PROGRAMS
# OF ALLIED HEALTH

DOLORES E. BATTLE

## INTRODUCTION

Cultural and linguistic diversity is a reality of contemporary American life. This fact has been confirmed by the 1990 Census which provides vivid documentation of the changing colors of what may be reasonably called the New America (U.S. Bureau of Census, 1990). The Census Bureau reported that over the last decade the rate of population growth for ethnic and linguistic minorities dwarfed the rate of population growth for White Americans. A marked increase in the number of immigrants (the greatest since 1920s) has been characterized by a dramatic change in the composition of the newcomers. While in the early part of this century, nearly 90 percent of the immigrants came from Europe, in the 1980s more than 80 percent of the immigrants came from Asia and Latin America (Scheslinger, 1991). As based on predictions from the 1980 Census and the study of immigration patterns, by the year 2000, the United States population is expected to be one-third minority.

The demographic change will impact the professional programs of allied health. The curricula will need to prepare for and address the specific needs of students, as well as clients, who are not of European descent (New York State, 1989). Since the people requiring the services of allied health professionals will be from the growing nonmajority cultures, it is important for faculty in the allied health professional education programs to effectively prepare all students to serve the new clientele of our nation.

With this challenge in mind, the chapter is intended to provide faculty with a description of the various approaches for broadening their academic curriculums to include multicultural content. Advantages and disadvantages for each approach are discussed. The application of these approaches to clinical training are also discussed.

## MULTICULTURAL EDUCATION

It is within the spirit of the Civil Rights Act of 1964, Title VI (1970) that multicultural education in the curriculums of the allied health professional education programs evolved; equity for persons to be judged and treated according to the rules and values of their own culture, be it the culture of the Deaf, the culture of poverty, or the culture of linguistically and ethnically diverse persons. During the 1960s and 1970s the importance of multicultural education was underscored by judicial actions brought about on behalf of those children whose rights to an education were violated under the Title VI of the Civil Rights Act of 1964. Several decisions of the Supreme Court in which minority handicapped children were denied an appropriate education (MILLS 1972; PARC, 1972) led to inclusion of provisions of nonbiased assessment in the Rehabilitation Act of 1973 and the Education of All Handicapped Children Act of 1975. The Bilingual Education Act of 1974 resulting from the judicial decision of Lau versus Nichols (1974) and the Ann Arbor decision (MLK, 1979; Bountress, 1980) were landmark cases in the progression toward multicultural and lingual education in the public schools.

In 1974, William Hunter, Director of the Multicultural Competency Based Teacher Education (CBTE) Project for the American Association of Colleges for Teacher Education stated:

> Education in the United States, to be relevant, must be multicultural. . . . The United States as a nation and as a society consists of many different people and products of behavior, all characterized by individual and group diversities within systems of relationships. This highly diversified and complex character of this **nation-society** sets forth its culturally pluralistic nature. If education in the United States is to meet the needs of its peoples, it must have a life blood of **multicultural content** in order to be sociologically relevant, philosophically germane, psychologically material and pedagogically apropos (p. 11).

Because a multicultural education is a **process** by which an individual develops competencies for perceiving, believing, evaluating, and behaving appropriately in different cultural settings, it must be considered in higher education. Multicultural education can be viewed as both an intervention and an ongoing assessment process to help institutions and individuals become more responsive to the human condition, to individual cultural integrity, and to cultural pluralism in society.

According to Bennett's (1988) model of multicultural education, there are important factors to consider when multicultural content and perspectives are incorporated into the academic curriculum. In the allied health professional education programs, faculty need to have a heightened awareness and knowledge of the historical perspectives and current cultural differences that may affect the provision of health care services; an understanding of cultural and intercultural differences of the consumers of health care services; an understanding of the attitudes and values that embody a commitment to reduce racism, prejudice, and discrimination; and finally the specific skills to teach all students the necessary content for providing effective health care services to persons from different cultural and linguistic groups.

Presently, professionals in allied health report that they have not had direct course work pertaining to the culturally and linguistic diverse clients that they service. For example, in the professions of audiology and speech-language pathology, the ASHA Omnibus Survey of 1988 (Shewan, 1988) indicated that 75.8 percent of the members of the American Speech, Language and Hearing Association (ASHA) reported having had no graduate coursework pertaining to communication disorders among multicultural populations, and 83 percent reported having had no graduate coursework pertaining to the limited English-speaking populations. Additionally, according to the data, less the 1 percent of the 64,000 plus members of ASHA were proficient enough in a foreign language to provide clinical services to foreign language speakers. Yet in 1988, 37 percent of the ASHA membership reported that they served clients for whom English was not their native language (Shewan, 1988).

There are two additional challenges to faculty and curricula in allied health programs. One is how to recruit and retain students of linguistic and cultural minority. The second is how to prepare nonminority students to most effectively serve minority clients. Four alternative curriculum approaches for multicultural education in the professional programs of allied health are presented as a means of achieving these goals.

# CURRICULUM APPROACHES TO MULTICULTURAL EDUCATION

## Pyramid, Unit, Infusion and Single Course Approaches

These curriculum approaches for multicultural education include: the pyramid, unit, infusion, and single course approaches (ASHA, 1987).

## The Pyramid Approach

The philosophy of the pyramid is that multicultural education must be presented through a curriculum that includes a series of courses, ethnographic experiences, and research endeavors presented at four different levels of the curriculum beginning with an introductory level, and building to interdisciplinary levels. In other words, the approach builds from a foundation of developing ethnic and cultural literacy and values (Level I) to the development of a professional knowledge base (Level II), to the application of the knowledge base to clinical and related activities (Level III), and finally to the expansion of the professional knowledge base through research (Level IV). Each of these levels will be described in detail in the following sections.

### Level I: Introductory Content

Level I of the pyramid approach strives to facilitate faculty and student's development of:
• Sociology of ethnicity, including issues of human behavior and learning.
• Knowledge acquisition of ethnic groups and their cultures, including linguistic knowledge;
• Understanding the concept of heterogeneity within racial and cultural groups;
• Recognizing the similarities among people of all races and cultures, as well as the differences;
• Understanding the differences between various multicultural concepts (e.g., understanding that race refers to biological characteristics, where as ethnicity combines the biological and cultural characteristics);
• Competencies for perceiving, believing, evaluating, and behaving appropriately in different cultural contexts (i.e., cultural literacy);
• Knowledge of how to combat racism;

• Value clarification and the pragmatic aspects of dealing with race, ethnicity, and cultural diversity within their personal lives;

• Skills for integrating multicultural knowledge into the academic curriculum;

• Development of teaching competencies for making curriculum content, clinical objectives, and learning activities meaningful to the experiential backgrounds and frames of reference of all students with regard to their culture values and beliefs, styles of cognitive learning and communication, and languages of origin;

• Recognizing that cultural differences significantly impact on the understanding and delivering of health care services (ASHA, 1987; Gay, 1983).

Courses which meet these introductory objectives can be included as part of the course offerings provided by allied health programs, such as audiology and speech-language pathology, or by other related programs such as education, linguistics, sociology, anthropology, or programs in the arts and sciences. Courses in cultural awareness are essential. However, care must be taken to assure that the content stresses both the explicit and the implicit characteristics of cultures so that students are adequately prepared to serve persons from diverse cultural backgrounds.

The cultural climate of the classroom is a critical component of Level I. How faculty deal objectively and comfortably in discussing racial and ethnic diversity in the classroom, is a key issue. The cultural climate in the classroom serves as a basis for interacting with persons from diverse backgrounds. In order for faculty to successfully present specific multi-cultural content, they must manage the differences in styles of communi-cation and learning, as well as language differences among students.

Level I of the pyramid approach provides an opportunity for faculty and professional staff to monitor and evaluate their own biases and assumptions by examining their own interaction style and interpersonal relations with students from other cultures, and by conveying informa-tion and feelings in ways that are appropriate for all students. Additionally, it involves a commitment to present a realistic portrayal of society, and of the communicatively, educationally, mentally and physically impaired populations within all of society, to students. Faculty who are clear in their own values and attitudes, and who are secure in understanding the nature of diversity, will present more effective curriculum content. The academic climate must reflect the idea of cultural understanding that goes beyond cultural acceptance. Students and faculty must be free to explore and face their own biases and prejudices with an end toward understanding.

Intercultural communication goes beyond teacher and student interactions. Other aspects need to be considered. Intercultural communication in the classroom is as critical as intercultural communication between student clinician and the client (and the caregiver) in the clinical setting. How do faculty address students from other cultures? Do faculty take as much time in considering the different needs of students as they do in considering the different needs of the clients they serve? Do faculty adapt their interactive style of teaching to meet the needs of their students as they do for meeting the needs of their clients? How do faculty perceive the learning ability of students from different cultures?

In 1987, the eminent American educator and expert in multicultural education, H. James Banks (1987), while addressing a conference sponsored by the American Association of Colleges for Teacher Education, expressed the view that the philosophy of ethnic pluralism must permeate institutions of higher education before specific multicultural curricula and materials can be effectively integrated into the educational curriculum.

## Level II: Professional Multicultural Content

The goal of Level II of the pyramid approach is to build on the general multicultural information acquired at Level I by providing information related to the specific allied health profession. For example, in audiology and speech-language pathology specific course work in communication disorders in various cultural groups is offered. Here the content of coursework for example, would be designed to bring an understanding of the various causes and effects of communication disorders among culturally different groups, and the effect that these differences have on assessment and intervention procedures. Course content and required readings at Level II must reflect current research related to cultural diversity as it pertains to the specific allied health profession, and to related areas such as education and medicine. Issues such as the role of various family members within different cultures, the family's perception of a handicap or a disorder, the family's perception of its role in the treatment process, the family's perception of the health care system, and other related issues are developed at this level. In addition to specific course work, independent study can afford students the opportunity to develop specialization in multicultural issues.

In discussing multicultural education, Hunter stated (as cited in Hunter and Masyesva, 1989):

> If my program could not provide specific information on differences in prevalence and symptomatology of various clinical syndromes and corresponding intervention strategies, then my minimal expectation was for some preparation in recognizing or dealing with the differing needs and sensitivities of individuals from culturally diverse backgrounds (p. 76).

It is important that students learn not to generalize behaviors of members of a particular group. Rather, they need to understand that differences and similarities exist across and within racial and cultural groups. Faculty should be careful to differentiate racial differences which are biological from those that are brought about by factors such as poverty, social class, educational status of the parents, family literacy, geographical area or urban/suburban environment.

## Level III: Application of the Knowledge to the Clinical Process

Level III of the Pyramid approach allows students the opportunity to apply their acquired multicultural knowledge to the clinical practicum setting. Critical areas of application include: the use of clinically nonbiased and bilingual assessment materials, the use of ethnographic interviewing techniques, and the use of interpreters. Specifics are elaborated in the clinical section of this chapter.

## Level IV: Expansion of the Knowledge Base Through Research

Level IV of the Pyramid approach encourages active research endeavors as a means of expanding the knowledge base of a particular allied health profession. Masters theses and student research projects can be used as a vehicle for engaging students in original investigations related to cultural diversity. The library holdings of the institution must be sufficient to support student and faculty research. For example, students in audiology and speech-language pathology can review and conduct ethnographic research projects related to communication behaviors among the culturally diverse.

Students must learn that ethnographic research goes beyond the notion of observation in natural settings. Students must be involved in the culture and the intricate ways that culture unravels itself in the study of their particular allied health discipline. Students need to develop an awareness of research paradigms used to determine standards of normalcy across behaviors and disorders so as not to equate ethnic and cultural diversity with socioeconomic status.

In order to maximize students' professional development and their later professional contributions to their discipline, multidisciplinary involvement with other disciplines such as anthropology, foreign language, sociology, linguistics, and child development can be fostered at this level. Cole (1986) maintains that multicultural research must stem from the vital needs and issues with the purpose of enhancing the quality of life of minority people. Thus, both student and faculty researchers must strive to maintain clarity of purpose and to interpret their findings relative to the culturally diverse.

### Application of the Pyramid Approach to Clinical Practicum

The Pyramid approach can be used as a framework within clinical practicum to provide students with opportunities for multicultural experiences. This can be accomplished by first providing students with opportunities for multicultural interactive experiences in real-life situations within the community where the student is an observer or minor participant, to later providing clinical services, and finally culminating with the design of culturally appropriate clinical research.

**Level I.** At Level I of the clinical practicum pyramid, observations begin with a nonclinical population to ensure that students are observing normal behavior. Observations and cultural norming are as critical to the delivery of nonbiased clinical services, as is learning the effective administration of specific tests and management procedures. Without cultural norming, student clinicians will filter observations through a mainstream American standard which may be inappropriate for a particular client, resulting in clinical judgment errors.

One of the primary benefits of exposing students to the normative behaviors of a cultural community is that it helps them to become more comfortable in interacting with the members of a particular cultural group. Additionally, it sensitizes students to their cultural biases and heightens their cultural awareness. Interesting locations for structured observations or volunteered participation include local restaurants, grocery stores, schools, community centers, child day care centers, senior citizen's centers, and other community agencies. In order to develop an understanding of the personal values, cultural insights, beliefs and practices for the persons that students will clinically serve, ethnographic observations should be systematic, supervised and complemented by supplementary lectures, educational films, publications, and other related activities.

**Level II.** At Level II of the multicultural clinical practicum, students should clinically observe professionals in their own particular discipline interacting with culturally diverse clients. Onsite visitations to nearby facilities with large multicultural populations can provide students with observation of the use of interpreters, ethnographic interviewing techniques, and nonbiased assessment tools, as well as observe the culturally appropriate interpretation of clinical assessment data with regard to recommendations and choice of treatment protocols. Observations should also include the very persons that the student will eventually clinically service. Videotaped or audiotaped clinical sessions, case studies or demonstration teaching such as ethnographic interviewing are also beneficial for students.

The ultimate goal at Level II is to prepare students to understand that the persons they will encounter in their clinical practicum setting may not share same cultural and social standards. For example, when is it typical for a Hispanic child to be weaned from the bottle? Is it unusual for the African American child to be spanked as a means of discipline? How does the Hispanic family see itself in preparation of their children for formal schooling? Do working class families have different expectations of therapy from those of middle class families? These understandings are as basic as knowing how to address a client, knowing which family member(s) is responsible for the client's progress and knowing which cultural designation a client prefers. The term **African American,** for example, may be quite inappropriate for clients who identify themselves as **Jamaican** or **Haitian,** but not for those clients who identify with their cultural roots in Africa. The term **African American** may also be inappropriate for a client who prefers the designation of his/her roots by his/her country of origin such as Kenya or Nigeria in Africa.

Level II of the clinical practicum pyramid in the allied health professions requires that students have an understanding of specific cultural beliefs, values, attitudes, and practices affecting health care, such as:

- What does the community designate as an illness or a disorder?
- What are the causes of disease and disability?
- How are illnesses, diseases or disabilities treated or cured?
- Who is responsible for their **cure?**
- What health foods are eaten and how are they prepared?

- And what is the literacy level of the significant person in the family and/or the community?

**Level III.** At Level III of clinical practicum, students should obtain direct clinical experiences with those culturally diverse clients that they have been exposed to and prepared to service. Given the demographics of this nation, it is highly likely that there will be a minority client base available for students to develop their clinical skills and awareness of cultural diversity. By formally establishing practicum settings, for example with head start programs, where minority clients are being serviced, guarantees that students will receive adequate clinical exposure to minority clients. Establishing exchange programs with urban universities provides another way to guarantee that students will be exposed to minority clients.

**Level IV.** At Level IV of the pyramid approach to clinical practicum, faculty should expand the professional knowledge base by having students conduct their own clinical research projects with culturally and ethnically diverse persons, as well as by having students evaluate the clinical research of others.

In summary, the philosophy of the pyramid approach holds that multicultural professional education be viewed as a series of experiences or opportunities that builds upon the knowledge and opportunities gained at previous levels. Since the acquisition of knowledge is an ongoing process, the pyramid approach is viewed as a means for continuing professional education throughout the life of the professional starting from a foundation of values clarification and commitment, leading to professional development and culminating in contributions to the multicultural knowledge base of a particular allied health profession.

## Unit Approach

The unit approach to multicultural professional education is based on the premise that within each course of a specific allied health discipline, there are one or more specific units of a course in which relevant multicultural information should be presented. For example, in a course on anatomy and physiology of the speech and hearing mechanisms, one unit might be devoted to the biological meaning of race and the cross-cultural anatomical differences that impact on speech and hearing functions. A course on language development might include a unit on language development in minority populations. The issues covered might include the perception of the family's role in the development of language among different cultures, the differences in the rate of phonological development among various languages, and the development of the specific linguistic features of a language or dialect. The unit may be taught by the faculty member who is assigned the course, or by an invited speaker who may be more familiar with the multicultural issues related to that aspect of the course. Each unit can include one or several lectures with accompanying reading assignments. Additionally, the assignment of a project or term paper, researching a particular topic, is beneficial. The ultimate goal of the unit approach is the **infusion** of multicultural content into the mainstream of the course.

There are several factors in the successful implementation of the unit approach. Faculty must demonstrate their knowledge of the multicultural content by showing students how this content relates to the course's total content. To be effective, the material should be presented as central, and not tangential to the course. Thus, the multicultural information should be introduced at a point in the course where the issues can be viewed as relevant. To add further credibility to the importance of the multicultural unit, content should be supplemented by required readings and should be included as content on examinations.

There are several advantages and disadvantages in using the unit approach. Since there are very few text books which have specific professional material related to cultural diversity, the multicultural units may be perceived as less important than other units in the course. This could yield the impression that the issues related to cultural diversity are tangential to other issues in a specific allied health professional discipline. There is also the possibility that students will perceive the multicultural information as being additive if the units are left to the later parts of the course, being covered only if time permits; if the unit is presented by a guest lecturer when the faculty assigned to the course is absent; if no reading materials are assigned, and if the information is excluded on an examination. Last, if only a single lecture covers multicultural content and students miss the lecture, the entire multicultural content and its relationship to the overall content of the course, is missed by students.

In spite of the main disadvantages of concentrating relevant multicultural information into one or two units of a particular course, there are several advantages to the unit approach. Students are provided with an awareness that multicultural content has an important relevance to the content and issues of a particular course. This awareness may generalize to other courses in the curriculum, serving as a catalyst for further student investigation of relevant multicultural and content in other courses. As the faculty assigned to a particular course become more aware of the multicultural content and issues involved as presented by a guest lecturer, they are then able to easily infuse relevant content throughout a particular course.

The development of the units takes a considerable of time and resources by both the faculty and the administration. In order for faculty to develop the necessary knowledge and expertise for teaching the multicultural units, requires administrative support for faculty to attend conferences and visit other professional preparation programs, as well as support for faculty exchange and visiting faculty programs. When individual faculty feel unprepared to competently teach multicultural content, the department's curriculum development committee can first take on the responsibility of developing course materials. In this way, the development of the unit material becomes a project for the entire department's faculty.

## The Infusion Approach

In the infusion approach, the multicultural information is **infused** or incorporated throughout a course as an integral part of the entire course content rather than being presented as a separate unit within a course.

In most allied health professional programs, virtually all courses have substantial multicultural information that can be infused. For example, differences in the incidence, causes and related variables of disorders/ disabilities/health conditions that may impact on clinical assessment management, are important issues to be infused. Specifically in speech-language pathology, the course content in craniofacial anomalies might include racial differences in the incidence of cleft lip and palate. In audiology courses, racial differences in the prevalence and causes of hearing disorders across the races might be infused into the course material.

For allied health programs, and especially those in audiology and speech-language pathology, *Communication Disorders in Multicultural Populations* (Battle, 1992) provides a comprehensive overview of culturally relevant factors related to each of the major culturally diverse groups in the U.S. It additionally includes an overview of the multicultural issues related to each of the major communication disorders (e.g., language, voice, fluency, neurogenic, and hearing disorders, and deafness). *Multicultural Literacy in Communications Disorders* (Cole, 1992) also provides a wealth of multicultural information for infusion into current coursework in audiology and speech-language pathology.

## The Single Course Approach

In the single course approach, students obtain a comprehensive and intensive educational experience with regard to developmental, etiologic, sociocultural, linguistic, and service delivery issues pertaining to minority populations. The course can be taught by a single faculty member who possesses extensive knowledge of the multicultural content, or can be taught by a team of faculty members, each representing their own area(s) of expertise.

In the curriculums of speech-language pathology and audiology, the multicultural topics might include:

- Cultural differences which may impact on adequate delivery of speech-language pathology and audiology services to members of specific minority groups;
- Pertinent sociolinguistic differences in bilingual and minority populations;
- Etiologies of specific speech, language and hearing disorders that impact on minority populations;
- Communicative disorders and behaviors among various multicultural populations;
- Procedures for nonbiased assessment and appropriate intervention of communicative disorders in minority and bilingual populations;
- Professional and public policies relative to minority and bilingual communicatively handicapped;
- Research designs and methodology that are appropriate for studying of multicultural populations (Cole, 1991).

The single course approach has the obvious advantage of being a comprehensive and intensive educational experience. However, when the course is placed in the elective category, students may complete the program without having benefitted from gaining multicultural and linguistic knowledge that is essential to their professional careers.

# EVALUATION OF THE MULTICULTURAL CURRICULUM

The approaches to multicultural professional education presented in this chapter can be implemented with flexibility and creativity, depending on the level of cultural literacy and competency of the program faculty and the commitment by both faculty and administration. Each or a combination of the four approaches presented may be appropriate at various stages in the development of multicultural curriculum for a particular allied health program. As the levels of competency and cultural literacy of the faculty develop, and as the curriculum changes, the use of the various approaches may also change. Whichever approach is chosen, however, must be accompanied by faculty involvement and a commitment of resources by the administration. By doing so, allied health professionals in this growing diverse nation can meet their obligation to provide the highest level of health care and education to all persons, not only for today but also for the years to come.

The issues is **not whether,** but **how** faculty will disseminate multicultural information in their program's curriculum, on their campuses and in their communities. The Multicultural Professional Education Program Administered Audit (ASHA, 1992) provides guidelines for program self-evaluation of the multicultural curriculum that can be applied to any allied health curriculum. Among the factors to be evaluated are:

1. Do assigned textbooks and research articles adequately cover multicultural information?
2. Do instructors make use of classroom examples that reflect cultural diversity?
3. Do class projects involve multicultural diversity?
4. What is the number and nature of student research projects that have a multicultural focus?
5. Is the most current multicultural research included in course content?
6. Do courses in research methodology include designs and paradigms for conducting multicultural research?
7. Are the clinical materials used appropriately with culturally diverse populations?
8. Do students have clinical exposure to clients from culturally diverse groups within culturally diverse settings?
9. Does the curriculum have an order of teaching which instills

multicultural sensitivity prior to imparting specific multicultural content?

10. Has the faculty been provided with the opportunity to develop multicultural sensitivity and resources for content information to aid in curriculum development?

11. Does the university administration have a stated commitment to multicultural diversity in the curriculum?

12. How does the program use interdisciplinary resources to strengthen multicultural education?

13. To what extent does the curriculum (e.g., coursework, research, clinical training) involve resources from within racial and ethnic minority communities?

14. Are there efforts to assure that students are placed in practicum settings where there is an appreciation for both the cultural diversity within the clinical population and for the racial and ethnic background of the students?

15. Does the curriculum provide opportunities to expose and familiarize students with nondisordered members of other cultures so as to increase awareness of normal behavior within the culture?

16. Are university resources utilized to develop the multicultural curricula through interdepartmental course offerings, conference, and guest speakers?

17. Are library holdings and other educational resources regularly updated to reflect the growing body of knowledge on multicultural populations?

18. Is there a plan for networking with other universities and programs with regard to curricular issues such as visiting faculty or student exchange programs?

19. Is there a mechanism for evaluating the effectiveness of the curriculum in preparing program graduates to work with the culturally diverse populations?

## CONCLUSION

Faculty in professional preparation programs of allied health are challenged in preparing students to see beyond themselves and to gain a better understanding of cultural diversity. By meeting this challenge, each new generation of allied health professionals will become educated and competent to provide quality professional services to persons of all cultures, racial and ethnic groups. Ernest Boyer, President of the Carnegie Foundation for the Advancement of Teaching stated in Dateline 2000 (Parnell, 1990):

> Our world has undergone immense transformation. It has become a more crowded, more interconnected, more unstable place. A new generation of Americans must be educated for life in this increasingly complex world. If the . . . college cannot help students see beyond themselves and better understand the independent nature of our world, each new generation will remain ignorant, and its capacity to live confidently and responsibly will be dangerously diminished (p. 3).

# REFERENCES

American Speech, Language and Hearing Association: *Multicultural Professional Education in Communication Disorders: Curriculum Approaches.* Rockville, Author, 1987.

American Speech, Language and Hearing Association: Multicultural professional education program administered audit, *Asha, 34* (5): 49–50, 1992.

Banks, J.: *Multi-Ethnic Education: Theory and Practice.* Boston, Allyn & Bacon, 1987.

Battle, D. (Ed.): *Communication Disorders in Multicultural Populations.* Reading, Andover Medical, 1992.

Bennett, C.: *Comprehensive Multicultural Education Theory and Practice,* Boston, Allyn and Bacon, 1986.

*Bilingual Education Act of 1974* 20, United States Supreme Court § 800b, 1975.

Bountress, N.: The Ann Arbor decision: Implications for the speech-language pathologist. *Asha, 22* (8): 543–544, 1954.

*Civil Rights Act of 1964.* 42, United States Supreme Court § 2000d, 1970.

Cole, L.: *Multicultural Literacy in Communication Disorders.* Rockville, American Speech, Language and Hearing Association, 1992.

*Education of Handicapped Children Act.* 20, United States Supreme Court § 1402, 1975, pp. 1411–1420.

Gay, G.: Curriculum for multicultural teacher education. In Klassen, F. & Gollnick, D. (Eds.): *Pluralism and the American Teacher.* Washington, American Association of College of Teacher Education, 1983, pp. 127–134.

Hunter, S. & Masayesva, A.: Multicultural professional education: Student perspectives. *Asha, 31* (9): 76–77, 1989.

Hunter, W.: *Multicultural Competency Based Teacher Education Project.* Washington, American Association of Colleges of Teacher Education, 1974.

*Lau Versus Nichols,* 414, United States Supreme Court § 563, 1974.

*Martin Luther King Elementary School Children Versus Michigan Board of Education,* 473 F. Supplement 1371 (E.D. Mich), 1974.

*Mills Versus Board of Education of the District of Columbia,* 348 F. Supplement 866 (D.D.C.), 1972.

New York State Department of Labor: *New York State Labor Industry Task Force Report.* Albany, Author, 1989.

Parnell, D.: *Dateline 2000: The New Higher Education Agenda.* Washington, Community College Press, 1990.

*Pennsylvania Association of Retarded Children Versus Commonwealth of Pennsylvania,* 343 F. Supplement 279 (E.D. Pa), 1972.

Schlesinger, A.: *The Disuniting of America: Reflections of a Multicultural Society.* Knoxville, Whittle Direct Books, 1991.

Shewan, C. (1988): Omnibus survey: Adaptation and progress in times of change. *Asha, 30* (8): 27–32, 1988.

United States Bureau of the Census: *Statistical Analysis of the United States.* Washington, United States Department of Commerce, 1990.

## Chapter 11

## PREPARING STUDENTS AS EFFECTIVE HEALTH CARE PROFESSIONALS: THE IMPORTANCE OF A CROSS-CULTURAL CURRICULUM

DAVA E. WALTZMAN

### INTRODUCTION

The increasing although not yet sufficient number of minority students in higher education, requires that the curricula of both undergraduate and graduate school programs become more sensitive to the needs of students who represent linguistically and culturally diverse groups. The chapters within this volume abound with and reflect the current philosophical statements regarding the importance of faculty and students becoming aware of their own cultural identity, and how this affects their intercultural perceptions. Violations of individual or collective cultural expectations of acceptable behavior in a given situation can stem from cultural misunderstanding and result in potential interpersonal conflicts (Gudykunst & Ting-Toomey, 1988). Because of this, there is a need to identify cultural attitudes that influence perceptions of others. A multicultural perspective recognizes an individual's culturally based beliefs, values and behaviors, and is sensitive to the individual's environment (Pederson, 1990). More specifically, in allied health professional education programs, it is additionally essential to be aware of the potential impact of culture upon faculty and students' perceptions of themselves as health care providers (Harper, 1990).

In order to not be merely politically correct, an understanding of cultural diversity, as well as how to best integrate cultural education across the curriculum needs to be identified and addressed. Harper (1990) provides a particularly appropriate definition of *curricula* to address this need as:

> . . . the content and courses of training that constitute the sphere of learning in schools of higher education. This implies not only courses but the philosophy,

243

assumptions, theories, goals, methods, and expected outcomes underlying the courses. The curriculum must also represent a comprehensive plan of action for accomplishing some end and for the growth and development of people (p. 16).

With this definition in mind, educational programs might then adapt curricula along the guidelines proposed by the National Association of Independent Colleges and Universities (NAICU) in *Understanding Campus Climate* (1991):

- Provide opportunities for students to read, study, and celebrate their own culture as well as those of others;
- Take a comprehensive approach to ethnicity, race, and gender rather than specific courses within isolated majors (i.e., ethnic studies; women's studies);
- Utilize a formal approach for monitoring the classroom environment to ensure a "healthy climate" for students within academic programs;
- Do not inappropriately expect students to speak for their entire cultural group;
- And provide tutoring and mentoring to facilitate competence in academic expectations and performance of those minority students deficient in basic skills.

This chapter will present suggestions for adaptation of cultural diversity in the curricula of professional education programs of allied health. It is hoped that these alternatives will facilitate the process for students in the allied health professions to receive the requisite skills for effective intercultural communication as health care providers.

## MINORITY REPRESENTATION IN
## ALLIED HEALTH PROFESSIONAL PROGRAMS

Basic to the issue of curricula adaptation to address pluralism within education is the recruitment of minority students. This is particularly important in order to "provide expertise in the area as well as a model for care" (Sakauye, 1990, p. 337). The National Association of Independent Colleges and Universities (NAICU, 1991) identifies the following important factors regarding the participation of minority students, faculty, and staff members: special efforts to recruit and retain minority individuals, action to improve the campus climate for people of color, and continued efforts to further the level of accomplishment regarding these issues.

Recruitment and retention concerns with which the NAICU members have grappled, are relevant to the professional education programs of allied health. These issues involve the paucity of matriculated minority students, the sparse representation of minority individuals in both the student body and as faculty role models, and the potential discomfort of being a minority student within a majority campus. Because of these issues and the fact that "multiculturism must be more than counting heads" (*Pluralism in the Professoriate*, 1991, p. 6), the challenge for faculty is the implementation of curricular adaptations in order to address the needs of culturally diverse students while educating all students regarding multicultural diversity. The Undergraduate Research Program at the Massachusetts Institute of Technology, as cited by NAICU (1991), provides examples of supportive and developmental activities for minority students. Recommendations include advise to:

> Work to develop an enhanced sensitivity to the legitimate concerns and interests of minority students in the established graduate faculty. This will make them better mentors, regardless of their own ethnic or cultural background. Faculty should be sensitive to minority-oriented research topics, to culturally influenced learning styles, and to co-operative work styles (p. 26).

Suggestions regarding minority faculty member recruitment generated by the NAICU are readily adaptable to student enrollment in allied health programs. These include:

- Working with high school guidance counselors in order to alert younger community members to the array of professions within the allied health fields.
- Collaborating to support "summer bridge programs" for high school students to stimulate retention of bright students.
- Offering inservice and professional development programs at the undergraduate level, as well as in high school and graduate equivalency diploma (GED) programs.
- Directly approaching and encouraging undergraduate students to encourage them to consider careers in health care professions. Personal contact can help students realize their potential. Candidate names can be generated through liaisons in liberal arts programs, as well as honors recipients and/or preprofessional club participants. Program graduates can also be a source of significant contact.

- Developing fellowship and/or forgivable loans programs to ease financial burdens and to heighten awareness of health care fields. Along with this, pursuing possible corporate support for services provided by minority individuals to their communities.
- Providing mentoring and tutorial assistance to facilitate academic success. Diverse educational backgrounds may not have properly prepared otherwise bright and capable individuals for the demands of professional education programs. The availability of strategies for learning and test taking, and the development of report writing skills may make candidacy more reachable and realistic.

It is difficult to discuss recruitment issues without also considering those regarding retention. The educational process is greatly influenced by cultural differences. Andersen & Powell (1991) define this as meaning, "The entire educational system, together with the rules and procedures for effective classroom interaction, reflects a cultural dictate rather than a universal mandate" (p. 209). Students who feel lost within the culture of the mainstream educational system and more specifically in its classrooms and lecture halls, will be thwarted in their pursuit of further education. As has been pointed out in previous chapters in this volume, Asian students, for example, as contrasted to their Anglo classmates, are traditionally reticent to verbally participate in classroom discussions and tend instead to listen and take notes. Hispanic/Latino students generally do not voice disagreement with an authority figure, nor do they respond to questions generated by someone who obviously knows the answer. Behaviors expected of students within the mainstream educational system may in fact transgress cultural barriers.

Andersen and Powell (1991) discuss factors that contribute to the intercultural context of the classroom. These include: learning style, teacher and student relationships, classroom rituals, intelligence assessment, value placed on formal education, time value and verbal, as well as nonverbal behavior. They suggest that a positive learning environment can be created through cultural understanding and sensitivity.

As a means of facilitating intercultural communication within academia, Collier (1991) provides rules for politeness, cultural appropriateness, relational appropriateness, and approaching tasks in interactions between Anglo advisors and Asian, African, and Hispanic/Latino American students. Table 11-1 as summarized from Collier (1991), demonstrates the similarities and differences in the requisite behaviors expected of Anglos as determined by the respective minority cultures.

Being aware of factors such as these can smooth the alliance between educators and students, and in turn create an environment that fosters the retention of minority students.

## CROSS-CULTURAL CURRICULA DESIGN FOR THE ALLIED HEALTH PROFESSIONS

Content and courses required in programs in the allied health professions should include an emphasis on the unique culture, lifestyle, history, needs and experiences of specific minority groups. The first task of the curricula in providing meaningful training programs is to sensitize health care providers to differences in working with particular minority groups, and to then become experienced in the problems of a specific group (Sakauye, 1990). Issues and topics to be included in curriculum content involve the need to (Harper, 1990):

- Identify and establish working definitions for the terms *minority, race, ethnicity, culture,* and *social-cultural.*
- Separate concepts such as, minority and ethnicity or race and culture.
- Define homogeneity versus heterogeneity of minority groups.
- Explore the impact of diversification within similar ethnocultural groups attributed to such factors as nationality and heritage, geographical region of origin, migration experience, social class and socioeconomic status, age, generation, urban/rural setting of origin, educational achievement, length of time in this country, ethnic neighborhood setting in the U.S., place of residence, language(s) spoken in the home, responsibilities to the household, household size and composition, upward mobility, rate of intermarriage, and degrees of acculturation (e.g., McGoldrick, 1982; Randall-David, 1989 as cited in Waltzman, 1993).
- Explore the impact of family patterns/structures including: size, interactional patterns, line of authority, decision making policies, attitudes toward women, men, older adults.
- Examine and analyze such terms and concepts as assimilation, acculturation, biculturalism and ethnic identity.
- Discuss the implications of various reasons for immigration to this country. Consider voluntary versus forced moves.

TABLE 11-1

RULE BEHAVIORS EXPECTED OF ANGLO FACULTY ADVISORS BY MINORITY STUDENTS

| RULE: | ASIAN AMERICAN | AFRICAN AMERICAN | HISPANIC/LATINO AMERICAN |
|---|---|---|---|
| Politeness | Manage time appropriately | → | → |
|  | Allow mutual talk time | → | → |
|  | Greet warmly | → | → |
|  | Attend nonverbally | Attend appropriately | →Attend appropriately through verbal and non verbal means |
|  | Avoid foul language | | → |
|  | | Show recognition and respect for student as an individual | Use a courteous manner |
| Cultural Appropriateness | Avoid overgeneralizing and stereotyping | → | → |
|  | Avoid criticizing ability or preparation for college | → | → |
|  | Avoid negative comments about accents | → | → |
|  | Allow adequate time for all students | → | → |
| Relational Appropriateness | Show respect | Act in a friendly and direct manner | Show support and respect verbally and non verbally |
|  | Avoid requesting too much openness | | |
|  | Avoid confronting or embarrassing | Build trust slowly | Take time to show concern and friendliness |
| Approaching the Task | Provide adequate advise throughout the meeting | → | → |
|  | Allow a mutual role in decision making | → | → |
|  | Prefer adequate advise throughout the meeting | Reassess information to avoid mistakes | → |
|  | | | Establish the relationship first through a warm greeting and small talk |

Courtesy of Author

- Formulate strategies for educating minority clients who are non- or limited-English speaking and/or without formal education.
- Devise methods for the provision of services to minority clients residing in the ethnic ghettos, inner cities, and rural areas.
- Explore the implications of the impact of a dual health care system (e.g., folk and Western medicine).
- And discuss the influence of various religious styles, expressions, practices, rituals, ceremonies, and symbols in relation to health care issues.

## Selected Examples of Essential Curricula

*Minority Aging: Essential Curricula Content for Selected Health and Allied Health Professionals* (1990), edited by Harper, provides curricula that are readily adaptable to the course content discussed here. Selected examples have been edited and are as follows.

### Asian Americans

Sakauye (1990) recommends that training programs in the health care professions include:

1. Courses on cultural and ethnic variation that address the following content areas:
   - general consideration of such aspects as attitudes, cultural norms, childrearing practices, and religion;
   - social issues of the ethnic group including family problems, underemployment, and family interactions;
   - variabilities (e.g., interaction with authority figures) in therapeutic relationships;
   - and racial bias.
2. Mandatory seminars on reading, writing, and speaking the ethnic language.
3. Provision of seminars on clinical issues and case supervision of minority clients.
4. "Supervised case experience with Asian minority patients should be a service requirement. Diagnostic experience utilizing a translator should be experienced to sensitize professionals to the problems inherent in language barriers" (p. 337).

## African Americans

Barresi (1990) summarizes the salient points regarding curriculum content for health professionals in providing care to African Americans as including:

1. Awareness of the difference between cohort age groups of majority and minority individuals, as well as diversity within groups.
2. Understanding the distinction between ethnicity and minority status.
3. Appreciation of the heterogeneity and wide variety of characteristics represented within ethnic and minority groups.
4. Understanding the demographic statistics (size and composition) of the ethnic and minority groups to be aware of the magnitude of the issues faced by these people.
5. Awareness that differences in family type and size, socioeconomic status, region, rural-urban location, marital status, living arrangements and acculturation levels, may contribute to the salient characteristics of individuals and their families.
6. Appreciation of the high level of reciprocal care available within extended kin groups, surrogate parenting arrangements, and regional proximity of family members.

Satcher and Thomas (1990) identify the following aspects for inclusion in curricula addressing the needs of older adult African Americans and other minorities. These recommendations appear appropriate for adaptation to minority groups across generations. Health professionals should be taught:

1. Historical and cultural background of specific minorities.
2. The relationship between cultural values and belief systems, and approaches to health and health care.
3. Specific health care needs of age cohorts as related to their unique physical, mental, social and spiritual conditions.
4. The impact of family and community setting upon health status, habits and response to care.
5. The importance of coping mechanisms in various age cohorts, and their impact upon health status and care.
6. The role of exercise, nutrition, and other activities that influence health care.
7. Resources available in the health care system for minorities.

8. Identification and description of the barriers to health and health care for minority individuals.

The following comments by Davis (1990) summarize the implications racial and cultural diversity have for the curricula:

> Health problems of the Black elderly are undoubtedly due to complex interactions among biological, environmental, psychological, cultural, social, structural, and economic factors. Future nursing curriculums will be challenged to provide content and clinical experiences so that nurses can deliver health care that is scientifically sound, humanistic, and culturally sensitive to the Black aged population (p. 481).

The implication for this synopsis to be generalized more broadly to allied health professions, and to include African Americans and other minorities across generations, is clearly apparent.

### Hispanic/Latino Americans

Valle (1990) cautions to avoid stereotyping when deciding what to include in curriculum. He offers the guidelines outlined in Table 11-2 as "a working curriculum development strategy for organizing ethnocultural phenomena from cross cultural-perspectives" (p. 442) in an attempt to objectify the way that the content is assembled relative to the Hispanic/ Latino cohort as a whole, and the Hispanic/Latino family in particular.

The approach in Table 11-2 offers the health professional a means of assembling a "culturally relevant/cross-cultural" curriculum described by Valle, as a way to approach the acculturation process from different directions as a factor of the variables being examined. He purports that this approach allows health professionals to additionally assess "gaps in the available knowledge base and focus on questions needing further attention" as well as, "distinguishing between social equality concerns relative to the family and culture-of-origin residual variables" (p. 442).

### American Indian and Alaskan Natives

With consideration for the approximately 500 different American Indian tribal groups and over 200 Alaskan villages in the United States representing unique languages, customs, values and geographical locations, Edwards and Egbert-Edwards (1990) offer a generalization of values applicable to a vast majority of these individuals. A curriculum to address minority needs should integrate these considerations (p. 146):

Table 11-2.
**The Acculturation Continuum Operating Guidelines for Cross-Cultural Curriculum Design**

| TRADITIONAL ⟵⟶ | BICULTURAL ⟵⟶ | ASSIMILATED |
|---|---|---|
| (Reflecting values, norms, language, customs of the culture of origin) | (Reflecting incorporation of both ranges) | (Reflecting values, norms, etc. of the host society) |

1. The assumption is made throughout the undertaking that the health professional has prepared himself or herself (and his or her team) with a preliminary "ranging" knowledge of the target ethnic group (in this case Hispanics/Latinos).
2. A further assumption is made that the health professional is knowledgeable about the norms and issues relevant to the topic at hand with reference to the general (Euro/Anglo) population.
3. The health professional uses the available literature, case examples, and so forth relative to the target ethnic group. The curriculum content and concepts are organized relative to the thematic requisites of the specific health profession.
4. The professional gathers and filters data/information with regard to the following:
   a. examination of cohort variances and commonalities emerging from the ethnic group's sociodemographic profile
   b. identification of residual values and normative expectations
   c. assessment/placement of the ethnic family unit, the elder, and the significant others, as well as subgroups and the cohort as a whole at different points of the acculturation continuum
   d. identification of possible socioeconomic status/social class multiple jeopardy confounds
5. This is done with reference to the different domains of daily living impacting the ethnic elder, the family, and so forth, and encompasses the activities of performance relative to the home, the workplace, the community, internal psychological states (e.g., depression, health self-reports).
6. The Hispanic curriculum content for the ethnic group is matched/compared with the appropriate clinical, research, and policy information available relative to the Euro/Anglo general population.
7. A cross-culturally appropriate curriculum is then assembled and communicated.

Adapted from Valle, R.: The Latino/Hispanic family and the elderly: Approaches to cross-cultural curriculum design in the health professions. (In Harper, M.S. (Ed.): *Minority Aging: Essential Curricula Content for Selected Health and Allied Health Professionals.* Health Resources and Services Administration, 1990, p. 441.)

1. Appreciation of individuality with emphasis upon an individual's right to freedom, autonomy, and respect.
2. Group consensus in tribal/village decision making.
3. Respect for all living things.
4. Appreciation, respect, and reverence for the land.
5. Feelings of hospitality toward friends, family, clanspeople, tribesmen, and respectful visitors.
6. An expectation that tribal/village members will bring honor and

respect to their families, clans, and tribes. Bringing shame or dishonor to self or tribe is negatively reinforced.

7. A belief in a supreme being and life after death. Indian religion is the dominant influence for traditional Indian people.

## CONCLUSION

The need for curricular adaptations and modifications to address the growing minority populations in both the academic and clinical environments in which students within the allied health professions are being prepared has been emphasized. As Johnson-Crockett (1990) stresses, "The health care professional and student must have a working knowledge of the cultural, religious, and ethnic beliefs and practices of the minorities in the community where service is planned" (p. 541). This knowledge is essential in order to interact effectively with minority individuals without violating their cultural norms. As health care providers, allied health professionals represent a group of individuals who are invested in sustaining a meaningful quality of life for others. In order to accomplish this, it is essential that faculty in the allied health professional programs both demonstrate by their own example, and convey to their students through their choice in course content, the requisite skills required in being intercultural communicators. Because intercultural communication occurs whenever a message produced by a person in one culture must be processed by an individual from another culture (Porter & Samovar, 1991), faculty should prepare their students for intercultural experiences both within the classroom and for their future professional encounters. Curricula adaptation can be the means to facilitate this process.

## REFERENCES

Andersen, J.F. & Powell, R.: Intercultural communication and the classroom. In Samovar, L.A. & Porter, R.E. (Eds.): *Intercultural Communication: A Reader,* 6th ed. Belmont, Wadsworth, 1991, pp. 208–213.

Barresi, C.M.: Diversity in Black family caregiving: Implications for geriatric education. In Harper, M.S. (Ed.): *Minority Aging: Essential Curricula Content for Selected Health and Allied Health Professionals.* Washington, Health Resources and Services Administration, Department of Health and Human Services. DHHS Publication No. HRS (P–DV-90-4), U.S. Government, 1990, pp. 297–311.

Collier, M.J.: Competent communication in intercultural unequal status advisement contexts. *Howard Journal of Communications, 1:* 3–22, 1988.

Davis, L.H.: The Black aged and the nursing curriculum: A historical perspective and implications for the future. In Harper, M.S.: *Minority Aging: Essential Curricula Content for Selected Health and Allied Health Professionals.* Washington, Health Resources and Services Administration, Department of Health and Human Services. DHHS Publication No. HRS (P–DV-90-4), U.S. Government, 1990, pp. 477–483.

Edwards, E.D. & Egbert-Edwards, M.: Family care and the Native American elderly. In Harper, M.S.: *Minority Aging: Essential Curricula Content for Selected Health and Allied Health Professionals.* Washington, Health Resources and Services Administration, Department of Health and Human Services. DHHS Publication No. HRS (P–DV-90-4), U.S. Government, 1990, pp. 145–163.

Gudykunst, W.B. & Ting-Toomey, S.: *Culture and Interpersonal Communication.* Newbury Park, Sage, 1988.

Harper, M.S.: Introduction. In Harper, M.S. (Ed.): *Minority Aging: Essential Curricula Content for Selected Health and Allied Health Professionals.* Washington, Health Resources and Services Administration, Department of Health and Human Services. DHHS Publication No. HRS (P–DV-90-4), U.S. Government, 1990, pp. 3–22.

Johnson-Crockett, M.A.: Home health care of the minority elderly: Implications for geriatric education. In Harper, M.S. (Ed.): *Minority Aging: Essential Curricula Content for Selected Health and Allied Health Professionals.* Washington, Health Resources and Services Administration, Department of Health and Human Services. DHHS Publication No. HRS (P–DV-90-4), U.S. Government, 1990, p. 535–547.

Pederson, P.: The multicultural perspective as a fourth force in counseling. *Journal of Mental Health Counseling, 12:* 93, 1990.

*Pluralism in the Professoriate Strategies for developing faculty diversity. Minorities on Campus Series.* Washington, National Association of Independent Colleges and Universities, 1991.

Porter, R.E. & Samovar, L.A.: Basic principles of intercultural communication. In Samovar, L.A. & Porter, R.E. (Eds.): *Intercultural Communication: A Reader,* 6th ed. Belmont, Wadsworth, 1991, pp. 5–22.

Sakauye, K.: Differential diagnosis, medication, treatment, and outcomes: Asian American elderly. In Harper, M.S. (Ed.): *Minority Aging: Essential Curricula Content for Selected Health and Allied Health Professionals.* Washington, Health Resources and Services Administration, Department of Health and Human Services. DHHS Publication No. HRS (P–DV-90-4). U.S. Government, 1990, pp. 331–339.

Satcher, D. & Thomas, D.J.: Dimensions of minority aging: Implications for curriculum development for selected health professions. In Harper, M.S. (Ed.): *Minority Aging: Essential Curricula Content for Selected Health and Allied Health Professionals.* Washington, Health Resources and Services Administration, Department of Health and Human Services. DHHS Publication No. HRS (P–DV-90-4). U.S. Government, 1990, pp. 23–32.

*Understanding Campus: Climate An Approach to Student Diversity Minorities on Campus*

*Series.* Washington, National Association of Independent Colleges and Universities, 1991.

Valle, R.: The Latino/Hispanic family and the elderly: Approaches to cross-cultural curriculum design in the health professions. In Harper, M.S. (Ed.): *Minority Aging: Essential Curricula Content for Selected Health and Allied Health Professionals.* Washington, Health Resources and Services Administration, Department of Health and Human Services. DHHS Publication No. HRS (P–DV-90-4). U.S. Government, 1990, pp. 433–452.

Waltzman, D.E.: Effects of cultural variation in communicating with minority older adults: Asian, African American, Hispanic. In Clark, L. (Ed.): *Understanding Communication Disorders in the Older Adult: A Practical Handbook for Health Care Professionals.* New York, Brookdale Center on Aging, 1993.

# INDEX